# VERBAL LEARNING
## AND
# VERBAL BEHAVIOR

PROCEEDINGS OF A CONFERENCE SPONSORED BY
THE OFFICE OF NAVAL RESEARCH AND NEW YORK UNIVERSITY

# McGRAW-HILL SERIES IN PSYCHOLOGY

## HARRY F. HARLOW, *Consulting Editor*

John F. Dashiell was Consulting Editor of this series from its inception in 1931 until January 1, 1950. Clifford T. Morgan was Consulting Editor of this series from January 1, 1950 until January 1, 1959.

# *VERBAL LEARNING*
## *and*
# *VERBAL BEHAVIOR*

Edited by

CHARLES N. COFER

with the assistance of BARBARA S. MUSGRAVE

PROCEEDINGS OF A CONFERENCE SPONSORED BY
THE OFFICE OF NAVAL RESEARCH AND NEW YORK UNIVERSITY

### PARTICIPANTS

Weston A. Bousfield    Charles E. Osgood
James Deese    Leo Postman
Albert E. Goss    Wallace A. Russell
James J. Jenkins    Denzel D. Smith
George Mandler    Benton J. Underwood
Arthur W. Melton    Barbara S. Musgrave
Clyde E. Noble    Charles N. Cofer

McGRAW-HILL BOOK COMPANY, INC.

New York     Toronto     London

1961

## VERBAL LEARNING AND VERBAL BEHAVIOR

11550

III

# PREFACE

In this volume are recorded the proceedings of a Conference on Verbal Learning and Verbal Behavior held in the fall of 1959 under the auspices of New York University and the U.S. Office of Naval Research. By way of preface to these proceedings, I wish to report on how the conference developed, what its plan of operation was, how the proceedings were prepared and what they represent, and to acknowledge the fact that the aid of several individuals and organizations was indispensable to the execution of the conference plan.

In the fall of 1958, when I was at the University of Maryland, Dr. D. D. Smith and I agreed that a conference in the general area of verbal learning was desirable. A great deal of research has gone on in verbal learning—75 years' worth—and the Office of Naval Research, as well as other agencies, has had an important supporting role in a good deal of it, under its policy of encouraging basic research. Dr. Smith and I made up a list of people whom we felt to be particularly active in the traditional field of verbal learning, most of whom were current or recent ONR contractors. We made these persons a committee, and from that time on these persons participated in the development of the plans for the conference program and participating personnel. Smith and I had agreed that the total conference group would be small, that the papers would consider problems of theory, issue, and method rather than be direct research reports, and that a series of papers on important topics would be prepared and distributed prior to the meeting.

With these agreements in mind, I wrote to the following committee members: James Deese, A. E. Goss, G. A. Miller, C. E. Noble, Leo Postman, and B. J. Underwood. They were apprised of the general plans which Smith and I had developed, and several topics for the conference were proposed. Nominations of potential participants were solicited. The response was enthusiastic. With two more exchanges of correspondence, the conference topics were settled, and the other participants were agreed upon. Invitations and assignments were then sent out to these other participants. One person, because of ill health, declined to participate. Later, two other people, one of them G. A. Miller, had to withdraw because of unanticipated conflicts with other commitments. A little further adjustment of topics and assignments was therefore necessary.

As planned, the seven assigned papers were prepared and distributed ahead of the conference; therefore, none was read or otherwise presented at the meeting. Each paper had a discussant, and the conference procedure was that a given discussant presided over the session concerned with the paper (usually not without interruption) and then led a general discussion. Discussion sessions lasted from two to three hours and were lively.

The proceedings which follow consist of the seven papers prepared ahead of the meeting, together with a paper prepared by the discussant of each paper. Except for minor editing and, in some cases, the addition of footnotes, the prepared papers are in the form in which they appeared at the conference. Some of the discussants prepared their papers before the meeting, and these papers are presented here with but minor changes. Other discussants wrote their papers after the meeting. Following each prepared paper and discussant's paper, there is a summary of the conference discussion. Dr. Barbara Musgrave, now of Smith College, served as the conference recorder, and these summaries were prepared from her notes by the writer, after conferences with Dr. Musgrave. These summaries do not represent in any way a verbatim account of the discussion, or even an accurate portrayal of the sequence in which items were talked about. They represent an attempt to outline the major issues that came up and what was said about each one. After the preparation of these summaries the participants reviewed them. Responsibility for their form and for errors they contain, however, must remain the writer's.

The remaining sections of the proceedings, the Introduction and the Commentary, were prepared by the writer from his own notes and Dr. Musgrave's notes and from his remarks at the final session of the conference, at which he attempted a summary. The references cited by each writer and discussant follow their papers; certain additional references were mentioned in the discussions, and these have been listed following the summary of each discussion.

It remains to acknowledge the role of those who made the meeting possible and who made it function so effortlessly. The conference was jointly sponsored by the Psychological Sciences Division of the Office of Naval Research, U.S. Navy Department, and the Department of Psychology, New York University, and was partially supported under Contract No. Nonr–285(47). Without Barbara Musgrave's notes certain portions of these proceedings would not exist.

Mr. Aaron Finesot, Director of the Office of Special Services to Business and Industry, New York University, was very helpful in making available the university's Frank Jay Gould House as a meeting and living place. We owe him our gratitude. Mr. Carol E. Spette, Resident Manager of Gould House, his wife, and his excellent staff provided meals and lodgings in such an effortless way that one hardly knew the staff was there. To them also our thanks are extended.

*Charles N. Cofer*

# CONTENTS

# Chapter 1

# INTRODUCTION AND SUMMARY

The experimental study of memory was initiated by Hermann Ebbing-haus, whose book *On Memory* was published in 1885. Ebbinghaus invented the nonsense syllable, defined by him as two consonants separated by a vowel which did not form a meaningful word. Using himself as his subject, Ebbinghaus learned, serially, list after list of such syllables, studying a number of variables whose effect on the processes of acquisition and retention of the lists he delineated. He made some comparisons between nonsense-syllable learning and the learning of poetry, but Ebbinghaus's chief concern was to study the basic proc-esses of learning and retention. He thought that this study could be accomplished best if the various complexities which meaningful words and organizations of meaningful words introduce were eliminated. And he believed that the nonsense syllable eliminated these complexities.

In the ensuing years, verbal learning, a term which designates the kind of study which Ebbinghaus carried out, has received the attention of innumerable investigators, and the papers published on problems of verbal learning number in the thousands. Many variations in technique and materials have been introduced. For example, the method of paired-associates learning is used as frequently as the method of serial antici-pation, which Ebbinghaus employed, and lists of meaningful words are approaching the popularity of lists of nonsense syllables. A host of variables has been added to those which Ebbinghaus considered, and experiments have been designed to explicate transfer and interference effects within and between lists as well as other problems beyond the range of Ebbinghaus's efforts. Nevertheless, all of this work bears Ebbinghaus's stamp: it has concerned the learning and retention of lists of discrete items in an effort to describe and to explain basic as-sociative processes and the conditions of which they are a function. The books by McGeoch (1942) and McGeoch and Irion (1952) represent this work well, up to the time at which they were published.

The Ebbinghaus tradition, then, has focused attention on associative processes, studied by means of the rote learning of verbal materials. It has tended to ignore or to neglect verbal characteristics and skills which a person's natural language has provided him and which may interact with the task set for him in the laboratory. Further, it has tended not to examine processes of "higher order" than elementary associations. Experimental controls have been carefully devised to minimize as much as possible the contribution to list learning of factors which might complicate the formation of independent or discrete associations, such as grouping, rhythm, mnemonic devices, and relationships among individual units.

There have, of course, been objections to this tradition from time to time. Almost thirty years ago, Bartlett (1932) denied that the nonsense syllable eliminates meaning as a factor, and he went on to carry out and to describe investigations whose stimuli, responses, and procedures were very different from those of studies in the Ebbinghaus tradition. Recent writers who have stressed coding or organizing operations (cf. Miller, 1956) seem more in Bartlett's tradition than in Ebbinghaus's, although they may have started from still different viewpoints, such as information theory. The description of the natural language characteristics of people and of languages themselves is having a growing influence on several aspects of psychological inquiry (cf. Carroll, 1953; Miller, 1951; Osgood and Sebeok, 1954), and that such characteristics have relevance to the study of verbal learning is abundantly demonstrated in the present conference (cf. also Underwood and Postman, 1960). This latter trend is the study of verbal behavior. Although the acquisition of first and of second languages is an important problem in the study of verbal behavior, the emphasis here is not so much on language acquisition as it is on description of the verbal behaviors which the individual has already acquired, how much and by what means they may be altered, and how these behaviors influence his relations with the world and his functioning in other areas, like verbal learning. On this basis, then, verbal learning and verbal behavior can be distinguished, although the two have much in common and interact.

In the present conference, all of these trends or traditions are represented. Although no participant can be classified simply, the work of some of them has fallen mainly in the Ebbinghaus tradition and that of others in the study of verbal behavior. Several have been interested in coding or organizing processes. The topics, too, represent these three interests. The papers by Deese and Goss are pertinent to coding and organizing processes, those by Deese, Bousfield, and Russell to verbal behavior, and those by Postman, Underwood, and Noble to verbal learning. In its concern for individual differences, however, Noble's paper departs from the traditional interests of students of verbal learning.

There follows an attempt to epitomize this conference. This will be done through a brief summary of each of the prepared papers and of the discussion which it engendered. In the Commentary, at the end of the volume, a statement is made of the more outstanding trends, agreements and disagreements, issues of method and of definition, and deficiencies of this conference.

## James Deese
### From the Isolated Verbal Unit to Connected Discourse

Professor Deese questions the idea that any verbal unit can be considered as an isolated one. However, he does suggest that the study of diverse kinds of material can contribute valuable information through the kinds of contingent relationships among segments which different materials display. His approach is essentially a correlational one; i.e., normative data are used to predict the individual's behavior in some situation in which restrictions on the behavior are imposed. Deese argues that the nonsense syllable is not a desirable unit because it involves certain complexities not found in meaningful words. The word, as a unit, encounters definitional problems which, however, he considers of little practical importance. Deese then describes studies in which the method has been a single presentation of a list of words followed by an immediate, free recall. His paper reviews three factors often presumed to influence the recall of a list of words.

The first factor is interitem associative strength. Lists of words which have a high index of interitem associative strength (i.e., words in the list are frequent associates of other words in the list) are more readily recalled than lists with low interitem associative strength. Intrusions of other (nonlist) words into the recall of the list are also predictable on this associative basis. Deese conceives the recall of such lists as involving the actual retention of but a few words, and the "recall" of additional words through "guessing" or "constructing" them by means of association to the words actually retained. Deese saw no reason to suggest that the subject edits or selects among his associations in this process.

Second, Deese presented evidence that leads him to doubt that word frequency is a factor which is related to the free recall of words. Once a word is encoded or well integrated, it should be readily recalled, no matter what its frequency of occurrence in the language. For example, *dog* and *giraffe* differ widely in frequency of usage, but if they are well encoded they should not differ in recallability.

The third factor is sequential dependencies among words. Recall of higher approximations to the English language is better than it is for lower approximations, not because more words are actually recalled from the higher approximations, but because the subject's knowledge of

English syntax allows him to guess or to construct the words which must be there in the case of the higher approximations. His recall score would be elevated by correct guesses.

In summary, Deese conceives the recall of lists of words as chiefly determined by interitem associative factors and by sequential features imparted to the material either by a text itself or by the subject. Both factors permit the subject to construct or to guess much of his performance in recall. In addition, the subject will tend to use the more frequently occurring words which are highly available to him. Recall of connected discourse can be very probably accounted for by these same factors, although certain additional complexities will arise.

In the discussion, criticisms were addressed to Deese's guessing-or-construction hypothesis, on the basis that importations do not appear frequently in delayed recalls and the subject's immediate recall of a list is usually only a fraction of the number of words the list contained. If the subject were guessing, it seems that he would produce more words than he does, including importations or intrusions. Further, the word *guessing* was criticized as not being descriptive of what the subject is probably doing. (In revising his paper, Deese tended to substitute *constructing* for guessing.) Deese's attack on the word-frequency variable was also questioned, and several kinds of evidence were advanced to suggest that it influences verbal behavior. Also mentioned was the need for better associative norms than those available, and the problem of contextual influences on associative responses was emphasized.

*Albert E. Goss*
*Acquisition and Use of Conceptual Schemes*

Coding and organizing processes were mentioned in the Introduction, and Professor Goss's paper is concerned with such processes under the term *conceptual schemes*. His paper reviews some of the historical antecedents to current interest in conceptual schemes, citing the work of Bartlett and of the Gestalt psychologists and that of theorists who have stressed the role of mediating responses and their consequent stimuli. Goss's paper then deals with the definition of such conceptual schemes, of which he gives several examples, and the possible ways in which such schemes are learned. He also developed, theoretically, the ways in which conceptual schemes may function in the further learning of stimulus-response relationships and how the conceptual schemes may themselves be modified. Central to his theoretical analysis as well as to his treatment of several examples, including an analysis of the act of writing something, is the idea that conceptual schemes have their value because they involve verbal labeling responses which serve a mediating role; in some instances they provide for transfer from one situation to another, and in other instances they serve the function of discrimination.

In the discussion which followed Goss's paper, perhaps the major point among those raised concerned the role of labeling in the use of grammatical rules in speaking and writing. There are really two points here. One is that native speakers and writers of a language achieve, at a very early age, considerable skill in using the grammar of the language and that they are able to apply the grammar correctly to words and phrases which they have not heard or seen before. The other point is that such usage goes on in the absence of explicit knowledge of the grammatical schemes themselves or of explicit (or implicit) labeling responses such as those which Goss suggests, particularly in many formal writing tasks. There was a good deal of agreement that simple associative processes alone cannot account for these phenomena of grammatical usage, but there was sharp disagreement as to how much language behavior non-associative mechanisms must account for and as to the nature of such mechanisms. It seems evident that the participants were differentially persuaded that the language of native speakers and writers is skillful, grammatical, and flexible, on the one hand, and repetitive, ungrammatical, and learned by rote, on the other. While some data exist concerning these points, it was agreed that much more study is needed. Language learning in the young child was seen as an area critically requiring study in order that knowledge of the acquisition of conceptual schemes or grammar be accumulated.

*Weston A. Bousfield*
*The Problem of Meaning in Verbal Learning*

Professor Bousfield's paper suggests that meaning is not a useful concept if by meaning is meant something other than verbal associations. His paper includes a number of demonstrations of the power which measures of association have in predicting transfer and generalization in verbal problems, together with a theoretical statement of his viewpoint and an analysis of the mechanisms involved in Osgood's semantic differential in his terms. Since it is Bousfield's contention that implicit or explicit verbal associative responses mediate transfer and generalization and function in the semantic differential, he sees no reason to invoke any other interpretation of meaning.

The discussion of this paper included attempts to clarify the theoretical differences between Bousfield and Osgood and to explore more fully the implications of the models. Data relevant to the adequacy of the models were reviewed. Problems he sees in Bousfield's model were outlined by Osgood. A major problem is that Bousfield's model, dependent as it is on verbal responses, cannot explain how the preverbal child learns meanings. On the other hand, successful predictions of verbal behavior in various situations support Bousfield's conception. There was considerable discussion of the adequacy of evidence which Osgood marshaled as supporting the necessity for a conception like the one that he has developed.

## Wallace A. Russell
## Assessment vs. Experimental Acquisition of Verbal Habits

The characteristics and processes of the natural language have an intrinsic interest and importance in themselves, and their significance further arises from the influences they may have on other psychological processes. Professor Russell points out that there are two strategies which have guided research in relation to these points. One is to assess the status of language characteristics by test procedures, e.g., by word-association tests, and then to examine experimentally either the influence of other variables on such test performances or the influence of characteristics ascertained by tests on processes like learning or perception in a laboratory situation. The other strategy is to attempt to build into the subject, through experimental operations, the kind of verbal characteristics in which the experimenter is interested and then to test, again experimentally, the influence of other variables on these characteristics or the influence of these characteristics on other processes. Two major questions arise. First, are the habits or characteristics developed in the laboratory comparable to characteristics which the natural language possesses? Second, can all significant language functions be simulated experimentally? Concerning question one, error in the estimation of individual characteristics by means of data from normative samples is always probable, and there is the problem of reliability in conjunction with efforts to obtain estimates of his characteristics from the experimental subject himself. Of more systematic importance, however, is the issue of validity of tests as indicators of the constructs in which the experimenter is interested. Russell gives several reasons for believing that test-inferred and experimentally introduced processes may not be the same thing. In answering his second question, Russell indicated that an affirmative answer is not yet possible, but he further suggested that modifications of and innovations in laboratory techniques offer some hope that many language functions, at least, can be studied appropriately in the laboratory.

In the discussion, questions arose as to the equivalence of measures which presumably get at the same variable, like different measures of association and of verbal fluency, and there was a note of considerable caution concerning the assumption of the identity of or the correspondence between experimentally established and test-inferred constructs.

Much discussion was devoted to the Mowrer (1954) paradigm for the acquisition of meaning and to the question of whether the acquisition of associations requires more than one trial. Basic to both of these issues was the conviction on the part of several participants that syntactical factors are not adequately taken account of in the Mowrer paradigm and that such factors may account for the apparent slowness in the acquisition of associations when several associations are acquired simultaneously in list learning.

## Clyde E. Noble
### Verbal Learning and Individual Differences

Professor Noble argued that correlational and experimental approaches to the study of verbal behavior are complementary. He summarized data consistent with the proposition that rate of acquisition in selective learning tasks is a positive function of initial ability level. Specific relationships between aspects of verbal learning and individual differences were brought out. Noble described Hull's approach to the treatment of the individual-difference factor, and, although he is in sympathy with this orientation to the problem, he indicated a number of problems which must be worked out before its adequacy can be evaluated. Problems of method that must be solved, including that of standardization, were illustrated by the task of establishing the association values of nonsense syllables and by the need for improved measures of personality and motivational characteristics. If steps are taken along these lines of method, a more complete integration of verbal learning and individual differences can be accomplished than is possible at the present time.

A point made in the discussion was that constructs presumably measured by test procedures are often unclear. It is possible that the abilities involved in verbal learning are multiple and not highly intercorrelated. There may be three kinds of learning in verbal learning: stimulus integration, response integration, and the association of stimuli and responses.

It was emphasized that it is not enough just to decide to study individual differences. There must be some basis for deciding with what individual-difference factor one will begin. Individual differences in the performance of individuals, as measured by various indices provided by learning tasks, and individual differences present before learning starts should be distinguished. The former can be related to the learning process itself. Some investigators find that prior measures of individual differences interact with measures of learning; others do not.

Some attention was paid to the distinction between stimulus-response laws (S-R laws) and response-response laws (R-R laws). The group had difficulty in making a clear distinction between these types of laws.

*Leo Postman*
*The Present Status of Interference Theory*

Professor Postman's paper is a reanalysis of the theory that failures of recall occur because of competition of responses at the time of recall. One postulate is the independence hypothesis. In the retroactive-interference paradigm A-B, A-C, for example, the A-B list was considered not to be affected during the learning of the A-C list; i.e., the strengths of the associations in the A-B list were independent of the A-C list. At recall, competition of response would explain forgetting; when the responses B and C were of equal strength, failures in recall would occur, but when the strength of C exceeded that of B, B could not be given and so would be deemed "forgotten." Recent evidence suggests that the independence hypothesis is incorrect and that there is actual unlearning or extinction of the first-list responses (B) during the learning of the second list (A-C); A-C is the interpolated list of a retroaction design. Recovery of the A-B associations may occur, and then there will be competition between B and C. In the case of similarity between responses (B and B') of the two lists, however, the first-list response may serve as a mediator between A and B' (the second list). Such mediation is also inconsistent with the independence hypothesis. In this case, facilitation of second-list learning may result. Differentiation of the two lists also is important to accuracy of recall, and this differentiation decreases as time after learning increases. Hence, retroactive interference should increase with time in the A-B, A-B' paradigm, an effect that is less marked in the A-B, A-C case.

Postman also brought out evidence for other factors in forgetting, like specific and generalized response competition. Specific competition is that between particular responses associated with the same or similar stimuli. Generalized response competition is the subject's tendency to make responses from the last list practiced. This should be greater in retroaction than in proaction. Other analyses concerning unlearning, mediation, list discrimination, and specific and generalized response competition brought out differences that should be expected between retroactive and proactive interference, from manipulation of temporal intervals, and from different values of other parameters of the learning situation.

Since proactive interference now seems to be the major factor in long-term forgetting, Postman devoted attention to factors which may act proactively on laboratory learning tasks. He analyzed and presented evidence concerning two such factors, letter sequences and unit (i.e., word) sequences which have their sources in the natural language. They act to interfere with the retention of tasks learned in the laboratory.

Discussion of this paper focused on several issues. One was whether interference can explain all forgetting. Is there "deterioration" of the memory trace in time, independently of interference? There was discussion of the learning of pairs of words which have differing degrees of prior associative linkages, as determined from associative norms, but which differ little in their difficulty of learning. Context in the process of recall, it was agreed, is an extremely important variable and deserves much more study than it has had.

*Benton J. Underwood*
*An Evaluation of the Gibson Theory of Verbal Learning*

In 1940, Eleanor J. Gibson published an analysis of verbal learning problems in terms of the concepts of generalization and differentiation, concepts derived from work on the conditioned response. As Professor Underwood observes in his paper, the theory was an influential one. Underwood's discussion is devoted to the question whether the theory has continued usefulness in the present. After outlining Gibson's major ideas and stating what now seem to have been defects in the original statement of the theory, Underwood examines the application of Gibson's theory to the problem of learning and retaining a single list and to the problem of transfer. In the former case he finds the theory holds in certain respects when geometric forms or nonsense syllables are used as stimuli but not when words are used as stimuli. Whether data on errors in list learning support the theory depends on how errors are measured, and certain predictions concerning recall in relation to intra-list similarity of stimuli are not supported. Underwood finds the theory to be valid for only a limited range of transfer phenomena and probably to be invalid for other transfer phenomena. A number of developments in the analysis of verbal learning have followed directions to which the theory is not relevant and concerning which it offers little help. In general, Underwood concludes that Gibson's theory now has little usefulness. Only a thorough revision could bring it up to date and give it viability.

In the discussion, there seemed to be no major disagreement with many of Underwood's evaluations of Gibson's theory, and perhaps because of this, the topics discussed diverged from specific concern with the theory. The concept of similarity was discussed in some detail, in an attempt to clarify its meaning, and there was an extensive discussion of the topics of meaningfulness, stimulus familiarity, and response integration, all in the context of relevant experimental work.

#### REFERENCES

Bartlett, F. G. (1932) *Remembering: A study in experimental and social psychology.* New York: Cambridge.

Carroll, J. G. (1953) *The study of language.* Cambridge, Mass.: Harvard University Press.

Gibson, Eleanor J. (1940) A systematic application of the concepts of generalization and differentiation to verbal learning. *Psychol. Rev.*, 47, 196–229.

McGeoch, J. A. (1942) *The psychology of human learning: An introduction.* New York: Longmans.

McGeoch, J. A., & Irion, A. L. (1952) *The psychology of human learning.* (2nd ed.) New York: Longmans.

Miller, G. A. (1951) *Language and communication.* New York: McGraw-Hill.

Miller, G. A. (1956) The magical number seven, plus or minus two: Some limits on our capacity for processing information. *Psychol. Rev.*, 63, 81–97.

Mowrer, O. H. (1954) The psychologist looks at language. *Amer. Psychologist,* 9, 660–694.

Osgood, C. E., & Sebeok, T. A. (1954) Psycholinguistics: A survey of theory and research. *J. Abnorm. Soc. Psychol.*, 49, Suppl. to No. 4.

Underwood, B. J., & Postman, L. (1960) Extra-experimental sources of interference in forgetting. *Psychol. Rev.*, 67, 73–95.

# Chapter 2

# FROM THE ISOLATED VERBAL UNIT
# TO CONNECTED DISCOURSE

*James Deese*

THE JOHNS HOPKINS UNIVERSITY

The title of this chapter may be objected to on at least two counts. First of all, it is, in the simplest empirical sense, close to nonsense. One of the certainties about verbal behavior is that there is no such thing as a verbal unit in isolation. For, however we may try to isolate a verbal unit in the laboratory, we must reckon with the inevitable verbal environment provided the unit by the individual when that unit is presented to him. In general, what we mean by "isolated unit" is that the environment in which the particular unit appears in the laboratory is not the environment likely to be provided by the individual from his own verbal repertoire.[1] Thus, paradoxically, we may "isolate" a unit (a word, a syllable, a letter) by presenting it before and after the presentation of other specified units; the catch is, of course, that these environmental units are statistically independent of the unit in question.

It is less clear that the phrase "connected discourse" does not have an objective referent. Here we are likely to point to samples of English prose. What we mean to imply by this operation is that the verbal units embodied in the material we present to an individual *do* have environments likely to agree with the verbal environments supplied by that individual. Thus, there is a correlation betweeen an individual's predictions about the sequences in the sample and the sequences actually presented. Connected discourse, of course, means more than this to the semanticist, but we are not concerned with semantic or content problems in this chapter.

Furthermore, the problem embodied in the title of this chapter may be objected to on the grounds that it is an artificial one. That is to say, the variation referred to is not one presented by nature; it is a problem arising out of the particular methods used by experimental psychologists to study more nearly natural verbal problems. In nature, verbal units usually have appropriate environments (by definition); it is only in the

---

[1] I am using the phrase "verbal environment" in the general linguistic sense.

laboratory that they do not. Nothing could be more dreary than a comparison of methods and techniques originally devised, not to be representative of natural processes and constraints in language, but to control and limit certain features of variation in verbal material, particularly those features thought to be important by early investigators.

Despite these considerations—considerations which make us approach the problem with some faint distaste—there are questions of very general importance which are raised by a comparison of different kinds of materials in verbal learning and memory. The essential feature of difference between kinds of verbal material—leaving aside certain physical aspects quite trivial for the present set of problems—is in the natural relationships between segments of the material presented to individuals. These natural relationships provide the verbal environment of particular segments of verbal behavior, and they are relationships discoverable in some form or another from the behavior of individuals. They usually take the form of contingent relationships; that is to say, they are of the form: Given the probability of verbal element A, what is the probability of B occurring in an individual's behavior?

While it is obvious, it is nonetheless important to note that the relationships discoverable in an individual's verbal behavior tell us nothing about how such relationships are built into that individual; we know only that they exist. It is an easy and, I think, a pernicious assumption to decide, without careful reflection on the matter, that the relationships discoverable in normative data reflect some simple, one-to-one transformation of an input into the individual.[2]

Thus, the most generally useful technique in the study of verbal behavior is to learn something, by the collection of normative data, of the verbal usage of a population of individuals. The information so obtained is then used to predict the effects of particular kinds of restrictions upon an individual's behavior in some testing situation. This, of course, exemplifies what psychologists generally know as the R-R paradigm of scientific investigation; the technique is limited, we all know, by the severe demands made upon inferential reasoning by the comparative lack of control in such a paradigm. In the study of verbal behavior, however, most important controls are readily available; thus the power of inferences from R-R investigations is rather great in this field.

Part of the tradition of sterility and the sense of weariness that attaches to the problem under consideration in this chapter is that investigators have not always clearly recognized that the problem necessarily is a correlational one. The correlational approach is most firmly established

---

[2] As a matter of fact, the interrelationships among associations suggest that the obtained frequencies reflect general schemata determined by the structure of the mind.

in the more recent experimental work on the problem. Because, in different ways, they have established the importance of intra-individual and interindividual correlations in the study of different kinds of verbal material in learning, memory, and verbal output, the studies of Bartlett (1932), Foley and MacMillan (1943), Miller and Selfridge (1950), and Noble (1952) are, in their various ways, significant landmarks in different areas.

Thus, a comparison between different kinds of verbal material is interesting only if we have some basis for predicting how such material should behave. We cannot, in most cases, discover the psychological properties of our material without normative data, though, it should be noted, some investigators have had notable success in using their own verbal behavior in lieu of norms. The earlier clustering studies of Bousfield (1953) provide a notable example.

The kinds of materials and methods used in studies of verbal behavior are, by and large, the inheritance of association theory, much as the materials now used in the study of perceptual memory are offsprings of Gestalt theory. The methods themselves are capable of almost endless variations, though some variations are of limited importance. The essential variations that carry us from the isolated unit to connected discourse are (1) variations in the type of material itself, (2) the order or method of presentation of the material, (3) the nature of the test of retention employed, (4) the instructions and/or reinforcement contingencies employed during presentation, and (5) the scoring system. This chapter will be almost entirely concerned with the variations in type of material, though we will touch upon some other methods of altering the experimental situation in verbal learning. We can, however, look at the entire collection of variations as a framework upon which we can hang the issues involved in going from relatively isolated material to connected discourse.

In addition, we will be almost entirely concerned with experimental studies in which free recall immediately follows a single presentation of the material. Despite the fascinating questions raised by a comparison of methods of producing recall, we shall be forced almost completely to ignore this problem.

## UNRELATED WORDS

The phrase "unrelated words" needs an explanation if only for the reason that, all other things considered, we would expect to begin with "the nonsense syllable" or something like it. The nonsense syllable, however, presents serious difficulties, and, I believe, these difficulties have carried it out of the main stream of the problem of going from the isolated unit to connected discourse.

The requirements of the nonsense syllable were dictated by association theory. Ebbinghaus (1885) tells us that he invented nonsense syllables because they lacked meaning, because they were simple and uniform. They could be used in any order or pattern, and, if you went through the same procedures with different syllables, the outcome would be the same. To be sure, Ebbinghaus expressed some doubt that his nonsense syllables had all of the virtues claimed for them, and, if subsequent research had done nothing else, it has at least vindicated Ebbinghaus's doubts.

In point of fact, though Ebbinghaus did not say so explicitly, nonsense syllables were intended by him to stand for ideas—ideas at the outset of an experiment that bore no relation to one another or to ideas outside of the set formed of possible three-letter nonsense syllables. Learning consisted in the formation of associations between the ideas represented by the syllables.

The subsequent history of the nonsense syllable as a methodological tool in verbal learning is an orderly but steady retreat from this position. The early calibrations of nonsense syllables were made because investigators realized that such syllables were not independent of other bits of encoded verbal behavior, and the normative studies were designed to assess the degree to which particular syllables were related to other syllables and words.

Their lack of independence is not the real difficulty with nonsense syllables, however, since they share this property with all verbal units. The real problem with them is that they are not encoded at the outset of an experiment. This problem did not plague the early investigators to the extent that it has the more recent ones since the earlier workers pronounced rather than spelled individual items. Pronouncing, no doubt, facilitates the encoding of the syllables, though, so far as I know, the implication of this assertion has not been studied directly.

When nonsense syllables are spelled, it immediately becomes clear that they are not integrated units but rather that they are, for the most part, collections of elements (letters) with varying degrees of transitional frequencies between the individual elements. Thus, the units out of which nonsense syllables are composed depend for *their* probability of occurrence in behavior upon their verbal environment. They do not all necessarily appear if the others appear (as is the case, with trivial exceptions, with the letters of common words).

This, I believe, makes nonsense syllables too complicated to serve as examples of isolated units. For example, consider the typical experiment in which nonsense syllables are used in learning by serial anticipation. For a 12-item list, the structure of the dependencies between elements and syllables becomes quite complicated. The analysis of an individual's output and the relation of this output to the material presented is made difficult by the duplication, in any one of three positions, of individual symbols, each with different transitional probabilities to adjacent symbols. The picture is made even more complicated by the item boundaries induced by the standard method of presentation and the instructions and reinforcement patterns administered to the subjects who learn such items.

Thus, instead of having 12 items, as we sometimes convince ourselves, we actually may have as many as 36. The nonsense syllable may be useful in studying the encoding process itself, and this usefulness has been vastly increased by the stage analysis of rote learning introduced by Underwood and his associates (Underwood, Runquist, and Schulz, 1959).

For our present purposes, however, I believe that we would do well to abandon the nonsense syllable. Nonsense syllables are not, in fact, closer to being isolated units than are properly chosen real words. And, by virtue of their incomplete encoding to naive subjects in the laboratory, they produce complications in analysis.

If we start with isolated units in the form of ordinary English words, we may, except for certain special problems, ignore the transitional relations between the elements—letters or phonemes—of words. Thus, when we use real words with native speakers of a reasonable level of intelligence and education, we can ignore many of the problems that plague the user of nonsense syllables. In the isolated word, unsupported by context, phonetic similarities (or similarities of spelling) may be important in experiments in which communication with the subject is through a noisy channel. This problem, however, is even a greater one with nonsense syllables, and by carefully choosing words it is possible to minimize the importance of noise in the channel between the source and the subject.

How do we recognize words? As a practical matter this is not a very great problem, though in theory it is. It is a problem because populations of speakers do not agree in their vocabularies, and furthermore, single individuals continuously change their vocabularies. Thus, any attempt to assess the number or distribution of encoded words for any given speaker is handicapped by the fact that there is a distribution of the limits of encoding across individuals in populations and within individuals across time.

While no linguistic technique gives us an unequivocal theoretical answer to the question of how to delimit the word, most generally we can rely on the criterion we have already mentioned, namely, the relative independence of words from their phonemic or literal environments. No part of a word is independent of its environment *without itself also being a word*. The word is not constrained absolutely by what follows and precedes it, as are the segments of the words.

This leaves a certain confusion between the morpheme and the word. I don't think this need be troublesome if we recognize that bound morphemes are not independent of their environments. Free morphemes are characteristically words; thus some words are free morphemes and others are free morphemes plus bound morphemes.[3]

These are questions not likely to trouble the typical worker in verbal behavior, however. Fortunately, he can rely upon the large mass of printed sources (limited here by English orthographic practices) or, more particularly, the Thorndike-Lorge (1944) word count. Or, alternatively, he can ask his subjects to generate words in lists, which they will readily do.[4]

The word is not a concept popular among linguists for the good reason that it is not always identical with the minimal unit of encoding. The linguist says that we encode by morphemic units. The validity of his assertion becomes most apparent when we examine certain difficulties in scoring recall protocols. Scoring problems most frequently center around bound morphemes. What, for example, does one do if a subject writes "pleased" when "please" is the word originally presented to him? If we avoid morphemic duplication (having both "please" and "pleased" in the material), we can solve the problem arbitrarily by making separate tabulations which, for some purposes, can be combined.

In general, we will accept the word as the fundamental unit in going from isolated units to connected discourse, though we recognize the difficulties this entails. The concept of the word is not clear-cut enough to prevent ambiguous instances. Under certain conditions spelling, word length, and intra-word and interword similarities may all be important. As a first approximation, however, the word will do nicely as a basic unit.

## THE PROPERTIES OF WORDS IN FREE RECALL

In studies of free recall, I have concerned myself with three modes of varying the verbal environment of given units of material. These modes may be thought of as the routes which carry us from the unit in a random environment to the unit embedded in a highly structured environment. They are (1) variations in the frequency of occurrence of the words comprising the material presented for recall, (2) variations in the sequential environment of words comprising the test material, and (3) variations in the associative environment of the test words.

If we collect sets of words at random from some convenient source, say the Thorndike-Lorge (1944) count, we will find that our sample sets

[3] This point of view was largely stimulated by Z. Harris's (1955) paper on morphemic boundaries.

[4] It is interesting to note that if this is done, English orthography is not always followed. Students, quite properly according to theory, regard "inasmuch as" as one word.

will differ from one another in each of these three characteristics. Occasionally we will find a set that, by chance, is composed almost entirely of very high frequency words. Also, by chance, we may find a sequence of words in such a set that is rather like a sequence in ordinary English.[5] Finally, if we choose words at random, we may find, more frequently than we would perhaps have thought at first, that several of the words are associates of one another. However, it is much easier to produce sets that are "organized" in one or all three of these characteristics by deliberately selecting nonrandom sets. That is the technique generally employed in the studies discussed in the balance of this section.

*Association as a Variable*

We can examine the most general case of associative relationships within sets of words presented to individuals for free recall by calculating the average relative frequency with which all words on the list tend to be elicited as free associates by all the others. Such an index of the associative relationships among words in a list may be obtained from a matrix in which the words as stimuli for free association appear in the rows and the same words as responses in free association appear in the columns. The index itself I have called interitem associative strength (Deese, 1959a), and it is the mean of the column sums. It varies from zero, when items are completely unrelated to one another associatively, to 100 per cent (which theoretically could be obtained by many different arrangements of the fixed sum of the column sums). In actual practice I have, thus far, constructed lists with a maximum strength of about 30 per cent. A relatively high interitem matrix is presented in Table 2-1. It so happens that all 15 of the words in this table are high-frequency associates to "butterfly" by the Minnesota (Russell and Jenkins, 1954) norms. They are also, as it is easy to see, on the average rather high frequency elicitors of one another.

I have correlated the interitem associative indices for 18 different lists of words with the mean free-recall scores from these same lists. The lists themselves were 15 words long and were balanced for Thorndike-Lorge frequency. The recall scores were based upon 144 subjects (each list presented to 48), and the associative frequencies were obtained from an independent sample of 50 individuals. The obtained correlation between associative strength and recall is .88; the tendency for items to elicit one another as free associates is accompanied by a proportionate increase in free-recall scores.

The same study establishes a tendency for the highly organized lists to produce fewer extra-list intrusions, though this correlation is much

[5] This occurs in several of the first-order (random) sequences presented by Miller and Selfridge (1950).

lower ($-.48$). The correlation suggests, however, that there is sufficient convergence upon intra-list words to exclude extra-list intrusions from occurring with any great frequency in highly organized lists.[6] The extra-

Table 2-1

Interitem Associative Matrix for Fifteen High-frequency Associates of Butterfly*

| | Moth | Insect | Wing | Bird | Fly | Yellow | Net | Pretty | Flowers | Bug | Cocoon | Color | Stomach | Blue | Bees | Average |
|---|---|---|---|---|---|---|---|---|---|---|---|---|---|---|---|---|
| Moth | | 2 | 2 | | 10 | | | | 2 | 10 | | | | | | |
| Insect | 4 | | | | 18 | | | | | 48 | | | | | 2 | |
| Wing | | | | 50 | 24 | | | | | | | | | | | |
| Bird | | | 6 | | 30 | | | | | | | | | 2 | | |
| Fly | | 10 | | 8 | | | | | | 18 | | | | | | |
| Yellow | | | | | | | | | 3 | | | 11 | | 16 | | |
| Net | 2 | 2 | | 2 | | | | | | | | | | | | |
| Pretty | | | | | | | | | | | | | | | | |
| Flowers | | | | | | 2 | | | | | | 2 | | 2 | 2 | |
| Bug | 2 | 36 | | 2 | 4 | | | | | | | | | | 4 | |
| Cocoon | 16 | 6 | | 4 | | | | | | 10 | | | | | | |
| Color | | | | | | | | | | | | | | 20 | | |
| Stomach | | | | | | | | | | | | | | | | |
| Blue | | | | | | | | | | | | 10 | | | | |
| Bees | | | | 15 | | | | | 5 | | | | | | | |
| | 24 | 56 | 8 | 81 | 86 | 2 | 0 | 0 | 10 | 86 | 0 | 23 | 0 | 40 | 8 | 28.3 |

* The numbers presented in the table are percentages.

list intrusions that *do* occur in highly organized lists are very likely to be the same ones for different individuals. This fact is established by a cor-

[6] As Cofer points out in the discussion of this chapter, this assertion involves the implicit assumption that subjects are constrained in some way by list length.

relation of .55 between interitem associative strength and an index of interindividual agreement in extra-list intrusions.

The ability of associations to converge upon *particular* words in recall is demonstrated in another experiment (Deese, 1959b). Here the lists were so devised that they possessed varying average probabilities of eliciting particular words as intrusions in free recall. This was done by tabulating the frequencies with which all of the words on the list elicited some particular extra-list word as a free associate. The average of such frequencies for a particular list was used to predict the frequency with which that word occurred as an intrusion in the free recall of that list. The predicted intrusions correlated with their associative strengths .87 across 36 different lists given to 50 subjects.

These data provide an account of the role of associative processes in the maintenance of integrity in recall of well-organized material. The data on intrusions are particularly important in this respect, and these bear on the extent to which the associative processes are independent of the deliberate choice of mnemonic devices.

If we assume that the obtained relationship between interitem strength and recall demonstrates that individuals do make use of their latent associative repertoires to increase output in recall, the question then arises whether or not there is a selective process involved. Do individuals *edit* their associations before emitting them in recall? Such editing would presumably make the output in recall conform more to some memory trace of the list. The data on intrusions make this an unnecessary assumption. The appropriateness or inappropriateness of recall for a particular set of words is determined by the associative structure of the words themselves, not by any selection on the part of the individual doing the recalling. If the list is an organized one, the associations between the words in the list tend to dominate and restrict the range of outside intrusions. If the words on the list serve as associative stimuli for particular intrusions in recall, these appear in recall and thus systematically alter memory for the material. If the list is chosen from unrelated words, there is usually no convergence upon items in the list; thus correct recall is somewhat reduced, the reduction probably depending in absolute amount upon the number of words presented. In addition, it is unlikely that the unrelated words on such a list will converge upon any particular extra-list intrusions; thus the intrusions that do occur are scattered and idiosyncratic. Rather than being systematically altered, the memory for such a collection of words would disintegrate statistically.

The interpretation is further bolstered by the fact that it is difficult, not to say impossible, to increase an individual's recall by giving him an associative mnemonic device *outside* of the collection of words presented to him (Deese, 1959a). Apparently, if associations are to influence recall in an ordinary testing situation, they must occur spontaneously much as they occur in the free-association testing situation.

## Word Frequency as a Variable

It is a common assumption in psychological research on verbal behavior that word-frequency counts based upon printed sources reflect the probability of emission of words by individual speakers. This is probably an assumption that is wrong in detail, but like the adoption of the word as the fundamental unit of verbal behavior, it is sound enough for most practical purposes. In other words, word-frequency counts may be used to predict the outcome in any situation in which frequency of usage by individual speakers would be important.

While it is widely recognized that word counts themselves do not constitute independent experimental variables (Solomon and Howes, 1951), nevertheless the assumption is sometimes introduced that the word-count frequencies act as predictors in the way in which they do *because* they reflect the result of prior frequency of exposure or prior frequency of usage or some combination of these (Solomon and Postman, 1952). This assumption is not made in the present account. Therefore, word-frequency count is assumed to operate as a predictor of verbal behavior under appropriate test conditions because the counts reflect the probability of words appearing in an individual's behavior under the test conditions. Such an assumption is very close to that made by Howes (1954); in the present instance this idea stems from the more basic assumption that the encoding of words is, to a first approximation at least, an all-or-nothing process.

In studies of "approximation to English" the zero order of approximation is defined as a random sampling of words in the language. The first order is defined as a sampling of words weighted according to the frequency of occurrence of the words sampled. The result is that first-order lists are (1) composed of very common words and (2) likely to have frequent repetitions of the most common words, particularly in longer lists.

It is now well established (Miller and Selfridge, 1950; Sharp, 1958; Deese and Kaufman, 1957) that the largest difference in free recall between orders of approximation to English is between the zero-order (first-degree) and the first-order (second-degree) approximations. The data presented in Table 2-2 are typical of the recall for zero- and first-order lists of 50 words in length.

As a first hypothesis, I will state that the difference in free recall after a single presentation between these two orders of approximation is almost entirely the result of guessing behavior. The other possibility is to suggest that the occurrence of a list presented to an individual differentially raises in strength high-frequency compared with low-frequency items in the list. One difficulty in deciding between these alternatives is in the determination of the level of performance expected from guessing. I have not entirely solved this problem, but I have produced some data which suggest very strongly that the largest portion of the difference between the zero-order and first-order recall scores can be described in terms of guessing habits or some similar concept.

Table 2-2 shows that the mean number of items recalled immediately after a single presentation of a 50-item list at zero order is 7.9. At first order, the mean number of items recalled is 12.7. These numbers come from a comparison of each individual's recall protocol with the list presented to that individual, which, of course, is the usual technique of scoring. In addition, however, I also compared each recall protocol for each subject with the list displaced one from the correct list in the data book. This comparison was always to another list at the same order of approximation. Since the 10 lists at any given order were randomly arranged, this provided a measure of chance agreement between the words emitted in recall and those present on a *different list.*

While importations do occur in the recall of zero-order lists, and while occasionally the same word will occur on two different lists, these happen so rarely that the recall scored by the mismatch technique is essentially zero for zero-order lists. If, however, the same technique of scoring against the wrong list is used with the recall of first-order lists, the number "correct" on the average is 4.6. This is almost the difference in recall between zero and first order. Thus, if we accept the mismatch technique as yielding an estimate of the extent to which recall is determined by chance coincidences between what individuals emit in recall and any collection of words the same length of the same order of approximation, almost all of the large difference between first order and zero order is accounted for by chance.

These results suggest that, in part, the subjects did not remember more words on the first-order list, but that they were able to emit words in some match of the frequency characteristic of what they heard on the list. As one might expect, most of the coincidences between the words emitted by the individual subjects and the words on the mismatched list belonged to the class of function words. Table 2-2 shows that the total number of content words in *recall* for the first and higher orders of approximation varies from about 45 per cent to 65 per cent.[7]

The results of the mismatch comparison led me to wonder exactly what the precise relationship between word frequency and free recall was. The mismatch comparison itself implies, rather strongly, that mean free recall

[7] I have included the verbal auxiliaries and the copula in the class of function words.

ought to be independent of the general linguistic frequency of the words recalled. There are several features peculiar, however, to the zero- and first-order approximations. While, on the average, they differ in frequency, they are nonetheless mixed with respect to frequency; there are occasional words of low frequency in the first-order lists and there are occasional words of high frequency in the zero-order lists.

Therefore, it seemed worthwhile to study the relationship between frequency and recall when pure lists, varying in frequency, were used. I have collected data for lists in which words vary in frequency from 100 occurrences or more per million to lists in which the words have frequencies of 1 or 2 occurrences per million. The lists also varied in length from 12 words to 100 words. The data from this experiment are now available and two facts are clear: (1) there is a great increase in mean frequency of recall as list length is increased, and (2) there is an interaction between list length and frequency. There is a very small difference between lists of different frequencies when the lists are short (less than a single word); the difference between lists of different frequencies is very large, however, when the lists are long.

These are not extraordinary findings, but in view of my basic assumption that words, once encoded, should be equally well recalled, they need a word of explanation. I am in the position of trying to find ways to account for the fact that there is an interaction between list length and frequency. Originally, I had hoped that I would be able to make many of the obtained differences in recall associated with frequency disappear by applying a correction to the recall scores.

After a single presentation, recall usually contains some items which are phonetically or phonetically and morphemically similar to items on the list but not identical with items on the list. A strict scoring takes no account of these. Therefore, I classified all words occurring in recall but not on the presented list into three classes. The classes are (1) words that are morphemically and phonetically similar to a word or words on the list (for example, "silence" for "silent"), (2) words that are phonetically similar but not morphemically similar to words on the list, and (3) a miscellaneous class, very obviously largely made up of associates to words on the list.

I had hoped, of course, that there would be more "similar" intrusions for low-frequency than for high-frequency lists, so that when the two classes of errors based upon similarity were added to the words correctly recalled, the relationship between frequency and recall for the longer lists would disappear. This, however, was not the case. There is virtually no difference in the frequency of "similar" intrusions for the lists of different word frequencies. Intrusions do, of course, become very much more frequent for the longer lists, and they constitute a larger portion of the total words emitted in recall for the longer lists.

There is, however, a more important correction that must be applied to the obtained recall scores. This correction is based upon the interitem associative index, which is, we have seen, a potent predictor of the average correct recall. Even when words are collected at random, it happens surprisingly often that a fair number of the words are associates of one another. This, of course, is more likely to occur if the list is a long one than if the list is a short one. Thus, among other things, the average interword association index ought to increase as one increases the length of a list composed of randomly related items. Therefore, one would expect that individuals could recall a larger number of words for longer lists than for shorter lists even when those individuals have a fixed memory span. To be sure, there are many other features of longer lists that would lead one to expect better recall for them. For one thing, they take longer to present; thus there is more opportunity for rehearsal of early items during the presentation of later ones. However, if a considerable portion of the regression of mean recall upon list length can be taken out by interword association, it would provide evidence for the control of interword association over the list-length–frequency interaction upon recall.

The fact that there is such an interaction between word frequency and list length in determining recall is in accord with the predicted influence of interword association. Associations are more likely to be between familiar words than between unfamiliar ones. This is largely because the responses in association are high-frequency words by and large. Thus, the probability of associations occurring between random collections of high-frequency words is greater than the probability of associations occurring between random collections of low-frequency words.

Thus, I do not believe that there is any essential relationship between word frequency and free recall. Other things equal, it should be no more difficult to recall the word "giraffe" than the word "dog," though these come from the extremes of the word-count distribution.

## Sequential Relations

Sequential contingencies are obtained by tabulating words with respect to their verbal environments. Approximations to English provide the convenient, though not the most analytically useful, technique for studying them. The story about sequential dependencies and free recall is by now a very familiar one; there is a nonlinear but monotonic relationship between number of items correctly recalled and order of approximation to English. The increase in recall associated with the higher orders of approximation seems to be the result of sequential encoding (Deese and

Kaufman, 1957). While statistically the contingencies in sequentially associated passages are independent of direction, in recall they are apparently not, at least for English-speaking individuals. If the encoding were completely sequential, mean recall scores should permit a recovery of the rank order of occurrence of items in the list. This is roughly the case for fairly long lists when the data from a large number of individuals are averaged. The behavior of any one individual on any one list is best characterized, however, as consisting of short bursts or runs of sequentially related items with the bursts tending to be in serial order, though not necessarily so (Postman and Adams, 1960). The evaluation of these runs is statistically difficult because of the problem of estimating the influence upon chance levels of runs of the effect of simply recalling a greater proportion of the available pool of items with higher orders. Intuitive judgment, however, supports the claim for such runs.

It is also worth noting that the essential effects upon recall found with sequential contingencies in English also occur in Japanese (Masuyama, 1959), though the fact that thus far only short lists have been tested in Japanese has made the separation of sequential organization in the higher and lower orders more difficult.

This covariation of recall and statistical dependency gives rise to the same basic question we considered in dealing with the influence of associative strength and word frequency upon recall. We are faced with deciding how much of the increase in the number of items recalled that occurs with higher orders of approximation to the textual language is determined by the trace of the list itself, and how much by the guessing habits of the subjects. That is to say, we wish to know how much better the subjects' guesses correspond to the presented list for the higher orders than for the lower orders. Put another way, the problem is to determine whether subjects organize the lists they are recalling into chunks such that when a part of a chunk is recalled, the whole chunk is recalled (the completely encoded case: "How do you do."), or whether some of the interstitial material is supplied by construction or reconstruction of the passage based upon the subjects' appreciation of the grammatical and associative characteristics of the language itself.

There is no simple way of supplying answers to these questions from existing data, and perhaps there is none at all. Considering the possibility that the better recall with higher orders may be largely the result of the better chance an individual has of reconstructing the material correctly has led me to some more detailed analyses of the recall protocols for higher orders of approximation to English.

First of all, I have studied the recovery of deleted words from passages at different orders of approximation. I have asked 10 subjects to guess the words that belong in blanks inserted in place of words. There were

5 deletions in each passage and 10 passages at each order of approximation, so there were available 500 deletions at each order of approximation.
From the guesses of the subjects I have computed two indices for each
order of approximation; these indices covary rather closely and are probably measures of the same thing, with one being perhaps more reliable
than the other. One index is a measure of agreement between different
individuals in the words they supply at any given deletion. If all individuals supply the same word for a particular blank, agreement is 100 per
cent; if all individuals supply a different word, the agreement is zero.
The other index is simply the percentage of individuals supplying the
word actually deleted from the passage in question. Since this seems to
be a less stable index for the number of subjects used, the index based
upon interindividual agreement is the one presented in Table 2-2.

Table 2-2

Index of Inter-$S$ Agreement in Supplying Deleted Words from Lists of Different Orders
of Approximation to English and Mean Recall Scores from the Same Lists. Each List
Is Fifty Words Long; There Are Ten Lists at Each Order of Approximation,* and
Ten $S$s Used for Each List

|  | Order of approximation | | | | | | | |
|---|---|---|---|---|---|---|---|---|
|  | 0 | 1 | 2 | 3 | 4 | 5 | 6 | 8 |
| Per cent content words in recall | 100 | 45 | 61 | 64 | 63 | 62 | 65 | 66 |
| Index of agreement | * | 4.1 | 5.8 | 10.6 | 13.0 | 18.4 | 18.5 | 17.8 |
| Mean recall | 7.9 | 12.7 | 17.8 | 20.2 | 21.8 | 26.7 | 21.1 | 23.3 |
| Mean intrusion | 2.2 | 3.7 | 3.6 | 3.1 | 4.0 | 4.4 | 4.1 | 5.6 |

* No data were taken for zero-order lists on deletion agreement. It is a safe assumption that an obtained index would be close to zero.

Table 2-2 shows both the index of agreement and the average recall
data based upon 10 individuals recalling each of 10 passages at each
order of approximation. Both the index of agreement in supplying the
deleted word and recall increase rapidly with lower orders of approximation but hardly at all for higher orders of approximation. (Indeed,
they actually decline.) Thus, the relationship between recall and agreement in guessing about a missing word is linear; recall increases only so
long as individuals can guess with some accuracy.

Secondly, I have inquired about the ability of individuals to reconstruct a passage at a particular approximation to English after only a
relatively few critical words have been left (with the spacings between
words left intact). I have begun to collect data using 5, 7, and 10 words

from 50-word lists. The results thus far clearly show that it depends upon the particular words left, as indeed it should theoretically. When the remaining words preserve a good deal of the associative structure of the material (determined, unfortunately, thus far by content analysis), there is a regression between free recall and number of items correctly reconstructed by this technique. As in the previous case, the regression is linear. This is also to say, the number of items reconstructed is curvilinear against orders of approximation.

Thus, it seems likely that the number of items in free recall of such sequentially structured material goes on increasing only as long as the ability to reconstruct the passage from a few elements goes on increasing. Note that I am implying that individuals actually do construct material (guess) during recall. There are several pieces of internal evidence that suggest this to be so. For one thing, an occasional individual will, in recall, rearrange the list so as to get all instances of a particular function word grouped together. Secondly, as more context is added, individuals add intrusions in the form of additional function words. Intrusions at zero order are largely, though not entirely, content words. The much higher absolute frequency of intrusions for the higher orders (see Table 2-2) is the result of the addition of extra function words.

Thus, I would regard the recall of sequentially contingent verbal material as much more closely duplicating the process of remembering described by Bartlett (1932) than does the recall of material that is only associatively organized. This is so in the sense that the recall of sequentially contingent material (or, perhaps more generally, material that has some of the functional characteristics of ordinary language) is in part at least a *constructive* process. That is to say, something is manufactured by the individual doing the recalling, and the raw material for his manufacturing comes from his appreciation of the language after which the sequential pattern was modeled. In the case of purely associative material, the subject emits the content of his verbal organization without constructing something which models the pattern of the language he is speaking.

In summary, the recall of sequentially organized material is complicated and, no doubt, reflects the occurrence of several different processes. First of all, there is probably an associative framework, based upon the organization implied by the interword associative index. Between the elements of this organization the subject adds material which has the effect of constructing sequences according to the pattern of that individual's native language. In addition, the material presented to him becomes transformed by his own verbal organization. There are additions and substitutions based upon associations from within the material to outside of it, and there is a regression in verbal habits to the more frequently used and more easily available high-frequency words (Marbe's law again).

The data obtained thus far do not justify so sweeping a picture of the verbal processes involved in the recall of sequentially organized material, but what we have found thus far does not violate the picture, and, in addition, it has inspired the techniques of analysis tried thus far and those planned for the future.

## The Relation of Free Recall to Other Methods

The preceding discussion has been limited entirely to free recall. Given the limitations imposed by space and my chosen topic, I cannot provide a comparison of this with other methods of studying verbal memory. Suffice it to say that there are reasons for expecting that many of the relationships holding in free recall will not be found in paired-associates learning of the traditional variety, nor will they be found in studies of learning by serial anticipation. Indeed there is indication that actual reversals will occur.[8] We would expect this to be the case if the underlying mechanisms determining the emission of verbal units in the various cases were the same. The changes in results are expected on the basis of the changes in reinforcement contingencies and scoring techniques, not on the assumption of different verbal processes in the subjects.

## ON TO CONNECTED DISCOURSE

Thus far we have concerned ourselves with words. These words have occurred in sets presented to individuals for free recall. The sets we have called lists for the good reason that they really do not constitute connected discourse. We have dealt with sets that vary in word-count frequency, sequential dependency, and associative dependency. We have suggested that the actual words emitted by individuals after they are presented with such materials with instructions for free recall are determined by associative structures, constructions by the subjects based upon their own linguistic habits, and a kind of regression towards the general and familiar items in the language—a regression based upon the subject's representativeness as a speaker of educated American English.

It is clear, then, that for those lists for which recall is high, individuals do not retain more. It is simply that their associations to and guesses about the generalized aspects of the lists are more appropriate and hence yield higher scores by the criterion of stringent word-by-word scoring.

It is not difficult to see how the experiments with lists of unrelated and related words suggest certain analyses of the recall of connected dis-

[8] This assertion is based upon the comparison between free recall and the reconstruction of serial order made by L. Horowitz (1960).

course. Some of these I have suggested elsewhere. For example, the experiments on associative processes in recall have suggested that, in the process of recollection, words and groups of words will appear and disappear according to their associative connections with other words in the material. I have suggested (Deese, 1959b) that the changes described by Bartlett and others as leveling and sharpening may turn out to be simply a matter of the strength of contextual associations. Likewise, it may turn out that whenever group or population differences are associated with differences in recall, the underlying mechanism may be different distributions of associations in the populations in question.

Without belaboring the point, it is clear that there is ample room for exploring the influence of word frequency, interword association frequencies, grammatical constructions, etc., upon passages of connected discourse. It requires only that we are ingenious enough to construct material with the desired properties and that we are careful to decide the criterion of scoring that will be used.

Nevertheless, it is objected by those who see more in language than collections of words, no matter how well structured by association, that the real heart of the cognitive processes people use in dealing with connected discourse is lost in the analyses suggested thus far. Connected discourse is meaningful, it is said, and its meanings are embodied not only in the words but in the contextual relations of the material as a whole. These are infinitely more important, it is said, in determining the dynamic cognitive processes in verbal memory than all of the experiments on "lists" could suggest.

Such objections are, of course, in the last instance unanswerable. For this reason if for no other, some investigators in the area of verbal learning have resolutely shut themselves off from these kinds of objections. Perhaps because I am more tender-minded than others, I have not been able to do so. Thus, for a number of years I have worried about the problem of meaningful analysis in recall of connected discourse. I have tried a variety of techniques of content analysis in a vain effort to get away from the humble process of counting words and word sequences. I have tried a number of devices for getting objectively from counting words to evaluating content. In all of this, it had never occurred to me to study the correlations, via individual differences between subjects, between content scoring and word scoring. Very fortunately, this has just been done.

King (1960) has concerned himself with the problem of the intercorrelations between various measures of recall of passages of connected discourse. He used seven different scoring techniques. These were (1) scoring by number of idea groups recalled, (2) a kind of "cloze" scoring, (3) number of sentences recalled, (4) number of content words recalled,

(5) total number of words recalled, (6) total number of words *in* recall, and (7) a criterion based upon scaled judgments. King has used several stories (including the ubiquitous *War of the Ghosts*) and either one or two presentations (with only one recall).

Under all of the conditions he has examined, King's correlations have been extraordinarily high. The tables of intercorrelations obtained by King can be described quite well by a two-factor orthogonal structure. The residuals after the extraction of two factors are negligible. The two orthogonal factors can very well be represented by a rotation such that the factor axes are very nearly through the test vectors for number of content words recalled and the total number of words in recall. Such a projection yields an almost completely positive loading structure and predicts nearly all of the variance in the criterion scores.

Part of the simplicity of King's factor structure must be the result of limitations imposed upon the ways in which his subjects could differ from one another. One could imagine that particular kinds of material would invite subjects to differ with one another in ways to generate a stable third factor. Consider the case familiar to readers of essay examinations. Most examination writers vary in King's two factors; that is to say, they either have the right words or they don't (usually this means the words they found in the textbook), and either they write at length or they write briefly. Every once in a while, however, one runs across a student who writes "in his own words"—sometimes highly idiosyncratic words, but which, in the eyes of a judge, constitute adequate recall. Probably the incidence of verbally idiosyncratic behavior in recall could be increased by the use of particular kinds of passages. It is interesting to speculate how much idiosyncratic alteration could be predicted from word-association data.

The point of King's results for our purposes, however, is that highly subjective judgmental descriptions of recall can be reduced very nicely to words and word counts. It appears that over the range of variations tapped by the measurement of individual differences in this situation, we are not missing something fundamental by the kinds of counting we do. Furthermore, since the evaluation of recall is a social problem in itself, we may wish eventually to study such things as the relation between the association hierarchies in the scorer compared with the emitter of recall. Or, more generally, between the reinforcers and the scorers and the emitters.

## IN CONCLUSION

At this point I would like to recapitulate briefly the points I have been trying to make. I believe that the amount of material retained after one presentation must be very nearly the same for a wide variety of conditions. The variations in emitted recall are, in large part, accounted for by the associations evoked by the material and by the individual's attempt to construct new material based upon his native language. The short-range sequential dependencies found in approximations to English are probably not associations in the usual sense but are determined by the constructive or guessing processes. That is to say, in dealing with short-range dependencies, the individual knows that there are some "right" function words which belong, and the only problem is to guess which. The associations—the true associations—seem to be more nearly controlled by hierarchical strength in a given stimulus situation for a particular individual.

What about the unanswered questions? What about, for example, the interactions and compoundings between associations? The predictive strength of single associations has been surprisingly good, particularly since it is known that associative compounding does occur, but eventually we must deal with the compounding problem. We must also face the problem of describing the origin of the associative structures that work so well in the prediction of recall. This, however, constitutes a new and very large problem.

### REFERENCES

Bartlett, F. C. (1932) *Remembering: A study in experimental and social psychology.* New York: Cambridge.

Bousfield, W. A. (1953) The occurrence of clustering in the recall of randomly arranged associates. *J. Gen. Psychol.,* **49,** 229–240.

Deese, J. (1959a) Influence of inter-item associative strength upon immediate free recall. *Psychol. Rep.,* **5,** 305–312.

Deese, J. (1959b) On the prediction of occurrence of particular verbal intrusions in immediate recall. *J. Exp. Psychol.,* **58,** 17-22.

Deese, J., & Kaufman, R. A. (1957) Serial effects in recall of unorganized and sequentially organized verbal material. *J. Exp. Psychol.,* **54,** 180–187.

Ebbinghaus, H. (1885) *Über das Gedächtnis: Untersuchungen zur experimentelen Psychologie.* Leipzig: Duncker & Humblot.

Foley, J. P., & MacMillan, Z. L. (1943) Mediated generalization and the interpretation of verbal behavior: V. Free association as related to differences in professional training. *J. Exp. Psychol.,* **33,** 299–310.

Horowitz, L. (1960) Free recall and the ordering of nonsense syllables. Ph.D. dissertation, The Johns Hopkins University.

King, D. J. (1960) On the accuracy of written recall: A scaling and factor analytic study. *Psychol. Rec.,* **10,** 113–122.

Masuyama, E. (1959) Personal communication.

Miller, G. A., & Selfridge, J. A. (1950) Verbal context and the recall of meaningful material. *Amer. J. Psychol.,* **63,** 176–185.

Noble, C. E. (1952) An analysis of meaning. *Psychol. Rev.,* **59,** 421–430.

Postman, L., & Adams, P. A. (1960) Studies in incidental learning: VIII. The effects of contextual determination. *J. Exp. Psychol.*, **59**, 153–164.

Sharp, H. C. (1958) Effect of contextual constraint upon recall of verbal passages. *Amer. J. Psychol.*, **21**, 568–572.

Solomon, R. L., & Howes, D. H. (1951) Word frequency, personal values and visual duration thresholds. *Psychol. Rev.*, **58**, 256–270.

Solomon, R. L., & Postman, L. (1952) Frequency of usage as a determinant of recognition thresholds for words. *J. Exp. Psychol.*, **43**, 195–201.

Thorndike, E. L., & Lorge, I. (1944) *The teacher's word book of 30,000 words.* New York: Bureau of Publications, Teachers Coll., Columbia Univer.

Underwood, B. J., Runquist, W. N., & Schultz, R. W. (1959) Response learning in paired-associate lists as a function of intralist similarity. *J. Exp. Psychol.*, **58**, 70–78.

# COMMENTS ON PROFESSOR DEESE'S PAPER
## *Charles N. Cofer*[1]
### NEW YORK UNIVERSITY

I have found Dr. Deese's paper a valuable and stimulating one, and I am in essential agreement with him on many points. I am impressed by and am generally sympathetic to his emphasis on associative and frequency factors, but there are one or two points in this development which need clarification, or concerning which the evidence does not seem to be as clear as he seems to think it is. My comments will deal first with these issues, then proceed to some remarks concerning generalized habits and associations, and conclude with consideration of the problem of using verbal associative, normative data in the construction of connected materials. I shall not be concerned with Deese's animadversions toward the nonsense syllable or with his practical justification of the use of the word as a unit. On the latter point I agree; on the former point I daresay that others of you may wish to argue with Deese more than I do. I would add that two-syllable nonsense words, which can be pronounced, might avoid many of the disadvantages of the nonsense syllable.

## THE GUESSING HYPOTHESIS AND THE SELECTION OF ASSOCIATIONS

I should like first to look at the guessing hypothesis and the related problem of the selection of relevant associations, or the question of the editing subjects may or may not do in using their associations to construct their "recalls." There are several questions here.

[1] Some of the points made in this discussion arose during conversations concerning Deese's paper with Dr. David Rapaport.

The first arises in connection with the discussion on page 20 in which the assumption is denied that the more common words of our language are already learned better than uncommon words at the time an experiment is begun. What Deese means here, probably, is that it takes only a little experience with words for them to be equally well encoded, and that further practice, as with the frequent words, makes no further difference. But the further statement that relationships between the frequency of a word and psychological variables "occur only because common words occur commonly"[2] seems to me to mean nothing theoretically, although it is perhaps empirically sound. Surely there must be some differential effect in the subject of the fact that various words are experienced with various frequencies. Some term like response availability seems to me pertinent here, and I would use this term to indicate a hierarchical arrangement of words in a person's repertoire, the hierarchy representing variations in response strength due to frequency of experience. Association norms would be at least one indicator or measure of such a hierarchy, at least under certain conditions of elicitation. One of the complexities of verbal behavior arises, however, from the fact that such hierarchies can probably shift, at least momentarily, under the influence of stimulation, sets, preceding experience, and perhaps other factors. What I mean here is the demonstrated influence on response emission of such factors as partial structure and the recency or priming operation described by Russell (1959; also Storms, 1957; Storms, 1958), stimulus compounding, as described by several workers, and instructions. Some of the major problems in the study of connected discourse would probably be solved were the laws governing the shifts of response availability under these and other conditions well understood. But more of this later.

Under what conditions would the frequency-of-response-availability variable be primarily determinative of what words the subject would emit? I would think that an approximation to this state would be provided by the instruction, "Say all the words you can think of for the next number of minutes." While no one would probably come close to exhausting all the AA or A words he knows under such circumstances, he should certainly emit many words. I would think, for comparable time periods (whatever they are), he would generate many more than an average of 9 words, which, according to data Deese presents, is the mean number of AA words emitted from a list 25 words in length presented a single time.[3] On a pure guessing hypothesis, one would think many words than this would occur. My comments suggest the need for tempering a pure guessing hypothesis by stressing that

[2] This particular phrase was deleted by Deese from the revision of his paper.

[3] These data were presented in an earlier version of Deese's paper; cf. Deese (1960).

recall of lists probably depends on (a) a strengthening process through list presentation itself and (b) a limiting process set up by the instructions to recall the list.

The interesting data on recall of approximations to English, especially where scoring is by means of the wrong list, suggest again that if guessing is operative it is a restricted sort of thing. The subject must learn that there are function words, for example. Then he instructs himself to produce several of these. This suggests the operation of some sort of ordering process; i.e., the person tries to break up the mass of material presented into more manageable chunks for recall. No doubt he codes the function words in some simple way.

In conjunction with recall of orders of approximation to English, I should like to mention the findings obtained by Deese and Kaufman (1957) and by Deese (1957) with regard to serial position curves. For randomly arranged words, Deese and Kaufman found a serial position curve primarily indicative of recency, but as sequential organization was introduced in the higher approximations to English, the serial position curve shifted to show more effects of primacy and ultimately to the bow-shaped curve of serial-anticipation learning. What I wonder here is what "cue" in the sequentially organized material leads to the shift of recall to the earlier part of the sequence from the later part? Is it the presence of function words or some other property of the material? Analytic experiments on this point might provide us with leads as to the ways in which response to the organization of fully connected material occurs.

In summary of what I have said so far, I would say that Deese's guessing hypothesis is probably true, but only within the limits provided by the differential strengthening of certain aspects of the response hierarchy, the instructions, and whatever ordering or conceptualizing or chunking practices the subject engages in. If Storms's demonstration of priming of associations is a generalizable phenomenon, the failure of word frequency to show much relation to recall is probably due to the effects of differential strengthening of words already available in the potential-response hierarchy.

The role of free associations in recall brings us up against what is essentially the same problem that we have just discussed but in a different form. Deese's evidence (1959a; 1959b) that interitem associative strength relates closely to recall and to the occurrence of intrusions and that intrusions can be predicted from the free-association frequency with which the intrusion occurs to the words in a list seems to me a very valuable finding, but one which requires again some limiting statements. Deese himself stated this limitation when he wrote (1959b, p. 21) that "the probability of occurrence of an intrusion in recall is proportional to the average association strength of that item *in the context of the material being recalled . . ."* [italics added]. In a paper published earlier but written later than the one just quoted, Deese argued (1959a) that in recall it is not necessary to assume that people edit their associations. "The appropriateness or inappropriateness of recall will be determined by the list of words itself" (Deese, 1959a, p. 311); i.e., the convergence of free associations to items on the list or to particular extra-list words and not to others is taken as the basis on which recall for highly inter-associated items is superior and on which the failure of many extra-list intrusions to occur is explained. I do not understand this convergence hypothesis, and would like to see it spelled out more fully, especially in relation to the question of editing or nonediting of associations. If it means that strong but nonconvergent associations (extra-list) are suppressed by the convergent ones, that is one thing. Or does it perhaps mean that there is comparison of the nonconvergent with the convergent associations? There are, I think, difficult but basic questions of mechanism here which somehow must be clarified. Controlled association poses similar problems. Perhaps lists should be set up to maximize the presence of strong extra-list associations.

It is also puzzling that the absolute levels of mean recall of 15-item lists are not very high (Deese, 1959a, p. 302, table 2). The high-frequency lists (15 frequent K-R associates) generated a mean recall of 7.35 items, the low-frequency lists one of 6.08 items, and the zero-frequency lists one of 5.50 items. One would think that the high-frequency list would generate many more items in recall than just under half the 15 presented. Why doesn't the subject just run down the associative hierarchy and increase his recall substantially? We know (Cofer, 1958) that continued associations do yield a fairly close approximation to the kinds of responses which a group of subjects give by means of single associations (cf. also Rosen and Russell, 1957). Also, we know that subjects can increase the number of popular-association responses when they are instructed to do so (Jenkins, 1959). What this evidence means in the present context is that the associative hierarchy present in the list is probably available in large majority of people. Yet the recalls are but partial. What I suspect happens is that as a subject runs down the associative hierarchy, he gets other, stronger associations to the words he is thinking of, and they block out the weaker associations which were on the list. This may involve a recognition that the stronger associations were not on the list, the "editing" hypothesis. What we need here, I think, is another study in which after list presentation the subject is required to produce as many responses as there were words on the list, or perhaps to give any words he thinks of up to some limit. Such a procedure might provide clearer evidence concerning the question of the editing process.

Another possibility, of course, is that the fact of presentation of words in a list provides the kind of contextual situation which other evidence (Howes and Osgood, 1954; Jenkins and Cofer, 1957; Musgrave, 1958; Cofer, 1959) indicates modifies the associative structure which words as "isolated" stimuli yield.

At any rate, I am not convinced that the high correlations Deese has reported between measures of associative strength, amount of recall, and intrusions are necessarily inconsistent with the editing of associations. A further account of the mechanism of convergence of associations would be helpful here.

The things I have said in this section represent, for the most part, matters of which Deese is fully aware and which he has even mentioned in the paper under discussion. I have but reemphasized them, largely for purposes of getting more discussion of them.

## GENERALIZED HABITS AND ASSOCIATIONS

I rather suspect that when a subject hears or reads a piece of connected discourse a single time, he does in fact what Deese's subjects are being asked to do in the experiment outlined on page 25. That is, they probably "attend" to only certain of the words which the selection contains and build their "recalls" from these words by filling in on the basis of associations and generalized habits. In one of our experiments (King and Cofer, 1960), King and I found that after two presentations recall was better for a story which had few adjectives modifying nouns than it was for the same story (same length) when it had many adjectives modifying the nouns. Scoring here was for common content words alone, i.e., chiefly nouns and verbs. This finding could be interpreted as showing that the modified nouns did not "stand out" as well as the unmodified nouns. We need much further work which would tell us how people typically select, if they do, the parts of the material around which they will construct the rest of the recall. Gomulicki (1956) has suggested the scheme of actor-action-effect as the basis for such selection.

Deese's experiment outlined on page 25 is one possible approach to this problem. Another would be to get subjects to recall, following a presentation, in any order just the main words they are sure they remember. They would probably have some trouble breaking up the grammatical organization in order to do so. If this were true, it would be a tribute to the strength of the ordering and selecting habits they have developed. It would have considerable interest if materials could be written in which normal sequences or positions of events could be systematically varied. For example, perhaps the main event of the story could come at the end or in the middle rather than at the beginning as it often does. Such material might be difficult to set up and the recalls might be difficult to score, but we certainly need better information than we have concerning these kinds of habits.

One experiment which Segal and I have recently done (Cofer and Segal, 1959) is pertinent here. We selected six strong noun associates to each of four category names from the Connecticut norms (Cohen, Bousfield, and Whitmarsh, 1957). Six sentences were written, in each of which one noun from each category appeared. These sentences were read in order after instructions that only "something" about the six sentences was to be recalled. The subjects were asked to recall the nouns in any order. The recalls were scored for four-category clustering and for clustering by sentence. We found, in immediate recall, reduced four-category clustering (as compared to suitable controls) and a substantial, though short-lived, clustering on the basis of the sentences. What I think this shows is two fold. First, that parts of highly organized material can be recalled. Second, the sentence association was fairly strong, even after a single presentation, so that it was able to survive briefly in the face of the very strong category clustering that was present. Had we used weak associates of the category names, category clustering might have been very inferior to sentence clustering.

What I have tried to do in this section is to be a bit more explicit than Deese was in relation to the problem of generalized habits which pertain to connected material.

## ASSOCIATION NORMS AND CONNECTED DISCOURSE

It is obvious that to test some of the notions in Deese's discussion, it is necessary to write connected discourse to specification such that the effects of associative relationships can be tested. Let me make two general comments here.

First, our presently available norms (Russell and Jenkins, 1954) need extensive supplementation for this task. I have tried to write sentences with high-frequency and with low-frequency transitions, based on the Russell-Jenkins norms. It can be done, but the results are often odd and defy linguistic usage. In such a case, it is difficult to be sure that the only variable being manipulated is the associative one.

The other comment is that our recent studies (Jenkins and Cofer, 1957; Cofer, 1959), as well as those of Howes and Osgood (1954) and of Musgrave (1958), have shown that associative-response distributions may change considerably under context conditions as compared with no-context conditions. I shall not pursue this matter further here except to say that in the representation of associative norms in connected materials we have problems.

## REFERENCES

Cofer, C. N. (1958) Comparison of word associations obtained by the methods of discrete single word and continued association. *Psychol. Rep.*, 4, 507–510.

Cofer, C. N. (1959) Associative studies of complex clustering effects. *Tech. Rep. No. 26*, Contract No. Nonr-595(04), Office of Naval Research and University of Maryland.

Cofer, C. N., & Segal, E. (1959) An exploration of clustering in the recall of nouns embedded during presentation in sentences. *Tech. Rep. No. 27*, Contract No. Nonr-595(04), Office of Naval Research and University of Maryland.

Cohen, B. H., Bousfield, W. A., & Whitmarsh, G. A. (1957) Cultural norms for verbal items in 43 categories. *Tech. Rep. No. 22*, Contract No. Nonr-631(00), Office of Naval Research and University of Connecticut.

Deese, J. (1957) Serial organization in the recall of disconnected items. *Psychol. Rep.*, 3, 577–582.

Deese, J. (1959a) Influence of inter-item associative strength upon immediate free recall. *Psychol. Rep.*, 5, 305–312.

Deese, J. (1959b) On the prediction of occurrence of particular verbal intrusions in immediate recall. *J. Exp. Psychol.*, 58, 17–22.

Deese, J. (1960) Frequency of usage and number of words in free recall: The role of association. *Psychol. Rep.*, 7, 337–344.

Deese, J., & Kaufman, R. A. (1957) Serial effects in recall of unorganized and sequentially organized verbal material. *J. Exp. Psychol.*, 54, 180–187.

Gomulicki, B. R. (1956) Recall as an abstractive process. *Acta Psychol.*, 12, 77–94.

Howes, D., & Osgood, C. E. (1954) On the combination of associative probabilities in linguistic contexts. *Amer. J. Psychol.*, 67, 241–258.

Jenkins, J. J. (1959) Effects on word-association of the set to give popular responses. *Psychol. Rep.*, 5, 94.

Jenkins, P. M., & Cofer, C. N. (1957) An exploratory study of discrete free associations to compound verbal stimuli. *Psychol. Rep.*, 3, 599–602.

King, D. J., & Cofer, C. N. (1960) Exploratory studies of stories varying in the adjective-verb quotient. *J. Gen. Psychol.*, 62, 199–221.

Musgrave, Barbara S. (1958) Context effects on word associations using one-word, two-word and three-word stimuli. Paper read at East. Psychol. Ass., Philadelphia.

Rosen, E., & Russell, W. A. (1957) Frequency characteristics of successive word-association. *Amer. J. Psychol.*, 70, 120–122.

Russell, W. A. (1959) Bi-directional effects in word association. In J. J. Jenkins (Ed.), *Associative processes in verbal behavior: A report of the Minnesota Conference*. Minneapolis: University of Minnesota, Department of Psychology. Pp. 1–11.

Russell, W. A., & Jenkins, J. J. (1954) The complete Minnesota norms for responses to 100 words from the Kent-Rosanoff Word Association Test. *Tech. Rep. No. 11*, Contract No. N8onr-66216, Office of Naval Research and University of Minnesota.

Storms, L. H. (1957) Backward association in verbally mediated learning. *Tech. Rep. No. 18*, Contract No. N8onr-66216, Office of Naval Research and University of Minnesota.

Storms, L. H. (1958) Apparent backward association: A situational effect. *J. Exp. Psychol.*, 55, 390–395.

## SUMMARY OF CONFERENCE DISCUSSION

A major part of the discussion concerned the assertion by Deese that word-frequency variation, as revealed in word counts of the Thorndike-Lorge type, is not a suitable indicator of different degrees of learning of the words in question. While he agreed that a concept like response availability is a pertinent one, Deese pointed out that degree of prior learning as the determinant of response availability is commonly superseded by the context in which the word appears. That is, once encoded, words of different degrees of prior learning are all equally available in the context in which they are used.

Jenkins suggested that word frequency may reflect the number of stimuli or occasions for the occurrence of a word. If this approach were taken, the difference in frequency between the words *dog* and *giraffe* would be interpreted to mean that there are many more stimuli which serve as the occasion for the response *dog* than for the less frequent *giraffe*. Deese's assertion, applied to this example, means that given the appropriate stimuli, these two words, both being well encoded, are equally available, despite their quite different frequencies of spoken usage or of occurrence in printed material.

There was an attempt at further clarification of these points because there was some confusion as to which of two possible meanings was involved in Deese's use of the word "encoding" (Russell, Osgood, Noble). One meaning is the probability with which a response is given to a stimulus word in the case in which the two words are different. For example, in a free-association situation, subjects, by instruction, do not overtly repeat the stimulus word. Instead, a variety of other words is given in response to each stimulus, and these different response words vary in frequency of occurrence over a group of subjects. The other meaning refers to the situation in which a subject repeats or reads or otherwise takes notice of a stimulus word which has been presented visually or auditorially. In the word-association task as well as in paired-associates learning, such repetition is thought to be the subject's first response to the stimulus but to take place covertly. Deese's use of the word "encoded" follows this second meaning. Furthermore, he suggested that words are either encoded or not; there is not a gradient of "encodedness." Deese also seemed to believe that the acquisition of such units is an immediate occurrence rather than a gradual affair. While word-recognition experiments using tachistoscopic presentation have demonstrated variations in the recognizability of word stimuli as a function of their frequency of occurrence, length, and other variables, Deese's argument seemed to be that in learning experiments this kind of variation is unimportant; i.e., the recognizability or pronounceability of the words is guaranteed by the experimental conditions *if the words are encoded at all.*

Other terms which were used in the discussion and which seemed to be near synonyms of the word "encoding" as Deese used it were "response integration" and "patterning." There was wide agreement that some such process as these terms designate must go on in many verbal learning situations and that such response integrations are independent of, different from, and perhaps necessary precursors of the formation of stimulus-response associations. For example, if one is to associate the response *XCPTL* with a stimulus, it may be first necessary to establish this group of letters as a unitary or integrated response. Such establishing of the unit seems to be what Deese calls "encoding."

In passing, it should be pointed out that it is possible to conceive a stimulus-integration process as well as a response-integration process. (Osgood presented a matrix showing the relationships involved.) Stimuli vary in perceptibility as a function of frequency, length, and other factors, at least under conditions of impoverished presentation (achieved by brief exposures, blurring, dim illumination, etc.). Although it is not ordinarily done in learning experiments, one could study the development of associations between impoverished stimuli and responses which are uncommon letter sequences such as *XCPTL*. If this were done, the subject would have to learn to "recognize" the stimulus as well as to execute the response, and both integrations would probably be precursors to the formation of an association between the two.

There was discussion of the validity of Deese's point about the word-frequency variable. Reference was made to differences in speed and correctness in speaking high-frequency and low-frequency words (Osgood), to the greater amount of stuttering on words with low-frequency initial sounds than on words with high-frequency initial sounds (Goss), to the fine distinctions in speech sounds which must be discriminated through learning (Bousfield), and to the difficulty of some response sequences as skills as compared to others (Noble).

Objection occurred to Deese's use of the term "guessing" to describe the process whereby a subject constructs his recall of the material presented. Deese agreed that the term is a poor choice, as he did not mean that the process is a random one. Alternative terms suggested by the group were "untutored answering," "construction," "approximations," "production." There were arguments against Deese's conception that in recall a subject simply runs off his associations ("guesses") to the few words that he does in fact remember from the list. Postman pointed out that with delayed recall (one week) performance goes down, and importations, i.e., words not on the original list, do not increase; if there is guessing in Deese's sense this should not occur. He also pointed out that incidental learners do very little guessing, whereas they should be motivated to do so. To the objection that if subjects are running off associations, the number of their "guesses" might frequently exceed the number of words on the original learning list, Deese suggested that they probably do have some impression of list length at the time of list presentation and that number of words "recalled" does have some relation to length of list. (Wide individual differences occur.)

Postman suggested an experimental test of the guessing hypothesis. One group would be asked to recall a high-frequency word list presented to them, and the control group would be asked to *produce* a high-frequency word list. Would there be high commonality between the two sets of words given by the two groups? Deese predicted there would be, provided the instructions sufficiently restricted the control group. It was pointed out (Mandler) that what Deese is saying is that a given list of words will activate a subject's generalized language habits.

Deese agreed that the cues for reorganizing a list of words in recall are probably related to the occurrence of function words and of sequences of which they are a part.

Deese pointed out that he was using the convergence of associations not as a process but as a way of constructing word lists. He would agree that processes other than associative ones enter into ordinary connected material.

There followed a general discussion of a number of points relative to association. Jenkins observed that when Kent-Rosanoff stimulus-response pairs are scrambled and presented in a list, subjects do tend to put the pairs back together in recalling the list. The frequency with which pairs are recalled together is a function of their normative strength (Jenkins, Mink, and Russell, 1958). However, he would think that the repetition of the words during list presentation would raise these strengths, but this does not seem to occur. Deese referred to devices for boosting associative frequencies, as indicated in the study by Howes and Osgood (1954). Bousfield reported that recalls of lists made by breaking up three-word sentences (e.g., "Wasps sting painfully.") into randomly ordered series of words tend to show verbs following nouns. This sequential order occurs despite the fact that in the free-association situation verbs are seldom given as responses to nouns. There was agreement that more association norms are needed. Reference was made to work by Sue Ervin, who has been using sentences to collect normative information on associations, to work by Roger Brown (1958), and to the comparison of the norms collected by Woodrow and Lowell (1916) for children with those for the Kent-Rosanoff as applied to adults. Children tend to give sequential associations rather than associations which fall in the same form class as do the stimuli, which adults tend to give. Bousfield pointed out that in reading we usually encounter verbs following nouns. It is a problem that in free-association data the associations are often of the same form class as the stimuli. (For example, nouns occur as responses to noun stimuli.)

Deese suggested tentatively that free associations provide the framework of verbal discourse; i.e., associates occur every so often in such material, separated, for example, by function words. The processes that produce the words that occur between the associates, he thought, are probably not associative ones. Mandler, apparently responding to this idea, stressed the importance of studying the acquisition of syntactic structure. He said that he doubts that such learning occurs through the reinforcement of contiguous units. On the other hand, he urged that the problem be treated in an analytic and empirical way.

### REFERENCES

Bousfield, W. A. (1944) An empirical study of the production of affectively toned items. *J. Gen. Psychol.*, **30**, 205–215.

Bousfield, W. A., Herman, P. N., & Whitmarsh, G. A. (1959) The conditioning of verbal associative responses elicited by non-verbal stimuli. *Tech. Rep. No. 33*, Contract No. Nonr-631(00), Office of Naval Research and University of Connecticut.

Brown, R. W. (1958) *Words and things.* Glencoe, Ill.: Free Press.

Estes, W. K. (1950) Toward a statistical theory of learning. *Psychol. Rev.*, **57**, 94–107.

Howes, D. (1957) On the relation between the probability of a word as an association and in general linguistic usage. *J. Abnorm. Soc. Psychol.*, **54**, 75–85.

Howes, D., & Osgood, C. E. (1954) On the combination of associative probabilities in linguistic contexts. *Amer. J. Psychol.*, **67**, 241–258.

Jenkins, J. J., Mink, W. D., & Russell, W. A. (1958) Associative clustering as a function of verbal association strength. *Psychol. Rep.*, **4**, 127–136.

Russell, W. A., & Jenkins, J. J. (1954) The complete Minnesota norms for responses to 100 words from the Kent-Rosanoff Word Association Test. *Tech. Rep. No. 11*, Contract No. N8onr-66216, Office of Naval Research and University of Minnesota.

Taylor, W. L. (1953) "Cloze procedure": A new tool for measuring readability. *Journalism Quart.*, **30**, 415–433.

Woodrow, H., & Lowell, F. (1916) Children's association frequency tables. *Psychol. Monogr.*, **22**, No. 97.

# Chapter 3

# ACQUISITION AND USE
# OF CONCEPTUAL SCHEMES

*Albert E. Goss*[1]

UNIVERSITY OF MASSACHUSETTS

A conceptual scheme may be defined as one or more sets of categories or two or more variables that stand in ordinal, classificatory, or functional relationship to each other. It is the thesis of this paper that once conceptual schemes are acquired, they function as sets of mediating responses and stimuli with respect to the many particular items that are "placed within," "organized by," or "represented by" the conceptual schemes.

The first of the three sections that follow outlines some of the important historical roots of psychologists' interest in conceptual schemes and notes the specific antecedents of the notions to be proposed. The second section elaborates the definition of conceptual schemes and analyzes their acquisition. In the third section two major uses of conceptual schemes as mediating responses and stimuli are considered. Existing psychological concepts, principles, and data are obviously insufficient in form and quantity to permit definitive statements about either acquisition or use of conceptual schemes. With regard to these problems, therefore, this paper has a more modest goal: to suggest and illustrate a framework within which analysis and experimentation might profitably proceed.

## HISTORICAL ROOTS AND CONTEMPORARY INFLUENCES

Current viewpoints among psychologists concerning the origin and use of conceptual schemes have their modern historical roots in Descartes's "innate ideas" (1911, pp. 442–443) and Kant's "categories" (1881, p. 71) and "schemata" (1881, pp. 121–130) and in the treatment of abstraction advanced by Locke (1850, pp. 269–279). Descartes and Kant

[1] Bruce Gregory suggested the use of the Hertzsprung-Russell diagram for representing the stars and contributed to the proposed analyses in many ways. Mary E. W. Goss and Barbara S. Musgrave contributed useful suggestions.

saw the bases of organization of particular experiences as more given or innate than acquired; Locke regarded the bases as more experiential in origin.

In part by way of Lotze (Northway, 1940), Brentano, and Act psychology (Ward, 1920, p. viii), these conflicting orientations converged in the views of Ward. Ward's significance is that he with Head apparently inspired Bartlett's interest in schemata both as objects of investigation and as what Bartlett considered an explanatory principle (Bartlett, 1932, p. vii; 1958, pp. 140–141; Northway, 1940; Oldfield and Zangwill, 1942). Bartlett, both directly and through Oldfield and Zangwill (1942) as well as Northway (1940), has been of significance in directing attention to conceptual schemes as phenomena whose acquisition and use require further analysis and investigation. In their emphasis on organizing forces and principles, Koffka (1935, pp. 564–566, 611–612), Köhler (1929, pp. 301–348), and Wertheimer (1945, pp. 189–192) have had a similar influence, as has Katona (1940). These forerunners, however, have tended to treat conceptual schemes and related notions as "givens" whose effects are of primary concern. Consequently, theory and experimentation on the acquisition of conceptual schemes have been neglected.

Two other contemporary influences are of greater significance for the analysis of the acquisition and use of conceptual schemes proposed here. The first of these influences comprises functionalistic-behavioristic accounts of rote-learning phenomena (e.g., Irion, 1959; McGeoch and Irion, 1952; Osgood, 1953; Underwood, 1949; Woodworth and Schlosberg, 1954). The second of these influences are stimulus-response explanations of conceptual behaviors involving mediating responses and stimuli. Included here, as is noted in greater detail elsewhere (Goss, 1961), are, one generation removed, Meyer, Watson, and Dashiell; more recently, Miller and Dollard and Cofer and Foley; and most recently, Baum, Kendler and associates, and Osgood.

The explanatory concepts and principles employed in the present analysis appear to be plausible extrapolations from other seemingly less complex and certainly better-investigated domains. Thus, their adequacy as such, or as supplemented by any requisite additional concepts and principles, must be demonstrated by means of studies in which subjects acquire and use conceptual schemes. Underwood's "exposition of an orientation around which certain research on thinking can be carried out" (1952, p. 209), which also consisted of plausible extrapolations and resultant proposals for experiments, was the model for the realistic objective of the present paper: exposition of an orientation around which certain research on conceptual schemes can be carried out. This orientation assumes, however, that conceptual schemes are acquired, though the process may be complex, and that, as conceptual schemes are used, they often function as sets of mediating responses and stimuli.

## ACQUISITION OF CONCEPTUAL SCHEMES

### Definition

As has been indicated, a conceptual scheme is defined as one or more sets of categories or two or more variables in ordinal, classificatory, or functional relationship. Because of the very general form of this definition, some illustrations may be in order. Ordinal relationships are exemplified in outlines for speeches which advise, "Say what you are going to say, say it, and say what you have said," in Lloyd and Warfel's (1956, pp. 137–145) "basic statement-patterns," and in Miller's (1958, p. 486) "finite state generator." Figure 3-1 shows one of many possible examples

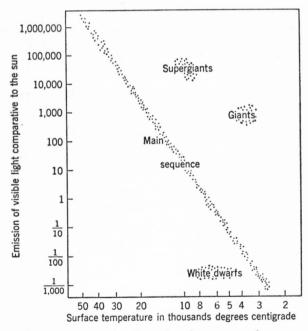

Fig. 3-1. Classificatory-functional relationship between surface temperatures and emission of visible light by stars. (*Modified from the Hertzsprung-Russell diagram in Hoyle, 1957, p. 163.*)

of classificatory relationships: there surface temperature and "emission of visible light comparative to the sun" are the dimensions of a classification of stars. Depending on their particular combination of temperature and light emission, stars are labeled "white dwarfs," "giants," "supergiants," or "main-sequence." The relationships in Figure 3-1 might also be regarded as functional relationships, in which the main trend is a direct relationship between temperatures and light emission to which the clusters of points labeled "white dwarfs," "giants," and "supergiants" are exceptions. More generally, in the simplest cases, functional relationships are exemplified by verbal, graphic, and logical-mathematical statements about the covariations of two sets of categories, a set of categories and a variable, or two variables.

From the definition and these illustrations it should be obvious that the components of conceptual schemes are sets of categories or variables as well as ordinal, classificatory, or functional relationships. Less obvious, perhaps, because so taken for granted, is that the sets of categories or variables may be relevant, irrelevant, or fixed with respect to the relationships. A set of categories or variables is relevant if it is involved in the relationships of a particular conceptual scheme, and irrelevant to that scheme if it is not so involved; it is fixed ("held constant") if, in the conceptual scheme, it is represented by only one category of the set of categories, or, in the case of variables, by only one value of the variable. Moreover, and quite apart from relevance, sets of categories or variables in conceptual schemes are designated by names, as are the subcategories or values of variables they subsume. For example, "sex" names the set of categories, and "male" and "female" name the specific subcategories; "temperature" and "light emission" name the variables, and "white dwarf," "giant," etc., name particular combinations of segments of each variable. More generally, numbers are the names for successive values of variables.

It should also be clear that ordinal, classificatory, and functional relationships can be—and generally are—represented by sentences in ordinary English (or any other language), by diagrams and models, and by statements constituted of the symbols of formal logic or in the form of mathematical equations. Thus, an ordinal relationship stated in ordinary English would have a form such as "Basic statement pattern one is noun, verb, noun." Diagrammatic representation of the sentence as *NVN* involves only a transformation to the letters or symbols $N$, for nouns, and $V$, for verbs.

Classificatory schemes can also be described in ordinary English. Thus, "Stars with surfaces temperatures from 5,000 to 10,000C which emit between one-thousandth and one-hundredth of the light emitted by the sun are 'white dwarfs.' Stars of lower surface temperatures which emit much more light and stars of higher surface temperature which also emit more light are 'giants' and 'supergiants,' respectively." The specific values for the ranges of surface temperatures and light emission involved in the latter two specifications might be given. In the graphic presentation of the classificatory relationship in Figure 3-1, the classification is by naming the swarms of points concentrated in particular areas of the figure. The mathematical form might be $L = aT + k$ ($L =$ light emission, $T =$ temperature), supplemented by specifications of three pairs of the ranges of $T$ and $L$ values for the three groups of exceptions, along with the names for each of these pairs of ranges. Thus Figure 3-1 can also be regarded as depicting a functional relationship between surface temperatures of and light emission by stars.

Classificatory relationships can be represented by "$n \times n$" tables as well as by "tree diagrams" (Kenemy, Snell, and Thompson, 1957, pp. 25–28) which begin with the one most general term and branch progressively as successive bases for differentiation are introduced. Functional relationships are, of course, often shown in tables or in both tables and figures. Atomic models in two or three dimensions, vectors, and circuit diagrams are among the additional devices for depicting both classificatory and functional relationships.

Conventional concept-formation tasks (Goss, 1961) and tasks requiring the serial reproduction of forms or stories (Bartlett, 1932) are often regarded as involving or exemplifying conceptual schemes. In two-stage paradigms of concept-formation tasks, the relationships of mediating responses to initiating stimuli and to each other can be considered conceptual schemes as that term has been developed here. However, the initiating stimuli have usually been relatively simple, directly observable things, properties, and relations or words labeling such things, properties, and relations. Conceptual schemes in this paper include not only such stimuli but also, and more importantly, sets of categories and dimensions which are relatively more abstract or derived. The analysis of acquisition that follows, therefore, draws little from the experimental literature on concept formation.

### Acquisition

In analyzing the acquisition of conceptual schemes at least three problems must be considered: (a) learning modes of representing conceptual schemes; (b) learning names for sets of categories and for categories of such sets, and names for variables and values of variables; and (c) learning to combine the modes of representation with names for sets of categories and variables in particular conceptual schemes. The first and second of these problems are, of course, embodied in the third. However, because some of the distinguishing features of modes of representation can be noted more readily, and because both modes of representation and names can be acquired somewhat independently of each other, these two problems are treated separately before combining them in the treatment of the third problem.

*Learning Modes of Representing Relationships.* That learning modes of representing relationships need not be related to learning specific names is suggested by courses in logic and mathematics, where modes of representing ordinal, classificatory, and functional relationships are presented to students and acquired by students largely without reference to specific sets of categories or specific variables. Further, in more advanced courses in logic and mathematics there is even less didactic use of specific illustrative sets of categories or variables.

Lloyd and Warfel's (1956) basic statement patterns have been cited as illustrative of ordinal conceptual schemes, and may be examined in terms of features which might be learned and procedures for such learning. The major categories of the conceptual schemes are $N$ for noun, $V$ for verb, $_LV$ for linking verb, $VG$ for verb group, $A$ for adjective, $A/$ for adverb, and *Prep.* for preposition. These categories occur in different combinations and orders which are the basic sentence patterns. Each of these conceptual schemes or basic sentence patterns, and also names for each one, could be learned without regard to the category for which each of the component letters might be considered a convenient abbreviation or symbol. In addition, certain relationships among them could also be learned. These are: $N$ always appears in the first position; $V$, $_LV$, or $VG$ always appears in the second position; with one exception, $N$, $A$, *or* $A/$ appears in the third position and always last; and the longest sequence has but five of the symbols. Acquisition of the basic statement patterns might be investigated by means of a paired-associates procedure in which the combinations and orders of the symbols were stimulus and response members on randomly alternating trials, and the number-letter labels $1$, $2$, $3A$, $3B$, $3C$, $4A$, $4B$, $5A$, $5B$, and $6$ on those same trials were either response or stimulus members, respectively. In this fashion the 11 combinations and orders of the symbols and the 11 labels would be acquired, as would bidirectional associations between the combination and label of each of the 11 paired associates.

Classification can be accomplished by means of matrices, tables, and tree diagrams which, along with ways of extending them from 2 to $m$ sets of categories or variables, can also be acquired. Functional relationships, as has already been noted, can be represented by means of tables, vectors, circuit diagrams, and other devices. But perhaps the most frequently used conceptual schemes are those based on rectangular coordinates and curves or on equations for such coordinates. They therefore deserve detailed consideration.

Rectangular coordinates can be represented and learned somewhat independently of the curves or equations for such coordinates. That is, the dimensions $x$ and $y$ and their graphic representation and also the concept of points can be developed prior to and without going on to equations relating $y$ to $x$ and to plots of those equations as curves.

Equations and the use of rectangular coordinates to plot curves based on those equations introduce the interrelated features of forms of specific functions (e.g., linear, exponential, or logarithmic), of characteristics of functions and curves (e.g., intercepts, slope, acceleration, asymptotes, maxima and minima), and of names for functions and curves which exhibit particular combinations of characteristics (e.g., negative growth, negative decay, sigmoidal). These features of equation and curves are learned, as are various relationships among them (e.g., inverse functions, combining functions). Further, responses of examining the equations for and identifying the constants which specify intercepts, asymptotes, and rates are also acquired. Thus, the acquisition of knowledge of rectangular coordinates and of features of equations and curves for such coordinates are well-established facts of human learning and performance.

These facts of learning and performance, however, constitute only a variety of phenomena which must ultimately be explained by means of concepts and principles of general learning theory, elaborated, perhaps, to deal with more relatively complex stimulus-response relationships. Although it may be possible to suggest some of the classes of variables which should influence acquisition of knowledge of rectangular coordinates and of features of the equations and curves for such coordinates, the details of the effects on acquisition of these variables, either separately or jointly, are largely unknown or speculative. Therefore, the suggestions for possible investigatory procedures and variables which follow are to be regarded more as programs for research to confirm the relevance of principles and to discover additional principles, rather than as explanations of the acquisition of modes of representing relationships.

Shown in Figure 3-2 are the materials for a task of learning various features of graphic representations of monotonic functional relationships between two variables, $x$ and $y$. The eight specific curves might be the stimulus members, the response members, or alternately the stimulus and the response members of a paired-associates task. For the eight curves as stimuli, the responses might be saying "positive slope, no change" for curve 1$a$; "negative slope, no change" for curve 1$b$; "positive slope, negative acceleration" for curve 2$a$; "negative slope, negative acceleration" for curve 2$b$; "positive slope, positive acceleration" for curve 3$a$; "negative slope, positive acceleration" for curve 3$b$; "positive slope, positive then negative acceleration" for curve 4$a$; and "negative slope, positive then negative acceleration" for curve 4$b$. Alternatively, the preceding responses could be stimulus members and the curves could be response members; drawings of the curves would then be the responses which were to be mastered. The task might be complicated by learning that the "curves" of 1$a$ and 1$b$ were "linear" and the remaining six were "complex," and also that the curves of *2a*, *2b*, and *4a* are sometimes called "negative-growth," "negative-decay," and "S-shaped" (ogival, sigmoidal) functions, respectively.

*Learning Names for Sets of Categories or Variables.* Names for sets of categories and subcategories can apparently be acquired with partial-to-complete independence of the learning of modes of representing relationships among the categories. Names for variables and for values of those variables can also be acquired with such partial-to-complete independence.

The stimuli for such learning may be instances of classes of relatively

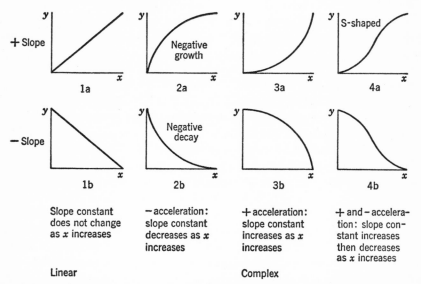

FIG. 3-2. Graphic representation of eight classes or prototypes of monotonic functional relationships between two variables *x* and *y*.

simple, directly observable objects, properties, and relations. Or the stimuli may be patterns consisting of such objects and properties in observable relations to each other. Very often, however, the stimuli are words referring to classes of observable things, properties, and relations, or to patterns of such words. Words that name patterns can themselves enter into patterns with other similar words. Thus, there can be generated "pyramids" or "hierarchies" of words (defined constructs, defined concepts) in which each of the words at a given level refers to two or more words in some relation on the level just below. The observable relations among objects and properties may be left-right, up-down, coincides–doesn't coincide, etc. For relations among words, in addition to logical terms such as "and," "or," "not," and "if . . . then," there may be mathematical terms for operations such as "$+$," "$-$," "$\times$," "$\div$," and "$\sqrt{\ }$."

When the stimuli presented are not words but directly observable things, properties, and relations, the paradigms for explaining the acquisition of names for each set of categories and their subcategories are those for concept-formation tasks with sets of initiating stimuli that are combinations of values along dimensions or combinations of common elements or relations with variable features. When the stimuli are words that refer to directly observable things, properties, and relations, the appropriate paradigms for explaining the acquisition of names for each set of categories and its subcategories are those for concept-formation tasks in which the initiating stimuli are sets of words whose subsets are specified by their arousal of common responses.

Analyses of the role of verbal mediating responses in the acquisition of conceptual behaviors with each of these three types of sets of initiating stimuli have been developed elsewhere (Goss, 1961). While those analyses are incomplete, they do provide first steps in explaining the various instances of acquiring names for sets of categories and subcategories and for variables and their values.

Other instances of the acquisition of such names, however, may not be as readily assimilated within such concept-formation paradigms. For example, sets of categories and variables are often defined by logical-mathematical equations in which the *definiendum* is on the left and the *definiens* is on the right in the form of two or more symbols in logical or mathematical relation to each other (Hempel, 1952). Accompanying such definitions is a series of further definitions of the symbols, and the entire definition may be repeated in what, except for technical terms, approximates ordinary English. Since there is only a single stimulus, the *definiendum,* and the primary task is the acquisition of a chain of responses which stipulates the *definiens,* this task is somewhat different from those considered in the concept-formation paradigms. The most pertinent principles are presumably those for the explanation of acquisition, transfer, and retention of connected material (Cofer, 1943; Miller, 1958; Welborn and English, 1937).

*Learning Particular Conceptual Schemes.* As has been suggested, modes of representing relationships of conceptual schemes are often acquired somewhat independently of learning a particular conceptual scheme. Also, names for sets of categories and subcategories and names for variables and their values are often acquired independently of the acquisition of both modes of representing relationships and particular conceptual schemes.

The degree of prior mastery of the representational modes and names of particular conceptual schemes, however, may vary widely, and there may be both positive and negative transfer to learning some particular conceptual scheme. At this stage of the development of analyses of con-

ceptual schemes, the role of varying degrees of prior mastery of representational modes and names, as well as the role of transfer from such
mastery to the acquisition of particular conceptual schemes, can be suggested most easily by means of a specific example. Selected for this purpose is the functional relationship between the temperature and light
emission of stars shown in Figure 3-1.[2]

In addition to a diagram, the relationships in Figure 3-1 could be
described entirely in sentence form or could be presented by means of
an equation, supplemented by a description of the "white dwarf," "giant,"
and "supergiant" exceptions to the main sequence given by the equation.
With respect to subjects' prior mastery of the components, there might
be differences among these three ways of representing the conceptual
scheme. For example, the verbal statement that "as temperature increases
light emission increases" might be more familiar than an equation of the
form $L = aT + k$. Conceivably, the verbal statement might even be more
familiar than the diagonal from top left to bottom right of Figure 3-1,
particularly since, by tradition, the abscissa values of this particular diagram decrease from left to right rather than increase.

Because of these varying degrees of initial familiarity, assuming that
the difficulty of the tasks is otherwise equal, differences in the number of
trials to master each mode of representing the relationship as well as
differences in the retention of those modes would be expected. To the
degree that prior training had involved experiences with transformations
from one to another among verbal, diagrammatic, or mathematical representations, mastery of the relationships in Figure 3-1 shown in a single
mode might involve almost complete transfer to mastery of the relationship expressed in the other two modes. There might then be no differences among modes with respect to retention.

However, some negative transfer to acquisition involving any of the
three modes might arise from at least three sources. One source is that
most relationships encountered previously will have had increasing
values from left to right along the abscissa. Because this more general
convention is not the convention for this particular conceptual scheme,
the direct relationship between temperature and light emission looks like
an inverse relationship. Thus, the two "increases" of the verbal statement,

[2] This example has several advantages. First, it can be regarded as involving classificatory or functional relationships. Second, these relationships are complex enough
to be interesting but not so complex as to be overwhelmingly difficult. Third, while
temperature and light emission are relatively familiar terms, specifications of the
temperature of and light emission by stars present problems not usually encountered
in specifications of the temperature and light emission of bodies on earth. Thus, an
understanding of specifications of temperatures of and light emission by stars requires
some new learning. A fourth advantage is that the components of this conceptual
scheme have already been described in some detail.

the implicit "+" of "*a*" of the equation, and the diagonal downward to the right might be subject to interference from the terms "decreases," "−," and a line upward to the right, respectively. A second source is the three exceptions to the main-sequence stars. They might prove troublesome because they are unusual. They might also cause difficulties because they are asymmetric both with respect to the number above and below the line and with respect to the shapes of those areas. A third source of negative transfer is that depicting the diagonal in terms of points alone might conflict with conventions of presenting points and a fitted line or just a fitted line without points.

The criterion of mastery of Figure 3-1 might consist of accurate reproduction of the trend and envelope of the points decreasing diagonally and also of the peripheries or contours of each of the three exceptions. There might be positive transfer to the reproduction of symmetric forms and negative transfer to the reproduction of asymmetric forms. Further, the curves of retention for reproductions of the symmetric and asymmetric forms might differ (Bartlett, 1932, p. 182; Woodworth and Schlosberg, 1954, pp. 773–776).

If just the names "temperature" and "light emission" (or the longer phrases for which these are abbreviations) were to be learned as labels for the abscissa and ordinate, this aspect of the acquisition of the conceptual scheme of Figure 3-1 would probably involve only positive transfer based on some prior familiarity with the terms. Were numerical values also to be acquired, the task could become more difficult, not only because of the larger number of responses but also because the numbers involved might be considerably larger or in a different form than the numbers usually encountered along the abscissas and ordinates of figures. Hence there might be some negative transfer. Were the temperature and light emission of stars differentiated from the temperature and light emission of other objects by mediating responses of "surface temperatures of stars" rather than "temperature," and "light emission by stars" rather than "light emission," such negative transfer should be minimized or eliminated.

The measurement—or, strictly speaking, estimation—of the temperature and light emission of stars requires equations and values obtained with instruments different from those used for the measurement of these features of terrestrial objects. If individuals who were relative neophytes with respect to physics and astrophysics were required to learn these estimation procedures, because of little positive transfer from prior learning to the acquisition of many components of the task, such learning would be slow. The complexity of the task and possible negative transfer stemming from other meanings of "temperature" and "light emission" might also result in relatively slow acquisition. The concepts and principles of learning involved would presumably be those applicable to the acquisition of long chains of responses of connected discourse, where positive transfer to segments of the chain is generally low; there might be some negative transfer to other segments of the chain or to the phrasing of the *definiens*.

## USE OF CONCEPTUAL SCHEMES

Acquisition of a conceptual scheme may be an end in itself. For example, all that a casual reader of Hoyle (1957) may wish to learn is accurate reproduction of Figure 3-1 and of any accompanying explanatory statements. Many conceptual schemes are learned for further use, however, and the further use often has two purposes.

The first purpose is to provide an arrangement within which many individual objects or events may be located or represented as particular cases of combinations of specific subcategories of sets of categories or of specific values of variables. For example, students just beginning to learn astronomy might wish to place individual stars new to them in their proper place in Figure 3-1, to label those stars as "white-dwarf," "main-sequence," etc., and to remember both their locations and labels. Seasoned astronomers might wish to do the same with newly discovered stars. The second purpose is to modify the particular conceptual scheme. Of various possible modifications, two are of interest here: changes in functional relationships between two variables and extension of a two-variable conceptual scheme to three variables.

Both uses of particular conceptual schemes involve acquisition and retention of additional stimulus-response relationships; the problem at hand is to specify the role of conceptual schemes in these processes. Provisionally at least, it is suggested that a primary function of conceptual schemes is as mediating responses and stimuli that influence both acquisition and retention of the additional relationships. This proposition is examined and exemplified below with respect to the two uses of conceptual schemes just noted, namely, characterizing objects and modifying schemes.

*Characterizing Particular Objects.* A few examples in which conceptual schemes serve as mediating responses and stimuli may be useful before turning to a more general statement of presumed sources of facilitative and inhibitory effects of such schemes on acquisition and retention of particular relationships.

Consider first a situation in which a seventh-grade child, who has had some training in English grammar and its use, is assigned the task of writing about some gift he received that he liked very much. Such a composition might well begin with a sentence that says the child has been given some gift by somebody. Writing the initial sentence entails the occurrence of written or typed responses: words or phrases for the "receiver," the "gift," the "somebody," and the "being given." Further, those responses must be written in some order—hopefully, in a "correct" order.

In the writing or composition of "thoughts" or "ideas" such as being given something by somebody, basic statement patterns may function as mediating responses and stimuli which influence the orders in which words or phrases are written.[3] Figure 3-3 diagrams the presumed me-

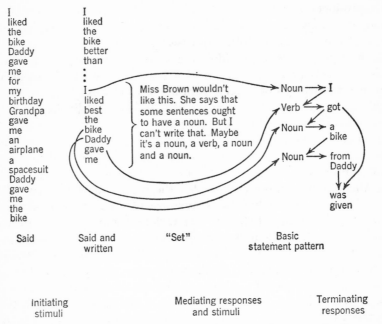

FIG. 3-3. Hypothesized chain of stimuli and responses of writing the first sentence of a composition about a gift which was received and liked. Successive responses which then serve as stimuli are downward from the top for the first two columns and for the sentences "Miss Brown . . . and a noun." For the last two columns the sequence weaves right, down left, right, down left, etc., and terminates with "was given."

diating role of basic statement patterns in the sequence of stimulus-response relationships involved in writing a sentence such as "I was given a bike by Daddy." The initiating stimuli are conceived as nouns, verb forms, adjectives, adverbs, etc., which are first said out loud or implicitly

[3] The "may function" recognizes that some sentences result from rote memorization or "chance" rather than from composition, and that composition of sentences by the young—and even by the more experienced—does not always or perhaps even frequently occur on the basis of partially or wholly explicit rules.

in varying combinations and orders. Some of these words may be written down, particularly after the child has had time to "think" and "remember" gifts that have been received. A tentative terminating response is writing a sentence from which the child proceeds to the composition of a further sentence. The child may, of course, return to rewrite each sentence before that sentence is left in what he considers final form. Such final forms are here regarded as completed terminating responses.

The first column of words in Figure 3-3 are words said out loud or implicitly as the child begins to "think" about and to "remember" words pertinent to the assigned theme in general and to an initial sentence in particular. (Probably this illustrative chain and those in the second column are much more orderly than most chains which occur when children are "thinking.") The second column in Figure 3-3 consists of two chains of words in which, as each word is said, the word is written. The child rejects the first of these written chains because it doesn't look like a "correct" sentence. The second chain is the point at which basic statement patterns might occur as mediating responses and stimuli. The child's cue might be the still unusual form of the chain of words which elicits a response such as "Miss Brown wouldn't like this. She says that some sentences ought to have a noun, a verb, and a noun.[4] But I can't write that. Maybe it's a noun, a verb, a noun, and a noun." At this point, the child has said an approximation of the basic statement pattern $N$ $VG$ $N$ $Prep.$ $N$, and he might then write "I," mediated by the response "noun"; "got," mediated by the response "verb"; "a bike," mediated by the response "noun"; "from Daddy," mediated by the response "noun" but, due to an already-learned preposition-noun sequence, written as "from Daddy." "Got" might then be changed to "was given" and, although grammatically incorrect, "from Daddy" might remain. After telling himself that the sentence " 'I was given a bike from Daddy' is like teacher says it should be," and perhaps checking against the "noun, verb, noun, noun" statement pattern, the child might proceed to the next sentence. Left at this point, "I was given a bike from Daddy" would be a tentative terminating response. Should the sentence remain unchanged in the completed composition, it would be a completed terminating response.

In actual fact, very few seventh-grade children may use such "basic statement patterns" consistently, and some, for all practical purposes, may never use them. Further, they will not have learned such patterns in the form of Lloyd and Warfel's symbols but rather as phrases such as "noun, verb, noun, noun" or "subject, verb, object, preposition, object." It is suggested, however, that when sentences are being composed rather than written down as products of rote memorization, some approximations of basic statement patterns function as mediating responses and stimuli

[4] The conventional noun-pronoun distinction is ignored.

which, in part, determine the order of words in tentative and completed terminating responses. Moreover, with more explicit training in the forms and uses of such basic statement patterns, it seems possible that children might be able to write grammatically correct sentences more often and with greater ease than without such explicit training. Should this seem unlikely in the case of first languages, it is Dunkel's suggestion that just such mastery of basic sentence patterns is prerequisite to effective use of second languages (1948, p. 54).

A more complicated example is found in Figure 3-4, which presents a

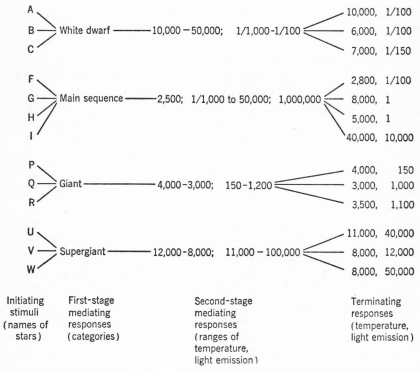

| Initiating stimuli (names of stars) | First-stage mediating responses (categories) | Second-stage mediating responses (ranges of temperature, light emission) | Terminating responses (temperature, light emission) |
|---|---|---|---|

FIG. 3-4. Paradigm of presumed stimulus-response relationships of acquisition of temperature (first) and light-emission (second) values for a set of individual stars. The second-stage mediating responses give the ranges of temperature and light-emission values for white-dwarf, giant, and supergiant categories. The second-stage mediating response for the main sequence gives pairs of values for the termini of the diagonal.

paradigm of the presumed stimulus-response relationships involved in the task of learning the temperature and light-emission values for a set of individual stars. The first step in acquiring these relationships is learning that stars A, B, C are "white dwarfs," that stars F, G, H, I are "main-sequence stars," that stars P, Q, R are "giants," and that stars U, V, W are "supergiants." Already learned, it is assumed, are second-stage mediating responses to stimuli produced by saying "white dwarf," "main sequence," "giant," and "supergiant." These second-stage mediating responses state the ranges of values of temperature and light emission for the four categories of stars. Accordingly, once the first-stage mediating responses have been learned as labels for individual stars, ranges of values within which the particular pairs of temperature and light-emission values for each star will fall are already specified. What remains is to refine the terminating responses to each star to specific pairs of values that fall within the narrowed ranges set by the second-stage mediating responses.

Involved in this paradigm are the following associations: (a) between initiating stimuli (names of stars) and (i) first-stage mediating responses (categories), (ii) second-stage mediating responses (ranges of values), and (iii) terminating responses (pairs of exact values); (b) between stimuli produced by first-stage mediating responses and (i) second-stage mediating responses and (ii) terminating responses; and (c) between stimuli produced by second-stage mediating responses and terminating responses. The greater the prior learning of the associations between initiating stimuli and first-stage mediating responses and of the associations between stimuli produced by first-stage mediating responses and second-stage mediating responses, the greater the expected facilitation of the learning of associations between initiating stimuli and terminating responses.

Although this paradigm resembles the two-stage paradigm for concept formation with sets of initiating stimuli whose subsets are specified by common responses (Goss, 1961), there are three important differences. First, unlike the concept-formation situation, in which associations between initiating stimuli and first-stage mediating responses have already been learned, the first phase of the realization of the Figure 3-4 paradigm is strengthening of associations between initiating stimuli and first-stage mediating responses. Second, the paradigm in Figure 3-4 has two stages of mediating responses, whereas the paradigm for the concept-formation task had only one such stage. (While the concept-formation task could have more than one stage, under most circumstances the further stages would probably involve synonyms and antonyms of first-stage words rather than grammatically unrelated responses such as those stating ranges of values of temperature and light emission. There is, of course, no ultimate difference in how these associations are acquired, but it seems likely that grammatical ones have greater initial average strengths.) Third, for each mediating response and stimulus of the concept-formation task, there is only one terminating response; as stated elsewhere (Goss, 1961), the mediating responses and terminating responses are isomorphic to each other. In the Figure 3-4 paradigm, each of the second-stage mediating responses is shown as leading to three or four terminating responses. Thus, while stimuli produced by the four different pairs of first-stage and second-stage mediating responses presumably increase differences among the four groups of stars, they also presumably decrease differences among the stars within each group. Should the names of the stars within a group be highly similar, there might be some retardation of the learning of associations between each initiating stimulus of a group and its terminating response. With dissimilar names for stars within a group, little retardation would be expected. Not all of the relationships in Figure 3-4, however, can be thought of as potentially facilitative.

Table 3-1

Presumed Sources of Facilitative or Inhibitory Consequences of Using Conceptual Schemes in Establishing Relationships between Initiating Stimuli and Terminating Responses

A. Reduction of extra-task interfering responses due to
    I. Intra-task relationships between initiating stimuli and mediating responses and among mediating responses
    II. Response-mediated differentiation of the particular task from other similar tasks
B. Division of the task into wholes, which
    I. Reduces intra-task response interference
    II. Provides a basis for linking parts
C. Response-mediated
    I. Dissimilarity and discrimination, which may be in part the bases for AII, BI, DII, EIV, EV, F
    II. Similarity and generalization, which may be in part bases for AI, BII, EI, EII
D. Greater consideration of combinations of categories or values, which
    I. Reduces omissions
    II. Assures differentiation with respect to both rows and columns
E. Trial-to-trial constancy in order of occurrence of stimulus-response relationships, which may
    I. Reduce omissions
    II. Reduce stimulus variability
    III. Facilitate distinctiveness based on different mediating responses to each different part
    IV. Reduce intra-task response interference
    V. Ultimately facilitate short-circuiting of nonessential stimulus-responses relationships
F. *Bits*-to-*chunks* recoding

Table 3-1 summarizes some of the presumed sources of facilitative or inhibitory consequences of using conceptual schemes in establishing relationships between initiating stimuli and terminating responses. It should be emphasized that, contingent on the relationships among initiating stimuli, mediating responses and stimuli, and terminating responses, the effects of a given factor may be facilitative or inhibitory.

A. *Reduction of extra-task interfering responses.* As Table 3-1 indicates, the first source of effects is a reduction in extra-task interfering responses. One reason for expecting such a reduction is that the mediating responses and stimuli of the conceptual scheme are already interrelated, so that on each successive trial each initiating stimulus will probably elicit the same mediating response or chain of mediating responses. Further, the chains of mediating responses might often be closed, so that each response leads back to itself. As a consequence, the numbers of extra-list responses elicited both by initiating stimuli and by mediating stimuli should be reduced. Another reason for expecting a reduction in interfering responses is that, because of common use of rectangular coordinates and apparently similar curves, many conceptual schemes can only be differentiated by noting the particular combinations of sets of categories or variables along the abscissa and ordinate. Naming these particular pairs of sets of categories or variables, or making other labeling responses which are unique to a particular conceptual scheme, should therefore reduce or eliminate extra-task responses due to generalization from other similar conceptual schemes.

B. *Part learning vs. whole learning.* Conceptual schemes may also be the bases for dividing fairly long tasks into a series of more readily learned parts (Miller, 1958, pp. 488–489; Sheffield, 1946). Despite the equivocal status of information about the relative advantages of learning wholes versus learning parts and their linkages (Woodworth and Schlosberg, 1954, pp. 782–786), one of the most adequate studies yet reported (Orbison, 1944) indicates that for paired-associates learning, at least, learning parts was superior to learning wholes. Conceptual schemes may assure the occurrence of parts which are relatively consistent from trial to trial. Further, because of already-established interrelationships among mediating responses, conceptual schemes provide bases for putting the parts together. The presence of bases for putting parts together should eliminate one of the apparent major disadvantages of learning parts as compared with learning wholes.

C. *Response-mediated dissimilarity and discrimination, similarity and generalization.* Empirical facts of the superiority—or, for that matter, of the inferiority—of part to whole learning, however, are not explanations of obtained differences between the two methods. One reason for expecting differences is that the several stimuli of each part come to elicit a common response as well as more specific responses, and that the common responses of each part, by differentiating that part from the other parts, reduce intra-task response interference. With conceptual schemes, the mediating responses that serve as bases for dividing the task into parts may also serve as the common responses to render the stimuli of that part less similar to the stimuli of other parts (Miller, 1958, pp. 488–

489; Sheffield, 1946). Without conceptual schemes as bases for specifying parts, the parts may vary from trial to trial, thus reducing any advantage due to a constant small number of stimulus-response relationships to be mastered. Within the parts of tasks separated by common mediating responses, the common mediating responses and stimuli may occasion increased similarity and generalization. In turn, such increased similarity and generalization may retard rather than facilitate acquisition of discriminative responses to the initiating stimuli of that part. Conversely, acquisition of a common terminating response to the initiating stimuli of a part should be facilitated by the presence of a common mediating response.

D. *Combinations of categories and values.* The presence of a conceptual scheme, particularly in the case of ordinal and classificatory relationships, may increase the likelihood that all possible pertinent combinations of categories, of sets of categories, or of values of variables are considered. Greater likelihood of considering most-to-all possible combinations should have two consequences. The first is a reduction in failures to make responses involving particular combinations of categories or variables among the combinations. The second is an increase in differentiation among the initiating stimuli. If only responses to categories or values along rows or columns occur, categories or values along columns or rows, respectively, are not differentiated. However, since each combination of categories or values is unique, by assuring that responses for combinations occur (and not just responses for categories or values along rows or columns), each cell of the conceptual scheme is differentiated.

Conceptual schemes involving functional relationships may function in a more complex fashion. First, such relationships limit the number of combinations of categories or of values which must be considered. Thus, errors of commission may be reduced. However, the successive points of the curves or equations are combinations of categories or values. Consequently, such curves or equations also assure the occurrence of combinations, and hence of greater differentiation than is possible with categories or values along only the abscissa or the ordinate.

E. *Constancy of trial-to-trial orders of occurrence of stimulus-response relationships.* Conceptual schemes may also increase the constancy of trial-to-trial orders of occurrence of stimulus-response relationships. Constancy in the order of such relationships, through lowered variability of external and response-produced stimuli, should minimize omission of essential relationships among initiating stimuli, mediating responses and stimuli, and terminating responses. Further, such constancy and consequent reduced variability should increase the distinctiveness of successive steps of the task, and thus not only enhance response-mediated dissimilarity and discrimination but also aid in short-circuiting nonessential stimulus-response relationships. In addition to minimizing omissions of essential relationships and contributing to the elimination of nonessential relationships, reductions in the variability of external and response-produced stimuli per se should facilitate acquisition.

Constancy in the orders of occurrence of stimulus-response relationships should facilitate the labeling of successive segments of the task with distinctive names, such as "first," "second," "third," etc. Contingent on the particular task, such distinctive names might add to or subtract from the effects of the discriminative mediating responses of the conceptual schemes. In general, since the latter would probably be a major determinant of the constancy of trial-to-trial orders of occurrence of stimulus-response relationships, names for segments and the discriminative mediating responses of the conceptual scheme should have effects which summate in the same direction.

Constancy of orders of occurrence should also reduce the numbers of terminating responses which are in close temporal contiguity to any particular initiating stimulus. Thus, amounts of intra-task interference of incorrect with correct terminating response should be lowered. Reductions in stimulus variability, as well as any further response-mediated dissimilarity arising from constancy of order, should also reduce intra-task response interference.

*F. Bits-to-chunks recoding.* Miller (1956) has shown that possible limitations on performances due to relatively short spans of immediate memory can perhaps be partly or wholly overcome by appropriate recoding of the stimuli or stimulus-response relationships which are to be remembered. Sets of $N$ stimuli or stimulus-response relationships are or can be practically partitioned into $k$ subsets (up to $k = 7 \pm 2$) of $n_i$ (up to $n_i = 7 \pm 2$) stimuli or stimulus-response relationships each. Each of the $k$ subsets is then labeled by a number or some other symbol, and the numbers or other elements of each subset are learned as responses to the label for that subset. The label for each subset is also learned as a response to the numbers or elements of the subset. In later tests of immediate memory with sets of $N$ ($12 \leq N \leq 40$) stimuli or stimulus-response relationships, immediate memory span was increased to 40 stimuli or stimulus-response relationships.

The distinctive names for the $k$ subsets might be regarded as a very simple conceptual scheme. By using each distinctive name as a response and then as a stimulus for the stimuli of the subsets, immediate memory was extended markedly.

Conceptual schemes could be regarded as bases for extending immediate memory for *bits* by converting *bits* into *chunks* and recoding the chunks. But this procedure is not an explanation. A possible explanation is that bits-to-chunks recoding introduces some of the preceding factors listed in Table 3-1 and, through their effects, increases immediate memory.

In addition to influencing acquisition, conceptual schemes should also influence retention of the specific relationships between initiating stimuli and terminating responses. The sources of such effects are also essentially those listed in Table 3-1. First, inhibition arising from extra-task interfering responses should be reduced or largely eliminated. Second, the breakdown into parts, based perhaps on response-mediated dissimilarity

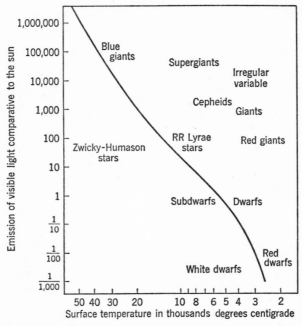

FIG. 3-5. Classificatory-functional relationship between temperature and light emission. (*Hoyle*, 1957, *p.* 163).

and discrimination, should reduce inhibition due to intra-task interfering responses. Third, by minimizing omissions and reducing stimulus variability, constancy of trial-to-trial orders of occurrence of stimulus-response relationships should reduce "spontaneous regression" (Estes, 1955). Thus, through reducing both stimulus variability and interfering responses, already-acquired conceptual schemes should facilitate retention of specific relationships between initiating stimuli and terminating responses. Conceptual schemes which have been partially acquired or which, due to the conditions of the particular task, are not present in stable form, might decrease retention of relationships between initiating stimuli and terminating responses.

*Modification of Conceptual Schemes: Changes in Functional Relationships.* The functional relationships of two-variable conceptual schemes may be changed because new and better data require such changes or because functions first presented in simplified forms are later presented in their more complex actual forms. For example, Figure 3-5 is the more complex actual form (Hoyle, 1957) which was modified to obtain the relationships shown in Figure 3-1. Two features have been changed: the

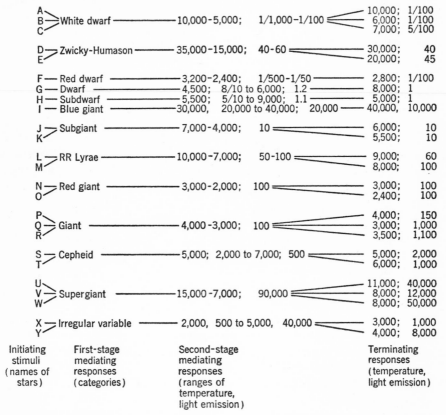

| Initiating stimuli (names of stars) | First-stage mediating responses (categories) | Second-stage mediating responses (ranges of temperature, light emission) | | Terminating responses (temperature, light emission) |
|---|---|---|---|---|

FIG. 3-6. Paradigm of presumed stimulus-response relationships of acquisition of temperature (first) and light-emission (second) values for the change from the functional relationship of Fig. 3-1 to that of Fig. 3-5. The second-stage mediating response for red dwarfs, dwarfs, subdwarfs, blue giants, cepheids, and irregular variables are those of the termini of trends expressing relationships within each of these groups.

main sequence is no longer exactly linear, and there are more exceptions to the main sequence than "white dwarfs," "giants," and "supergiants." Figure 3-6 shows some of the stimulus-response relationships involved in learning the conceptual scheme shown in Figure 3-5 after the presumed stimulus-response relationships of the conceptual scheme in Figure 3-1 have been learned.

Some of the relationships among initiating stimuli, mediating responses and stimuli, and terminating responses in Figure 3-6 will have already been learned and need not be changed. These are the relationships of Figure 3-4 for which the initiating stimuli are stars A, B, C (white dwarfs); stars P, Q, R (giants); and stars U, V, W (supergiants). The relationships between initiating stimuli and terminating responses for stars F, G, H, I also need not be changed. But the first-stage mediating response, "main sequence," and the second-stage mediating response of values for paired temperature and light-emission ranges need to be changed to include first-stage mediating responses of "red dwarf," "sub-dwarf," "dwarf," and "blue giant," as well as their associated second-stage mediating responses of values for termini of temperature and light-emission trends. The further relationships to be acquired are those among the remaining stars as initiating stimuli and the first-stage mediating, second-stage mediating, and terminating responses to those stimuli.

The prior learning of the relationships in Figure 3-4 should have assured substantial mastery of about half of the relationships in Figure 3-6. Accordingly, relative to controls for warm-up, performance set, and other nonspecific sources of positive transfer, acquisition of the relationships in Figure 3-4 should result in some facilitation of the learning of the relationships in Figure 3-6.

Although net positive transfer from learning the relationships of Figure 3-4 to learning the relationships of Figure 3-6 is expected, there are possible sources of negative transfer which might reduce the amount of facilitation to some degree. One source would be replacement of the common first- and second-stage mediating responses to stars F, G, H, I with different first-stage and second-stage mediating responses to each of the four stars. Such more discriminative first-stage and second-stage mediating responses should eventually facilitate the occurrence of a different terminating response to each of the four initiating stimuli. For a few trials, however, conflict between the old and the new mediating responses might occur. This would increase variability of mediating response-produced stimuli, and thus occasion some decrement in occurrence of correct terminating responses to those initiating stimuli.

The acquisition of new relationships might change the orders of occurrence of previously acquired relationships and thereby constitute another source of negative transfer. For example, new relationships might be interposed between stars A, B, C and F, G, H, I; between F, G, H, I and P, Q, R, and between P, Q, R and U, V, W. Such changes should disrupt serial associations, and thus at least temporarily increase both stimulus variability and intra-list interfering responses. Each of these changes should have some inhibitory effects on the already-learned stimulus-response relationships.

A further source of negative transfer is increased similarity of the terminating responses. Whereas the values of the paired ranges of temperatures and light emission for "giants" and "supergiants" are relatively dissimilar, introduction of the other groups of stars should increase the similarity of responses regarding temperature, light emission, or both, with the result that, through increased response generalization, response competition might increase.

Retention of the relationships between the initiating stimuli and terminating responses involved in this modification should be analyzed in terms of effects of conceptual schemes on each of the three kinds of changes in stimulus-response relationships which occurred. No changes occurred in relationships among some initiating stimuli, mediating responses and stimuli, and terminating responses. For these relationships, any further trials occasioned by learning the modification were overlearning or relearning trials. Accordingly, regardless of any effects of the conceptual scheme per se, better retention of the constituent stimulus-response relationships would be expected. Taking the conceptual schemes into account the situation is that which has already been considered, namely, the influence of conceptual schemes on retention of characteristics of particular objects.

In the case of other initiating stimuli, relationships to terminating responses were not changed, but those to mediating responses were changed. Should the changes in mediating responses occasion some initial negative transfer, retention after such amounts of training would be reduced. With no or positive transfer either initially or after a number of trials, however, the situation becomes essentially that for those relationships of the task which were not changed.

The remaining stimulus-response relationships are those involving the new initiating stimuli and their mediating and terminating responses. Once associations between initiating stimuli and terminating responses have been mastered, the situation for these stimulus-response relationships also becomes that for those relationships which were unchanged. Thus, in general, the influence of conceptual schemes on the retention of this modification can be analyzed in terms of those sources of effects which presumably influence retention of the stimulus-response relationships of characterizing particular objects.

*Modification of Conceptual Schemes: Addition of a Third Variable.* Figure 3-1 as such, or as modified in Figure 3-5, could also be modified by adding a third variable. Figure 3-7 shows such a modification: contours of equal stellar radii relative to the radius of the sun have been added (Hoyle, 1957). With this added variable, the first step might be to learn to reproduce these contours and their values. That size is inversely related to temperature and light emission would also be learned.

A second step might be learning the sizes of the stars in Figure 3-6 as new terminating responses to the names of the stars. For such learning, the old terminating responses in Figure 3-6 should function as mediating responses and stimuli. In general, both for acquisition of these new stimulus-response relationships and for their retention, the potential sources of facilitation or retardation listed in Table 3-1 would have to be considered. Extra-task interfering responses should be almost nonexistent. The task would be divided into parts with already-established relationships among the parts, and there should be constancy in the trial-to-trial orders of occurrence of the stimulus-response relationships. While some

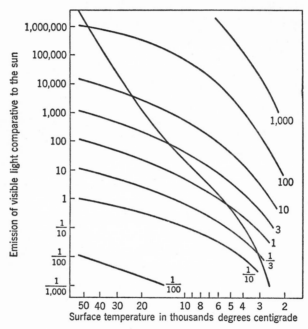

Fig. 3-7. Classificatory-functional relationship between temperature and light emission with contours of equal stellar radii comparative to the sun as a third variable. (*Hoyle,* 1957, *p.* 128.)

of the new mediating responses would have the same or similar values for temperature and light emission, the combinations of values should be more dissimilar. The magnitude of dissimilarity relative to the dissimilarity among the names for the stars might have some effects on the direction and amount of transfer to acquisition of the relationships between initiating stimuli and the new terminating responses. As suggested above, however, net transfer effects would probably be positive.

## SUMMARY

The objective of this paper was to provide a framework for analyses and experimentation concerned with conceptual schemes. A conceptual scheme was defined as one or more sets of categories or two or more variables that stand in ordinal, functional, or classificatory relationship to each other.

The first section outlined some historical roots of and contemporary influences on interest in acquisition and use of conceptual schemes. Descartes and Kant, who leaned toward a more innate origin, and Locke, who favored a more experiential origin, were considered the more remote modern antecedents. Bartlett's notion of schemata and Gestalt psychology's emphasis on organizing principles were identified as contemporary influences, particularly with respect to use of conceptual schemes. Functionalistic-behavioristic treatments of learning and stimulus-response analyses of conceptual behaviors which included mediating responses and stimuli were identified as additional, more important contemporary influences.

The first part of the second section presented a more detailed treatment of the definition of conceptual schemes. Then considered were problems of (a) learning modes of representing conceptual schemes; (b) learning names for sets of categories and for subcategories of such sets, and names for variables and values of variables; and (c) learning to combine modes of representation with names for sets of categories or variables in particular conceptual schemes.

The third section analyzed the use of conceptual schemes as mediating responses and stimuli with respect to acquisition and retention of the stimulus-responses relationships involved in characterizing particular objects or events which could be placed or located within conceptual schemes. Also analyzed were effects of already-acquired conceptual schemes as mediating responses and stimuli on acquisition and retention of the stimulus-response relationships of two kinds of subsequent modification of the conceptual schemes.

### REFERENCES

Bartlett, F. C. (1932) *Remembering: A study in experimental and social psychology.* New York: Cambridge.

Bartlett, F. C. (1958) *Thinking.* New York: Basic Books.

Cofer, C. N. (1943) Analysis of the errors made in the learning of prose materials. *J. Exp. Psychol.,* **32**, 399–410.

Descartes, R. (1911) Notes directed against a certain program. In E. J. Haldane & G. R. T. Ross (Trans.), *The philosophical works of Descartes.* New York: Cambridge.

Dunkel, H. B. (1948) *Second-language learning.* Boston: Ginn.

Estes, W. K. (1955) Statistical theory of spontaneous recovery and regression. *Psychol. Rev.,* **62**, 145–154.

Goss, A. E. (1961) Verbal mediating responses and concept formation. *Psychol. Rev.,* **68**.

Hempel, C. G. (1952) Fundamentals of concept formation in empirical science. In *International encyclopedia of unified sciences.* Vol. II. Chicago: University of Chicago Press.

Hoyle, F. (1957) *Frontiers of astronomy.* New York: New American Library (Mentor).

Irion, A. L. (1959) Rote learning. In S. Koch (Ed.), *Psychology: A study of a science.* Vol. II. New York: McGraw-Hill. Pp. 538–560.

Kant, I. (1881) *Critique of pure reason.* Vol. II. F. M. Müller (Trans.) London: Macmillan.

Katona, G. (1940) *Organizing and memorizing: Studies in the psychology of learning and teaching.* New York: Columbia University Press.

Kemeny, J. G., Snell, J. L., & Thompson, G. L. (1957) *Introduction to finite mathematics.* Englewood Cliffs, N.J.: Prentice-Hall.

Koffka, K. (1935) *Principles of Gestalt psychology.* New York: Harcourt, Brace.

Köhler, W. (1929) *Gestalt psychology.* New York: Liveright.

Lloyd, D. J., & Warfel, H. R. (1956) *American English and its cultural setting.* New York: Knopf.

Locke, J. (1850) *An essay concerning human understanding.* Philadelphia: Troutman & Hayes.

McGeoch, J. A., & Irion, A. L. (1952) *The psychology of human learning.* (2nd ed.) New York: Longmans.

Miller, G. A. (1956) The magical number seven, plus or minus two: Some limits on our capacity for processing information. *Psychol. Rev.,* **63**, 81–97.

Miller, G. A. (1958) Free recall of redundant strings of letters. *J. Exp. Psychol.,* **56**, 485–491.

Northway, M. L. (1940) The concept of the "schema": Part I. *Brit. J. Psychol.,* **30**, 316–325.

Oldfield, R. C., & Zangwill, O. L. (1942) Head's concept of the schema and its application in contemporary British psychology: Part III. Bartlett's theory of memory. *Brit. J. Psychol.,* **33**, 113–129.

Orbison, W. D. (1944) The relative efficiency of whole and part methods of learning paired-associates as a function of the length of list. Unpublished Ph.D. dissertation, Yale University.

Osgood, C. E. (1953) *Method and theory in experimental psychology.* New York: Oxford.

Sheffield, F. D. (1946) The role of meaningfulness of stimulus and response in verbal learning. Ph.D. dissertation, Yale University.

Underwood, B. J. (1949) *Experimental psychology.* New York: Appleton-Century-Crofts.

Underwood, B. J. (1952) An orientation for research on thinking. *Psychol. Rev.,* **59**, 209–220.

Ward, J. (1920) *Psychological principles.* (2nd ed.) New York: Cambridge.

Welborn, E. L., & English, H. B. (1937) Logical learning and retention: A general review of experiments with meaningful verbal materials. *Psychol. Bull.,* **34**, 1–20.

Wertheimer, M. (1945) *Productive thinking.* New York: Harper.

Woodworth, R. S., & Schlosberg, H. (1954) *Experimental psychology.* (Rev. ed.) New York: Holt, Rinehart & Winston.

# COMMENTS ON PROFESSOR GOSS'S PAPER
## *James J. Jenkins*
### UNIVERSITY OF MINNESOTA

Because Goss's paper has only recently been distributed and is a long and complex paper, I think perhaps the best way for me to initiate the discussion of it is to present, as best I can, an oversimplified account of the paper. This will refresh your memories of the content of the paper and should give us grounds for immediate discussion, since I am sure that no one man's simplification is ever accurate when it deals with another man's paper.

The paper, you will recall, is divided into three parts: the historical roots of conceptual schemes, the definition of conceptual schemes and an analysis of their acquisition, and finally, two major uses of conceptual schemes, that is, as mediating responses and stimuli and as bases for larger schemes.

Now if we all agree that conceptual schemes are acquired rather than "given," as I presume that we all would agree here since this is a conference on learning, we may dispense with the history for purposes of discussion and proceed directly to the second and third parts of the paper.

I would like first to treat the question of definition. Dr. Goss has defined a conceptual scheme in the following way:

"A conceptual scheme may be defined as one or more sets of categories or two or more variables that stand in ordinal, classificatory, or functional relationships to each other."

It seems to me that there are some minor points for disputation here. I would raise them, not because they are crucial issues, but because I think that it is important for us all to be talking about the same thing. In the first place, Goss has said that the scheme must involve one or more sets of categories or variables. I believe that this is not essential as he discusses conceptual schemes later. There must indeed be more than one *category*, but there do not necessarily need to be two or more *sets* of categories; that is, we can't have a one-category system because that would include everything or nothing and would, therefore, represent no conceptual scheme at all. A conceptual scheme, I believe Goss is saying, must involve at least two groups. It *may* involve many more than this. Perhaps we might rearrange the definition to say that a conceptual scheme is defined as two or more categories or variables or sets of categories or variables. We really want two implications here. One is that there must be at least two classes, and the other is that these categories or classes may themselves be further subdivided in some fashion or according to some system other than that on which the primary categories were divided. We want to embrace the notion of classes as well as the notion of classes of classes.

I would quarrel somewhat with the second half of the definition specifying that the categories be in ordinal, classificatory, or functional relationship. I believe that our major division here should be between classificatory relationships and functional relationships in general. The functional relationships ought then to include the ordinal as well as other special functional relationships. In the most general sense, I suspect that, aside from the purpose of instruction or conveying a clearer picture, the definition itself could do away with specifying the relationships of the categories in three classes and could simply say that the categories or sets of categories may bear variously specified relationships to each other. The limiting case at one end would be pure classification where the only relation between the categories might be exclusion. The limiting case on the other end is difficult to specify but could be as complex a functional relationship as one would like.

For purposes of stimulating discussion and to see if I understand his meaning, I have tried to formulate Goss's definition in a somewhat different sentence. I would simply ask whether it is fair to say we could define a conceptual scheme as the arrangement of differentiated responses and classes of those responses to discriminated stimuli. I am not sure that this says the same thing, but it is a more "psychological-sounding" sentence if we care to look at it.

I think we might find it instructive before going further to take Goss's example and look at it diagrammatically. I refer here to the advice to public speakers, "Say what you are going to say, say it, and say what you have said." Goss looks at this as a simple ordinal conceptual scheme. We might in this instance look at this scheme as a computer program or a "plan" following the notion that Miller, Galanter, and Pribram (1960) are developing in their book. The first category in our conceptual scheme is an instruction which says, "Go to category 2. Get the list of names of subclasses in category 2 and present those names in execution stage 1. When this has been done, proceed to category 2." Category 2 is a message consisting of some $n$ parts, each of which is labeled and has a final instruction directing the speaker to the next part and so on through all $n$ parts. The $n$th part directs the speaker to category 3. Category 3 then has an instruction similar to category 1 directing the speaker to list the names of the parts of category 2. These are repeated again as they were in 1 with appropriate differences indicating that this is a summary rather than an introduction. The conceptual scheme is rather clearly a program for proceeding, and the parallel to the computer case is very close.

However, if we now take the second case which Goss presents here, the plotting of the set of visible stars in terms of their emission of light and their surface temperature, we are talking about clusters of variables or categories which are determined by the intersection of two continuous variables. This is not a case of the ordering of units as much as it is a scheme for the *finding* of the units in the first place. An interrelated scheme like this makes available to us further discriminated stimuli; that is, the "clumps" of stars that can be seen in the covariation chart, to which we learn to make further differentiating responses. This is quite clearly a different kind of scheme than the one given above. One wonders whether the scheme for *finding* new conceptual categories, which this seems to have been in its original form, is not in essence an attempt to embrace all the activities of science. In a simpler sense, we can say that, given these variables and these instructions, we have a conceptual scheme which has been mapped out for us in some way; and we now look at the variables, read off their values, and we know how to label the objects involved. Or given a label, we know where the objects are to be found in the chart and something about their general characteristics.

As an aside, I think that we might note in passing that if a scatter plot does not change our stimulus-discrimination level, we regard it as fruitless. This is somewhat like Goss's irrelevant category. This was a new way to me to look at a scatter plot.

Goss then proceeds to an analysis of the acquisition of conceptual schemes and splits his analysis, as we have been splitting variables already here in the conference, into two different sets of learnings. The first is designated by him "learning modes of representing conceptual schemes," and is, so to speak, learning what the relations are between terms before the terms have a set of referents in the world. Thus, it is possible for us to learn a coding scheme without knowing yet what it is that is going to be coded or what the particular code assignment will be.

We can consider here three examples which Goss has given us. The first is an ordinal system in which we learn sequences or orders. We can learn these independent of having things to order or independent of the particular things that we are going to have to order in some particular situation later. The example treated here, that of combinations in grammar, is a somewhat unlikely one as we may see later, and seems to me to be more of a classificatory scheme. The general notion that one can learn orders before assigning the elements in the order to referential categories, however, is obviously true. We can learn code numbers in appropriate combinations or code sequences, such as the alphabet, which are then applied to situations in which these code symbols are to designate events in the world before we know what the events are to be.

The second set of examples refers to systems of classifications which involve matrices, tables, tree diagrams, and the like. Here again, one can certainly learn the model before he learns the content to be put into the model. Finally we have functional examples, circuit diagrams, vectors, and so on, in which we may enter complex facts about things. I think the questions that Goss raises here about the learning of functions are good questions to raise, but I think that his proposals for studying them are relatively aside from the actual questions asked. The proposals refer to a much lower order approach than the questions suggest.

Now obviously the kind of learning going on here can be rote learning, "dumb" learning, noninsightful learning; or it may involve great amounts of transfer, moving into more complex relational schemes which depend on knowledge of previously learned relational schemes.

The second kind of learning being talked about here is the learning of names or sets of categories or variables. This raises some real problems for us when we have to learn what the characteristics are which identify instances of classes and then learn to apply the correct response, labeling responses, to those instances. In more complex reference systems, we have to learn something about relations or patterns and learn how to isolate them and label them.

Now when one talks about learning particular conceptual schemes, I think the statement by Goss is too strong. He asserts that modes are *usually* acquired independently and that names are *usually* acquired independently. I would suppose that we are almost continuously acquiring modes of representation and names simultaneously.

It is obviously true, as Goss contends, that the degree of learning of each of these will affect the learning of complex combinations; and here he presents again the example from the star chart with the added problems of transferring from one domain to another: verbal description, equations, visual representation, etc. The relationship being expressed in all cases is the same, but one's ability to move from one to the other depends on his familiarity with the mode and the rules for converting from one system to the next. Transfer certainly does vary from one domain to another, and one would doubt that it is symmetrical from one to another.

Goss then moves to a consideration of the use of conceptual schemes. The first use he says is to place something in the scheme so that it can be labeled. The scheme serves here by providing mediating responses which serve as stimuli leading the individual to behave in a given way with respect to something.

The examples here, however, are particularly weak. It is almost certain that no child ever learned to write in the fashion that Goss seems to present here. Any mature speaker (and by mature we mean here any speaker of the language who is over five years old) who is speaking a native language follows a host of rules and conventions (most of which he cannot report to you) concerning categories for elements in the language (most of which he cannot name or label). The approach which Goss has taken throughout has implied that the response which is made in categorizing is a labeling, and presumably a verbal labeling, response. We *know* in the case of language behavior that this is not *true*. One of the *last* things a child is likely to say to himself, I would suppose, is something of the sort that Goss has him saying: "Some sentences ought to have a noun and a verb and a noun." We may be able to train children to talk like that, but this is certainly not the way they learn the language. Nor is it the way that the language appears to be used, even by seventh graders writing essays.

Language itself seems to be a prime example of a category system of elaborate complexity which is adequately used but cannot be described to you by the vast majority of the people who use it. Goss implies that in some cases sentences are simply rote-memorized so they appear in a given form, or are generated by chance rather than by composition. However, the argument which was advanced by Chomsky (1957) and which is repeated in Miller, Galanter, and Pribram (1960) is very impressive on this point. Even a reasonable number of sentences available to a child (out of the infinite set possible) is so great no one would have time to learn these sentences in his whole lifetime. Some sort of categorical conceptual *system* is learned, but it is clearly not labeled by the learner.

A beautiful example of this can be found in the very sophisticated group we have around the table here. Practically none of us can verbalize the rules for ordering adjectives in English without first ordering the adjectives and then looking to see what we have done. It is easy to say, "I want five big round red furry pillows," but it is a difficult task to specify what the set of rules is which determines the order of the adjectives which modify the noun. If one starts switching the adjectives around in the sentence, it is quite obvious that the "meaning" of the utterance changes, or it becomes "meaningless" or at best queer. It is hard to specify why this should be. The obedience to the rules is automatic and complete. Errors in this kind of behavior are almost never made by speakers of the language, and yet no speaker is taught these rules even in our classrooms, and the vast majority deny that such rules exist.

The fact that one must learn sentence patterns to learn to speak a second language and that learning is often facilitated by deliberate analysis of the language, to which Goss refers, is interesting, but I would urge strongly that this is not part of the behavior of the native speaker.

In his second example, returning again to the star chart, Goss presents a case in which the use of a conceptual scheme narrows the class of responses and thus makes it easier for the user of the schemes to learn certain items of information or get within the range of certain items of information. I think that most of the benefits that are attributed to the scheme in this case are related to the benefits that he gives later on in the paper; and if one were to classify them roughly, I suppose that the single statement which would be most appropriate to embrace them would be that conceptual schemes serve to minimize interference. They make available local responses with less competition from other responses.[1] I think we might ask ourselves whether we need a conceptual scheme of the sort that we have been talking about here in order to achieve this. It may be that the minimization of competing responses has little to do with the relationships between the categories but simply reflects the nature of the categorization involved.

Two examples may be useful here. The first is an example taken from a Pete Smith Specialty. It is an old (and I believe anonymous) mnemonic device. It proceeds as follows. The subject first learns a rhyming series to go with a number series:

> "One is a bun
> Two is a shoe
> Three is a tree" . . .
> Etc.

The subject then is instructed in learning a list of 10 objects to bring each object to be learned into some bizarre relationship with the rhyming object which is associated with the appropriate number in the series. Thus, if the first thing in the list is (as it was in the specialty) a trip to the dentist's, the subject imagines a dentist enclosed in a superlarge hamburger bun. This bizarre relationship or image is sufficient to maintain the association. When one recites, "One is a bun," this is sufficient cue to recall the dentist.

Miller, Galanter, and Pribram (1960) report that other work at Pennsylvania has shown that very large numbers of pairs may be retained with this bizarre-association attack on the problem. (In these studies order is neglected; only pairing is studied.) Presumably, this is due to the fact that, if the associations are indeed bizarre, there is little interference. The more common the association developing between two terms, the more likely the interference would be. It is not clear then whether this is a

---

[1] Two studies bearing on this are the interesting recall studies by Ravenna Mathews Helson. She has demonstrated that the more specific the labels given to the same recall material (e.g., "physicists" versus "scientists"), the more items the subjects can recall. See Mathews (1954) and Helson and Cover (1956).

categorizing scheme which by putting things into separate cells makes them available or is a system which by being unlike anything else, i.e., bizarre, preserves the item from interference from other items. I think we ought to give some consideration to this while we are talking about this whole procedure of reducing interference.

With respect to Goss's final section concerned with modifying a particular conceptual scheme, it seems clear that once a conceptual scheme is well learned and exists, it can be modified in ways which seem to be fruitful. If one has a partial structure which begins to separate things which the subject needs to keep apart, he can more easily add a third structure to it than he can build an entirely new structure.

It seems to me that for purposes of the conference we can talk about several questions here. One would be to discuss the definition of a conceptual scheme as it is offered by Goss. Does it in fact add anything to say that some relations are ordinal, some functional, and some classificatory?

Secondly, I think we might discuss again whether one learns modes and names independently. I think we would want to say sometimes yes, sometimes no; and we would like to know something about the situations in which we do one and situations in which we do the other. I believe that we also should be particularly concerned here with the directions of associative arrows. If stimulus-response directionality is at all important, we have to ask ourselves whether one can get from the categories to their contents, from the contents to the categories, or whether all such learning is bidirectional.

Thirdly, I think we want to disagree rather sharply with Goss's implicit contention that all categories are labeled. It seems to me that there is good evidence indicating that many, many unlabeled categories exist and are used with a high degree of success. Language may well be the supreme example of this.

### REFERENCES

Chomsky, N. (1957) *Syntactic structures.* The Hague: Mouton.

Helson, Ravenna M., & Cover, A. (1956) Specificity-generality of classificatory categories as a variable in recall. *Percept. Mot. Skills,* 6, 233–236.

Mathews, R. (1954) Recall as a function of number of classification categories. *J. Exp. Psychol.,* 47, 241–247.

Miller, G. A., Galanter, E., & Pribram, K. H. (1960). *Plans and the structure of behavior.* New York: Holt, Rinehart & Winston.

## SUMMARY OF CONFERENCE DISCUSSION

The major issue of the discussion was raised by Mandler, who argued that, while the star-classification example was useful for describing how a science develops, the functioning of conceptual schemes which cannot be ascribed to the mediation of verbal labels is also of great interest. This point was stressed in relation to verbal behavior, especially with reference to syntax. That is, syntactical rules are followed by young children and by adults who are ignorant of such rules and terminology. Objection was voiced in this point to Goss's emphasis on verbal labels as mediators for conceptual schemes.

Jenkins mentioned that even linguists have had difficulty in defining classes of words like adverbs. The words we are taught in school to label as "adverbs" do not function consistently in the way in which we are taught that they do. Furthermore, there are some constructions which we do not or cannot use, such as "He went slowly quickly," even though, in this case, the second adverb modifies the first adverb, which, by definition, is a proper function for an adverb.

Osgood gave a different example, illustrative of usage which is obviously unacceptable although permitted by the usual definitions. One can say "the two green silk stockings," whereas one cannot or does not say "the green two silk stockings." His point was that speakers and writers would assent to the first and reject the second phrase despite being unable to specify a rule governing the relative acceptability of such cases.

Other examples were given to support the objection to Goss's emphasis on verbal labels. For instance, Jenkins reported that children can replace nouns in connected discourse when the spaces occupied by the nouns are left blank, but when asked what these words are, do not call them "nouns." The work of Brown (1958) has shown that if grammatical tags are attached to a nonsense name in one situation, young children will change the tags appropriately when shown the nonsense-named object in another situation.[1] Osgood reported a study in which one group (I) was presented nonsense syllables, another (II) nonsense syllables which had syntactic cues in the right places (e.g., "The wugs noxed the glifs zuggly."), and the third (III) nonsense syllables with syntactic cues in the wrong places. Recall was best for Group II, next for Group I, and worst for Group III.

Another way in which this general point was made was by the statement that a person's use of a word in a particular linguistic situation is not dependent on his ever having heard the word used in that specific sit-

[1] Many times the discussion implies that grammatical or syntactical rules find errorless expression in speech and writing. This is not always the case. For example, a number of Brown's subjects (1958, p. 252) made "errors." Musgrave reported at the conference that college students fill a given cloze blank with words from a variety of form classes, some of which are appropriate (but which the experimenter had not seen as possibilities) and some of which are ungrammatical. The plaint of English teachers should be mentioned here. (Ed.)

uation or on his having been taught labels or rules for its use in such situations. Instead of imitation or instruction, what seems to be operating is some sort of analogic transfer. Presumably such transfer frequently results in correct speech or writing and hence is of importance in a full account of verbal behavior. However, correct usage usually does not permit excluding the possibilities that either imitation or instruction, or both, are causative variables. On the other hand, analogic errors—errors produced by using a word in conformance with the wrong rules—cannot be dismissed as the result of imitation or instruction. An example may occur in the case of a verb like *take* which a child hears for the first time. In transferring this word to a linguistic situation requiring the past tense, he is likely to change it in ways appropriate for other verbs, producing *taked* or possibly *tooked*, or to progress from *have taked* through *have tooked* and *have tooken* to *have taken*.

A number of conference participants agreed that the foregoing points and examples represent an important problem in verbal behavior and in verbal learning. Jenkins, Osgood, Deese, and Mandler were most explicit. They felt that associative processes, at least in the sense of word-word associations, could not presently deal with this problem. A different process is perhaps involved. As evidence for the latter point, Osgood indicated that analysis of a tape recording of a conference (Maclay and Osgood, 1959) showed that speakers pause before they start a phrase (e.g., the phrase "to the houses") and then pause again before emitting the final word of the phrase. Osgood suggested that the pauses evidence two processes: one a syntactic process involved in "selecting" the phrase form; the other a lexical process involved in "selecting" the word with which to complete the phrase. Neither process seems dependent on labeling.

Goss was not in complete disagreement with the points just summarized. He indicated that he agrees that simple word-word associative processes cannot do the entire job in this area. However, he suggested a number of points which might explain part of the phenomena and thus reduce the amount of explanatory burden to be carried by conceptions of syntactical rules. To begin with, he said that his definition of conceptual representation and of content is certainly not invariant. He emphasized that his paper deals with writing, not with speaking. Writing is not easy, he pointed out, and it requires frequent alteration or revision to avoid grammatical errors, repetitions, and so on. On re-reading what has been written, one explicitly checks for errors, which he then corrects. This point was advanced in favor of the notion that there is self-conscious use of labels in abiding by grammatical rules and categories. If rules concerning such style points as using synonyms instead of repetitions were less vague, i.e., if the schemata were more discriminable and hence more usable in an overt way, learning to write would be easier.

In relation to verbal performance generally, including speaking, Goss stressed several issues. One may be paraphrased by saying that language is not used as skillfully, correctly, and flexibly as the foregoing discussion implies. Many people may not speak, at least very often, in sentences. He urges that function words like prepositions, conjunctions, articles, and certain adjectives (e.g., "some," "all") may serve as cues for the occurrence of words which are from syntactically correct form classes.

Often, also, the environmental situation itself provides support for referential speaking in a certain sequence (which may appear to be grammatical). For example, the garage mechanic, in describing what is wrong with an engine, may simply follow the parts of the engine in talking about it; the order in his utterance is under the control of the sequence of external stimuli. A young child may see his father and say, "Daddy." The father may go out through the door, and the child says, "Go bye-bye," or "Daddy go bye-bye." When the father gets in the car, the phrase "in car" may be added to the previous one, giving an apparently ordered and grammatical sequence but a sequence which is, in fact, under the control of environmental variables.

Goss emphasized the repetitiousness that occurs in speech, especially in the form of phrases, implying that such units, once learned, are endlessly repeated. Imitation with social reinforcement, Noble suggested, might account for some patterns. In response to this, it was pointed out that even Skinner (1957) has been forced to say that the child learns speech patterns analogically.

Syntax and accidence, it was agreed, constitute problems, and the difference between Goss and the other vocal participants is largely one of the extent to which such skills must be invoked to account for speech and writing. It was agreed that much experimentation is required on these problems, especially with young children and perhaps with artificial languages. The experiments by Esper (1925; 1933) and by Wolfle (1932) were described by Jenkins and Postman, respectively, as examples of the use of artificial language learning in the investigation of problems of verbal behavior.

Mandler and Deese were asked to write out a more formal statement concerning the syntactical problem than is provided by the various examples in the discussion. Their statement follows:

"The occurrence of a new word in a syntactic structure determines its position and possibly form in most other syntactic structures in that language.

"This constraint cannot be explained in terms of the distribution of response probabilities or contingent probabilities between encoded units."

Goss was asked to comment on this statement. He said that the cues would probably be the position of the word, and particular preceding (e.g., "I") or succeeding (e.g., "is") words along with, in some cases, the forms of those words (e.g., with or without an "ed"). Primary stimulus generalization based on similarity between the original and subsequent "syntactical structures" may be sufficient to account for some subsequent uses of the word. In other cases, the word might evoke responses such as "follows 'I,'" "second position," and "verb" which had been associated with the word in the original sentences and which would now function as mediating responses to determine, in part, the word's position and form in new sentences. The form of the new sentences would also be important. For example, should a different tense be indicated by, say, a temporal adverb or phrase, the word might be used as a verb but its tense ending changed from that of the original tense to that consistent with the adverb or phrase.

During the discussion, Mandler expressed a point of view with which there was considerable agreement. He was asked to write a statement expressing his view. He wrote as follows:

"The question we have been raising is not whether associative theory is irrelevant to 'grammatical' behavior, but rather whether *some* syntactical problems can be adequately handled by such an orientation. Certainly, associative phenomena are important variables in the use of phrases, clichés, simple sentences, and so forth. On the other hand, I do not believe that conceptual schemas which depend on verbal labels will explain the general problem of syntactic structure. The comprehension of syntactic 'cues' by the pre-verbal child and the use of grammar by the uneducated adult, who knows nothing of grammar in terms of labels, seem to argue against such an approach. On the other hand, though, the glib invocation of 'schemas,' 'structures' or 'organizations' does not seem to contribute to an explanation or analysis of these phenomena. Furthermore, the analyses and critiques of the linguists have contributed little toward an understanding of the *development and acquisition* of syntactic structures. Little research is available which attempts to isolate the important determinants or antecedents of syntactic behavior. I strongly believe that in the long run it will be the psychologists who have worked analytically in the field of verbal learning who are likely to develop the necessary techniques to provide a better understanding of these problems. Associationist work in the field of verbal learning has developed some laboratory techniques and analytic tools which could be fruitfully applied to syntactic behavior; other research methods will have to be adopted or developed. But the answers will, I am sure, come from careful analysis and investigation in the laboratory. Research on the use of syntax and on syntactical learning must consider possible associative explanations, as well as provide controls for the already well-known and undoubtedly important associative phenomena. A psychology of syntax will come from the laboratory, not from facile criticism and the mere postulation of new processes."

### REFERENCES

Brown, R. W. (1958) *Words and things.* Glencoe, Ill.: Free Press.

Cohen, B. H., Bousfield, W. A., & Whitmarsh, G. A. (1957) Cultural norms for verbal items in 43 categories. *Tech. Rep. No. 22,* Contract No. Nonr-631(00), Office of Naval Research and University of Connecticut.

Esper, E. A. (1925) A technique for the experimental investigation of associative interference in artificial linguistic material. *Language Monogr.,* No. 1, 47 pp.

Esper, E. A. (1933) Studies in linguistic behavior organization: I. Characteristics of unstable verbal reactions. *J. Gen. Psychol.,* 8, 346–379.

Maclay, H., & Osgood, C. E. (1959) Hesitation phenomena in spontaneous English speech. *Word,* 15, 19–44.

Skinner, B. F. (1957) *Verbal behavior.* New York: Appleton-Century-Crofts.

Taylor, W. L. (1953) "Cloze procedure": A new tool for measuring readability. *Journalism Quart.,* 30, 415–433.

Wolfle, D. D. L. (1932) The relation between linguistic structure and associative interference in artificial linguistic material. *Language Monogr.,* No. 11, 55 pp.

# Chapter 4

# THE PROBLEM OF MEANING
# IN VERBAL LEARNING

## W. A. Bousfield

UNIVERSITY OF CONNECTICUT

This paper presents two general propositions for consideration. The first is that verbal associative responses may be regarded as meaningful. The second is that the problem of meaning in verbal behavior may be investigated on the basis of suitable analyses of verbal associative responses. It is appropriate to indicate that the theoretical rationale and its supporting evidence are mainly by-products of an ONR project in which I have depended on a group of able graduate students. These colleagues include Burton H. Cohen, Gerald A. Whitmarsh, Joseph J. Danick, Wendell Kincaid, and Paul Herman. They should not be held responsible, however, for such weaknesses as may exist in the theorizing.

At the onset I feel it necessary to state a bias. It seems to me that meaning is not only an unnecessary concept for verbal learning but a concept bound to lead to confusion. Like the concept of emotion it is ambiguous, and it is tied up with philosophical considerations going beyond the domain of psychology. It is evident, however, that meaning has joined the family of psychological concepts because it has able and influential friends. Perhaps it can attain greater acceptance if it can become domesticated. In other words, those who consort with this concept should provide a theoretical rationale for clearly relating it to the operations employed for its measurement. For the verbal learning theorist, the most useful operations are verbal in nature.

Since it is the admitted purpose of this discussion to present a theoretical interpretation, it is necessary to define its basic terms and to state its basic assumptions. The present account amounts to an elaboration and extension of an interpretation presented by Bousfield, Whitmarsh, and Danick (1958). First, it is useful to assume that a repeated, particular stimulation results in the development of a representational sequence. Such a sequence comprises both a representational response and a representational stimulus. The representational response is a

81

fractional part of the total reaction to a given stimulus. It has the characteristics of being stable and conditionable. The representational stimulus is a stable pattern of feedback stimulation consequent on the occurrence of a given representational response. New responses can be attached to it by conditioning. Perhaps these conceptions can be described as what resulted from a uniting of certain features of Hebb's (1949) cell assembly and of Osgood's (1953, pp. 680–727) representational mediation process that took place without their knowledge or consent. By way of explanation, it may be said that the stipulation of a repeated, particular stimulation for the establishment of a representational sequence is Hebb's requisite for the development of a cell assembly which he regards as a representational process. On the other hand, though Osgood has done much to make *mediation* respectable, the term is deliberately avoided in describing the representational sequence because it may or may not be mediational. This statement follows from the assumption that at least two separate learnings or conditionings, as they are generally dealt with, are needed for mediation to take place. In other words, it would appear that the term mediation should not be used unless the conventional mediation paradigm may clearly be applied, and it does not apply to a simple first-order conditioning.

One more assumption may now be proposed as useful in dealing with verbal behavior. It is that the representational response to any given word may be labeled as the word itself which the subject emits either implicitly or observably.[1]

In order to demonstrate the application of the foregoing assumptions, consideration will be given to the development of a meaningful response to a verbal stimulus. The example is that of a situation in which a subject learns a meaningful response to the word *evil*. The necessary conditionings are represented in Figure 4-1. Suppose a naïve and naughty child hears the word *bad* and is spanked. The US is a pain stimulus which elicits its conditionable representational response. The CS is the word *bad* which elicits its representational sequence. This includes the representational response which involves the child's saying *bad* either implicitly or out loud. Its consequent representational stimulus is what becomes conditioned to elicit the representational response to the pain stimulus. The resulting new habit is labeled $H_1$.

At a later time our child hears the word *evil* followed by the word *bad*. Perhaps he asks his parent the meaning of *evil* and he is told, "*Evil* means *bad*." The word *evil*, which is the CS, elicits its representational sequence. Now, however, the word *bad*, functioning as the US,

---

[1] The processes assumed to be involved in the implicit emission of a verbal response are not restricted to those of purely motor or peripheral types.

not only elicits its representational sequence but also the earlier-established $H_1$, so that the representational response to the pain stimulus also occurs. As a result of this learning, we should expect that when the child subsequently hears the word *evil,* he should say *bad* either implicitly or out loud. This is a consequence of the new habit labeled $H_2$. The representational response to the pain stimulus should also occur as a result of the representational sequence of *bad* which functions mediationally. Perhaps the representational response of the pain stimulus

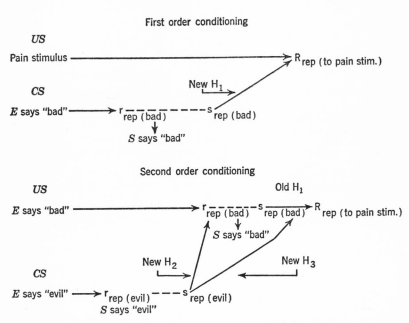

FIG. 4-1. The development of a meaningful response.

may also occur because of the possibility of the new $H_3$ representing its direct connection with the representational response *evil.* If this analysis is valid, it may be said that *bad* is a mediating response and the *pain,* perhaps describable as a negative feeling, is a mediated response. Which of the two merits the label meaningful? It may be submitted that the verbal behavior theorist, who uses verbal methods in dealing with meaningful responses, would be well advised to favor the assumption that *bad* is a meaningful response to *evil* because *bad* has acquired mediational properties. Though a case may be made for regarding the representational response to the pain stimulus as a meaningful response to *evil,* this incurs a penalty for the verbal behavior theorist who wishes to manipulate and to measure meaningful responses. While verbal responses are distinctive and their strengths are more or less measurable, we simply cannot at the present time identify distinctive nonverbal response patterns for different verbal stimuli. Certainly the child, whose training has been considered, should show a PGR and changes in heart rate when the word *evil* is presented and such changes are measurable, but can it be shown that such response patterns vary distinctively when different verbal stimuli are presented?

Returning to the child whose training has been considered, it would be expected that he should learn a variety of verbal responses, associative in nature, to the word *evil*. Each of these would be distinctive, and each would be meaningful because of the good grounds for supposing they would also be mediational. Noble's (1952) *m* may from the present point of view be justified as a measure of the meaningfulness of a given word, though his rationale differs from what is proposed here.

In order to indicate some of the consequences of the proposed interpretation, it may be helpful to apply it to the semantic differential. This is especially appropriate since Osgood should have something to say about it. The scales he has developed for appraising certain types of meaningfulness have amply been justified, and I would propose no criticism of this method. I am proposing, however, that the word-association rationale here developed adequately accounts for the process of making ratings of the semantic differential scales.

Let us suppose that the child who has undergone the training indicated in our example is capable of following the instructions for rating the meaning of *evil* on the *good-bad* semantic differential scale. The prediction is that he will rate *evil* at the *bad* end of the scale, and he will do this because *evil* elicits *bad* as a fairly strong associative, and therefore meaningful, response. The results of several recently conducted pilot studies appear to be consistent with this interpretation. They may be summarized as follows:

1. The semantic differential scale ratings are unaltered by rephrasing the instructions to those calling for word association; e.g., "To what extent does the word *music* make you think either of the word *good* or the word *bad*?"

2. The semantic differential ratings appear to be unaltered when the results obtained from the following two steps are averaged. These two steps may be illustrated as follows: (a) "To what extent does the word *music* make you think of the word *good*?" (b) "To what extent does the word *music* make you think of the word *bad*?" In each case the end points of the seven-point scale are labeled respectively "not at all" and "very strongly."

It should be noted that ratings of word pairs obtained in this way correlate highly with information available from free-associational norms. Thus, the word *table* elicits the associative response *chair* at a relatively high cultural frequency, and Ss give relatively high ratings of the extent to which the word *table* makes them think of the word *chair*. On the other hand, the word *table* elicits the associate *cup* at a relatively low cultural frequency, and Ss give relatively low ratings of the extent to which the word *table* makes them think of the word *cup*.

3. In another study a list of words was selected from free-associational norms on the basis of their eliciting either *good* or *bad* at a frequency of at least one occurrence. For each of the words the frequency of *good* was subtracted from the frequency of *bad*. The correlation between these differences for the words and their semantic differential ratings was significantly high.[2]

The results of these pilot studies, though not definitive, appear to justify the word-associational interpretation of the semantic differential. Furthermore, such an interpretation in no way detracts from the usefulness and validity of these scales.

To indicate how the word-associational approach may be applied to relatively simple learning situations, the liberty will be taken of reviewing several studies undertaken on the ONR project with which I have been associated.

The pair *wok-white* represents a nonsense syllable followed by a word. The theory here described indicates that the word *white* should elicit its representational sequence and a composite of meaningful associative responses. If this pair becomes learned, it may be assumed that connections should have become established not only between *wok* and *white* but also between *wok* and the composite of meaningful responses elicited by *white*, such as *black, snow, red, cloth*, etc. The data of a recently conducted study by Kincaid, Bousfield, and Whitmarsh (1959) support the prediction.

In another study, by Yavuz and Bousfield (1959), Turkish words were substituted for the nonsense syllables, and the subjects learned what were purported to be their meanings in English, e.g., *demet-nice*. One week

[2] It should be noted that so-called free-associational responses are obtained under conditions of minimal restriction. The operations for obtaining semantic differential ratings, on the other hand, may be described as imposing the highest possible restriction in that they in effect require only that judgments of associative strength be made of given adjectives as responses to given stimuli. In these terms, an intermediate degree of restriction would be represented when subjects are asked to give only the adjectives the given words make them think of. It appears highly probable that the magnitude of the correlation between the semantic differential scale and the estimated associational strengths of the adjectives of the scale as responses to the given words should vary positively with the degree of restriction employed in the measuring of the associative strengths of the adjectives as responses to the given words. If this reasoning is valid, the use of unrestricted free-associational responses for testing the word-associational interpretation of semantic differential ratings is at best a somewhat crude undertaking.

was allowed for forgetting to take place. The subjects were then given the Turkish words and asked to recall their supposed translations. They were also asked to rate the Turkish words on the *good-bad* semantic differential scale. It was found that the subjects tended to retain the connotative meaningful responses assumed to have been acquired by the Turkish words when they were unable to recall the supposed translations. The present explanation of this type of recall is that, even though the subjects were unable to recall the supposed translations, a sufficient number of the acquired implicitly produced meaningful responses remained to enable them to give the appropriate ratings.

In another recently conducted experiment by Bousfield, Herman, and Whitmarsh (1959), subjects undertook to learn a list of words, including *needle* and *sour,* which each appeared 14 times. One of these words was followed immediately by the nonverbal stimulus of a flash of light on 9 of its occurrences. The prediction was that the learning should result in the acquisition of demonstrable connections between *needle,* for example, and the verbal associative response elicited by the nonverbal stimulus. The data justified the prediction.

The type of experiment that has not been conducted but will soon be undertaken by us may be described as follows. Suppose a shock-elicited withdrawal of the hand is conditioned to a flash of light, and no verbal reference is made to these stimuli during the training. The prediction is that this learning should result in the establishment of a variety of meaningful verbal associative connections. Not the least of these would be the connection between the word *flash* and the word *shock.* It might also be ventured that the word *flash* would be connected with the word *bad,* so that *flash* would be said to have acquired a negative connotative meaning.

It appears appropriate in this discussion to consider the problem of verbal generalization. Much research in this area remains to be done, and it provides a nice testing ground for alternative theories. The conditions under which generalization is readily tested may, for the present purposes, be stated as follows. Suppose some type of observable response is trained to the meaningful word *needle,* and the meaningful word *scissors* is then presented. The extent of the tendency for the observable response to occur may be regarded as the measure of the amount of generalization of the observable response. While several different applications of associational theory have been used for purposes of prediction, the one here proposed, though it probably can be refined, has stood up relatively well. Table 4-1 shows how the Minnesota norms (1954) for free-associational responses may be used for making a prediction of the extent of the expected generalization. According to the theory under discussion, in the learning of the observable response to *needle,* connections become established not only between the stimulus *needle* and the observable response but also between the stimuli provided by the meaningful associates of *needle* and the observable response. The strengths of these stimuli are inferred from the cultural frequencies of the responses, which were based on a population of 1,008 subjects. All these subjects are assumed to have given the representational response of *needle.* The associational responses are those elicited in common by both *needle* and *scissors* at a cultural frequency of six or more. When *scissors* is presented in the testing situation, its representational response is not mediational but its associative responses are. The extent to which

Table 4-1

Computation of Index of Generalization for the Use of *Needle* as a Trained Word and *Scissors* as a Tested Word

| Trained word—*Needle* | | Tested word—*Scissors* | |
|---|---|---|---|
| Responses | *f* | Responses | *f* |
| Representational: | | Representational: | |
| Needle | 1,008 | Scissors | 1,008 |
| Common associational: | | Common associational: | |
| Sharp | 55 | Sharp | 90 |
| Thread | 464 | Thread | 13 |
| | | Needle | 9 |
| Sew | 64 | Sew | 8 |
| Sewing | 18 | Sewing | 8 |
| Σ common associational | 601 | Σ common associational* | 128 |

* Index = Σ common associational responses to tested word divided by the total number of associational responses = 128/1,008 = 0.127.

*scissors* should elicit the observable response is predictable on the basis of the decimal fraction representing the proportion of the associative responses to *scissors* that had in the earlier learning become effective, because of their representational stimuli, in eliciting the observable response. This proportion is 128/1,008, or 0.127. If *scissors* were the trained word and *needle* the tested word, more generalization would be predicted since the fraction is 601/1,008, or 0.596. The important factors incorporated in this treatment may be noted. First, the mediation of the observable response is contingent on multiple meaningful responses. In the second place, what has been referred to as directionality is clearly recognized. It is obvious that this method predicts a considerable amount of generalization for responses learned to antonyms. No such prediction would be made, however, on the basis of a measure of similarity of meaning since antonyms elicit relatively few common associative responses. It should be reported that our comparative studies indicate that generalization is to an appreciable extent predictable from the use of the most frequently occurring associative responses, and this confirms the findings of Mink (1957), who worked under the direction of Russell and Jenkins. On the other hand, the inclusion of the multiple associative responses appears fairly consistently to give better predictions, as was shown in the as yet unpublished dissertation of Dr. B. H. Cohen, with whom I have collaborated.

Since the problem of concept learning may be said to involve the learning of a type of meaningful response, it merits consideration in this discussion. The interpretation from the present point of view is that a conceptual response may be regarded as a type of meaningful associative response which is elicited in common by a group of stimuli. According to Underwood and Richardson (1956), the higher the dominance level of a given descriptive response, the quicker the learning of the concept it represents. There is no reason that response dominance should be limited to responses representing the sense impressions with which they worked. A dissertation study currently undertaken by Alan J. Lieberman sheds some light on the relationship between concept formation (though he did not use this term), the semantic differential, and free-associational norms. The stimulus items he worked with were three lists of 60 words each. Each such list was divided into two sublists. The words of each sublist, in turn, were selected so as to have extreme ratings at one or the other end of a particular semantic differential scale. The scales used were *good-bad*, the *active-passive*, and the *angular-rounded*. Precautions were taken to see that the various sublists were properly matched. Thus the means of the *good, active,* and *angular* ratings were similar, as were the means of the *bad, passive,* and *rounded* ratings. Furthermore, the sublists comprising a given experimental list differed along one semantic differential scale only. The differences along the other two scales were insignificant. The 60 words comprising any given list were randomized and presented one at a time to subjects in individual sessions. The task was to place the cards on which they were printed in one or the other of two racks. It was decided beforehand that the words belonged in one or the other of the racks on the basis of the concepts represented by the words; e.g., one rack was for the *good* words and the other for the *bad*. Errors were corrected as the cards were sorted. The progress of the learning was indicated by the percentage of the correct placing of the cards for six successive blocks of 10 words each. The results indicated a non-overlapping of the learning curves, with highest percentages for the correct placings of the *good* and *bad* words and the lowest for the *angular* and *rounded*. Learning significantly above the chance level was found for all lists except the *angular* and *rounded*. Since these differences could not have been predicted from the semantic differential ratings on which the words had been equated, it was suggested that the findings might have been predicted from the free-associational responses to the words. Free-associational norms were then obtained for all 180 words used in the experiment. How these meaningful associates were treated is indicated in the following example. For all the *good* stimulus words, counts were made of the cultural frequencies with which *good* was given as an associate. Counts were also made of the frequencies of occurrence in the norms of synonyms of *good*. The counts were combined to make weighted scores. These weighted scores appeared perfectly to predict the difficulty of the learning. Thus, the highest weighted scores were found for the *good* and *bad* words and the lowest for the *angular* and *rounded*. These findings certainly do not imply that semantic differential ratings lack validity, but they do suggest the advantages of working directly with word associations in certain types of studies of the formation of meaningful concepts.

In this consideration of concept formation, I am taking the liberty of outlining a testable interpretation of a significant study undertaken by Judson and Cofer (1956). Their method involved the presentation of groups of four words each, as illustrated by *skyscraper, temple, cathedral, prayer*. The subjects were asked to check the word in each group that was not related to the other three. In the example given it would be predicted, from the present point of view, that *skyscraper* should elicit a group of associative responses that would include *building* and its synonyms, but the associate *religion* would be absent or infrequent. The words *temple* and *cathedral* should elicit both *religion* and *building*. The word *prayer*, in turn, should elicit *religion* but not *building*. It may be said that as far as the associative responses are concerned, *skyscraper* and *prayer* are unambiguous, while *temple* and *cathedral* are ambiguous. For this group of words the subjects tended to check *prayer* as the unrelated word. To explain this finding, Judson and Cofer proposed that the response category represented by the first unambiguous word tends to be the dominant one in that it tends to inhibit alternative response categories. The point of reviewing this study is not to disagree with the proposed interpretation, but to point out that conceptual response categories may be treated as meaningful associative responses, and that associational responses elicited by given words may usefully be employed in this type of experiment.

In concluding this discussion it appears in order to offer some speculations regarding some factors meriting more attention than they appear to have received. The interpretation here proposed is to the effect that any meaningful stimulus should exert what might be termed a priming effect on a composite of responses to which it has become attached as a consequence of earlier learning. In so far as these responses are mediational, they are also meaningful. It is obvious that the habits representing these connections must vary in strength. What might be called the manifest response, however, is not determined exclusively by its previously acquired strength. When a stimulus occurs, it must occur within whatever context is present at the time, and this context should markedly affect the probability of occurrence of any given response. Context is here used as a generic term to refer to a variety of factors which may be described as set, motivation, nature of instructions, responses that have been elicited earlier, and ambient stimulation. These factors are not equally controllable. In so far as they tend to facilitate the occurrence of specific responses, the effect should be most potent on the responses with relatively low habit strengths. The effects of context must be evident in the data provided by free-associational norms. This is why the norms should be based on as large a population as possible. These speculations indicate that, since meaningful responses are determined to an appreciable extent by context, this factor merits further study. On the other hand, the more the control over factors of context, the less variable the experimental data.

Perhaps the title of this paper should have been "An Attempt to Justify Research on Verbal Associative Responses." Actually the term meaning need not have been introduced in describing any of the research here reported If we are to talk about meaning, however, it appears possible to make a case for regarding verbal associative responses as meaningful. At the same time, those who do not wish to talk about meaning can be optimistic about the usefulness of verbal associative responses and S-R theory for studying verbal learning.

## REFERENCES

Bousfield, W. A., Herman, P. N., & Whitmarsh, G. A. (1959) The conditioning of verbal associative responses elicited by non-verbal stimuli. *Tech. Rep. No. 33*, Contract No. Nonr-631(00), Office of Naval Research and University of Connecticut.

Bousfield, W. A., Whitmarsh, G. A., & Danick, J. J. (1958) Partial response identities in verbal generalization. *Psychol. Rep.*, 4, 703–713.

Hebb, D. O. (1949) *The organization of behavior.* New York: Wiley.

Judson, A. J., & Cofer, C. N. (1956) Reasoning as an associative process: I. "Direction" in a simple verbal problem. *Psychol. Rep.*, 2, 469–476.

Kincaid, W., Bousfield, W. A., & Whitmarsh, G. A. (1959) The parasitic reinforcement of verbal associative responses. *Tech. Rep. No. 32*, Contract No. Nonr-631(00), Office of Naval Research and University of Connecticut.

Mink, W. D. (1957) Semantic generalization as related to word association. *Tech. Rep. No. 17*, Contract No. N8onr-66216, Office of Naval Research and University of Minnesota.

Noble, C. E. (1952) An analysis of meaning. *Psychol. Rev.*, 59, 421–430.

Osgood, C. E. (1953) *Method and theory in experimental psychology.* New York: Oxford.

Russell, W. A., & Jenkins, J. J. (1954) The complete Minnesota norms for responses to 100 words from the Kent-Rosanoff Word Association Test. *Tech. Rep. No. 11*, Contract No. N8onr-66216, Office of Naval Research and University of Minnesota.

Underwood, B. J., & Richardson, J. (1956) Verbal concept learning as a function of instructions and dominance level. *J. Exp. Psychol.*, 51, 229–238.

Yavuz, H. S., & Bousfield, W. A. (1959) Recall of connotative meaning. *Psychol. Rep.*, 5, 319–320.

# COMMENTS ON PROFESSOR BOUSFIELD'S PAPER

## Charles E. Osgood

UNIVERSITY OF ILLINOIS

I am glad that Professor Bousfield states his bias—that meaning is an unnecessary concept for verbal learning—right at the beginning of his paper, and thus firmly plants himself on the side of the angels with B. F. Skinner. It is easier to deal with an acknowledged opponent than with a doubtful ally. As for myself, I am convinced that meaning is the single most important variable in human learning, verbal or otherwise— that human adjustment is mainly a matter of acquiring and modifying the significances of signs and learning how to behave in ways appropriate to these significances. I would like to think that at a conference like this, for example, most of the human participants will learn something more than a new arrangement in their word-association hierarchies, although this will also happen.

It seems to me that Bousfield, as well as Skinner and others of their disposition, walk a very narrow line between the virtue of parsimony and the sin of omission. In the closing pages of his *Verbal Behavior*, Skinner (1957) admits that there may be such things as nonobservable, symbolic responses to signs and even that such events may be necessary for a full account of verbal behavior, but he prefers to let other people worry about them. The sin of omission, you see, can come very close to repression of the unpleasant, the confounding, the complicating. Bousfield, however, decides to face the issue more squarely, to grapple with "meaning" directly—but in doing so convinces himself that meaning is not merely elusive but actually nonexistent, a phantom. He thinks that meaning has joined the family of psychological concepts "because it has able and influential friends," but I think that meaning always has been, and always will be, an influential relative just simply because the family has found that it cannot get along without him.

Bousfield feels that "meaning" is a concept bound to lead to confusion. With this I most heartily agree, although I think much of the confusion has come from attempts to circumvent the notion. I find confusions in Bousfield's paper, but I know that I have contributed my own full share. So let us start by trying to clear up some of these confusions.

Central to Bousfield's theoretical analysis of the role of meaning in verbal behavior is the notion of a "*representational* response, $r_{rep}$" which is said to be part of the total reaction to a given stimulus. Now this sounds very much like what I have called a "*representational* mediation process, $r_m$," and Bousfield says that he has borrowed this notion from me; we both agree that such processes have self-stimulational properties, and hence may have *mediational* properties. But closer examination shows that we are *not* talking about the same thing, that in fact we are involved in two old confusions in this field—confusions, incidentally, that also confounded an earlier SSRC conference at Minnesota on word association (Jenkins, 1959). One confusion concerns *the nature of the representational process* itself; the other concerns *the nature of the mediation process* in verbal behavior. We will not be able to communicate effectively with each other until these sources of ambiguity have been made explicit; then we may still disagree, but at least we will be clearer as to why.

First, then, *the nature of the representational or symbolic process.* Bousfield and I definitely agree that some kind of representational processes must be postulated in order to handle what we can directly observe about verbal behavior, e.g., mediated or semantic generalization, but we have entirely different conceptions of the nature of this process. This comes out most clearly if we compare Bousfield's diagram of primary sign learning (which he calls "first order conditioning") with the one I have used (see Figure 4-2). In the first place, Bousfield says that the US "elicits its conditionable representational response"; I have always assumed that in *primary* sign learning unconditioned stimuli simply elicit unconditioned (though admittedly complex) responses. If pain is assumed to elicit a symbolic process, and hence itself has the status of a sign, we must ask what is pain a sign *of*—what does it refer to? In the present example, I find no obvious answer to this question. I think we must start somewhere with stimuli that are *not* signs and responses that are *not* representational; otherwise the notion loses all of its discriminative force.

But even more importantly, look at the nature of the representational response in the two models and their derivation from observables. According to Bousfield, the representational response to the verbal sign "bad" is simply the child's saying "bad" overtly or implicitly, presumably on the basis of mimicry. The important thing to note about this conception is that it specifies the *form* of the representational response as being the same as the overt vocal production of the word, even if reduced in amplitude. In my own conception, the representational process is assumed to be some reduced portion *of the total behavior made to the thing signified;* under the condition of repeated pairing of the sign stimulus (the word "bad") with the significate stimulus (painful spanking), the sign stimulus comes to elicit those most readily conditionable and least interfering components of the total behavior to the significate (e.g., autonomic anxiety reactions, avoidant postural sets, and the like). It is precisely because this representational process *is* part of the actual behavior made to the thing signified that the sign has its discriminative

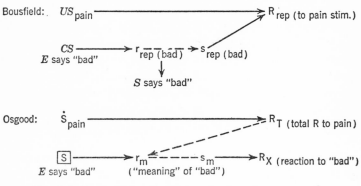

FIG. 4-2. Conceptions of primary sign learning compared.

semantic or symbolic capacity. The important thing to note about this conception is that it specifies that the form of the representational response is not the same as the overt vocal production of the word. Its occurrence and strength depend upon the presence of the sign and the frequency with which sign and significate stimuli have been paired; its nature or form depends upon the total behavior made to the significate.

Is there any way we can choose among these two alternative conceptions of the representational process? I offer two sources of evidence, one very old and one very new. In the early decades of this century, under the impetus of Watson's dictum that thinking is just implicit talking to one's self, a considerable number of studies were made, with gradually increasing sensitivity of apparatus. The ultimate refinement of vacuum tube amplifiers made it possible for Max (1937) and Jacobson (1932) to record changes in motor nerve potentials in millionths of a volt, with the express purpose of demonstrating a correlation between the form of implicit motor activity during thought and the form of overt speech. There is not one shred of positive evidence in that whole literature.

The very new evidence is a most ingenious experiment by Wallace Lambert at McGill, described in a manuscript he sent me just a couple of weeks ago (Lambert and Jakobovits, 1960). Lambert is studying "semantic satiation." Following massed presentation and overt presentation of some verbal stimulus, he has subjects judge the stimulus against a short semantic differential form, appropriately using reduction in polarization (i.e., shift inward toward the origin of the semantic space) as his index of satiation of meaning. In one experiment three groups of subjects were treated as follows: Group I repeated each test word out loud for 15 seconds and then rated it; Group II saw each test word and then had 15 seconds of silence before rating it; Group III repeated a *different* word (meaningfully unrelated) for 15 seconds and then rated the test word. The only group showing satiation, and it was significant beyond the 1 per cent level, was that repeating the test word. So far so good, but we have no differential test as to the form of the representational process. In a second experiment, nonsense and meaningful materials were compared. Group I repeated nonsense items like "groni'" and "nu'ka"; Group II repeated nonsense items like "tro'ga" and "bla'tu"; Group III repeated meaningful words like "Negro" and "canoe." The only group to show *any* satiation—and again this was significant beyond the 1 per cent level—was that which repeated the meaningful words "Negro" and "canoe." But now observe the fact that when a person is rapidly repeating "groni'," he is actually producing the identical overt vocalization as "Negro"; and when he repeats "nu'ka," he is producing the form of "canoe" over and over again. Now, *if* the response form of the representational process is *the same* as the overt expression of the sign it represents, as Bousfield would have it, then why isn't "meaning" satiated as much by massed repetition of "groni'" as by massed repetition of "Negro"?

Now, then, what about the other confusion, what about *the nature of the mediation process?* A significant experimental literature is rapidly accumulating on what is usually called "mediated generalization" but which, for reasons that will become apparent, I think should be termed *mediated verbal transfer*. The operations for demonstrating this phenomenon are readily stated. One verbal stimulus is paired with a novel response (e.g., *joy*-$R_x$) until a sufficient habit strength is built up; then a different verbal stimulus is presented, and we observe whether or not the novel response transfers to the new stimulus (e.g., *glee*-$R_x$?). It is necessary, of course, that the test stimulus not have been associated with the criterion response in the subject's past history. The nature of the criterion response itself is quite arbitrary and variable: it can be a flexion movement of the forefinger, saying a certain word as in lists of paired associates, or even saying a nonsense syllable. Although the studies with which we shall be mainly concerned *do* deal with transfer from one verbal stimulus to another, even this is not essential: many experiments have studied mediated transfer from significate to sign (e.g., from color *blue* to word *blue*), from sign to significate (e.g., from word *blue* to color *blue*), and from significate to significate (e.g., from *lace handkerchief* to *smell of perfume*). There is one additional requirement if *mediated* (as opposed to *primary*) *transfer* is to be demonstrated: the test stimulus must not be physically similar to the training stimulus.

If the conditions for demonstrating mediated verbal transfer are easy to state, the underlying mechanisms which do the mediating certainly are not. The experimental findings to date make it necessary for us to postulate at least two—and probably at least three, as I shall try to show later—entirely different kinds of mediating mechanism. One of these is what I would call *verbal response chaining*. This mechanism operates to the extent that either (a) the training word as a stimulus is already connected with the test word as a response or (b) training and test words as stimuli have been connected already with some common word as a response in the previous learning history of the subject. This is the kind of mechanism whose effects would be predictable from word-association norms. To get around the fact that subjects in these experiments almost never overtly produce the associated test word during training (situation a) or any common associates during testing (situation b), we must assume that such response chaining can be implicit; and this, of course, is where Bousfield's kind of representational process comes in. We simply assume that while learning the new habit *joy-window*, the subject is implicitly saying *glee*, hence *joy-glee*rep-*window*. Now I haven't the slightest doubt but that such a chaining mechanism as this is at work, continuously and pervasively; experiments like those of Bastian (1957) and Mink (1957) from the Minnesota laboratories are entirely convincing on this point. I object, however, when it is claimed that this is the *only* mechanism contributing to mediated verbal transfer, as Bousfield is forced by his theory to conclude.

The second mechanism is what I would call *semantic generalization*. This mechanism operates to the extent that training and test stimuli, as signs, have acquired similar representational mediation processes (in my sense) in the previous history of the organism. This is the kind of mechanism whose effects should be predictable from the multivariate distances (Ds) between words as judged on appropriate semantic differentials—and I say "appropriate" advisedly because a differential whose factors account for only a small proportion of the variance in word meanings is bound to yield a large margin of error. It should be noted that this mechanism includes the notion of *gradients of generaliza-*

*tion* (in this case, among the self-produced stimuli in the representational processes), and hence could be expected to yield *graded* amounts of transfer within the individual subject rather than the all-or-nothing transfer in individual subjects required by the chaining model.

Is there evidence for such a mechanism? In the first place, I would refer you to the very extensive literature on semantic generalization, including many Russian studies, in which transfer is demonstrated from signs to their significates and vice versa, among significates, and so on. This literature has been summarized, at least up to the dates of our publications, by both Razran (1949) and myself (1952). Second, I would point to the cross-modality metaphors (e.g., "My candle is flickering out," to refer to one's approaching death) and cross-modality synesthesias (e.g., representing *fast* music by colors toward the *red* end of the spectrum and the reverse for slow music) that are the flesh which graces the bare bones of aesthetics. Under psychological analysis, these fall out rather directly as instances of semantic generalization. But I doubt if you would very frequently find *death* among the associates to *candle* (unlit or otherwise) or *blue* among the associates to *slow*. (I looked up this last one, and it doesn't occur at all.) Third, we have the study by Dicken (1958) in which significant amounts of mediated verbal transfer were obtained within groups of words having reasonably small semantic distances among them but very low or nonexistent associative strengths.

As a final bit of evidence—and one which has an intriguing additional twist to it—I cite the results of a recently completed thesis by Baxter (1959). He selected the words *home, nurse, money, bleak, fraud,* and *starve* as being widely separated over the evaluative factor as determined from the *Semantic Differential Atlas.* (He used the measured meanings of these words on his own subjects.) The novel response was the GSR produced by shock as the US. Group I subjects were assigned one of these words at random as the training stimulus and were tested for generalization to all of the other words. The results were inconclusive. Baxter then ran two additional groups to try to find out what was happening, with these modifications: Group II subjects were given their most positively evaluated word as the training stimulus; Group III subjects were given their most negatively evaluated word. The results are shown in Figure 4-3. Note that for Group III we get an almost perfect generalization gradient as a function of semantic distance. Now, recalling that the unconditioned stimulus here was a just barely bearable shock and realizing that the training situation (*word-shock*) is precisely that in which Arthur Staats would talk about the "conditioning of meaning" (particularly if a nonsense item has been the CS), it becomes evident that here Baxter was intensifying an already negatively evaluative representational process and recording GSR as an index of it. This is a semantically uncomplicated situation. Now look at the results for Group II, where the most positively evaluated word was associated with *shock:* here the most similar word in meaning shows the least generalization, while the words which already had a negative evaluation show more generalization. Here we have a complicated semantic situation, in which an opposite meaning is being foisted upon the training stimulus. I began talking about words of opposed meaning being based on reciprocally antagonistic mediation processes almost fifteen years ago and tested the idea with some verbal retroaction experiments, but here is the first experimental evidence from someone else to support the idea.

Is such evidence sufficient to justify postulation of a semantic generalization mechanism as separate from verbal response chaining? I think

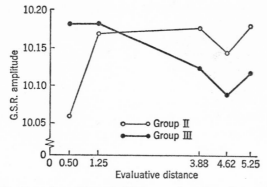

Fig. 4-3. Generalization of conditioned GSRs as a function of semantic distance from positively evaluated conditioned word and from negatively evaluated conditioned word. (*After Baxter,* 1959.)

it is, but Bousfield, Cohen, Whitmarsh, Noble, Cofer, and maybe even Jenkins would say that these cases can be handled by their (b) alternative, that is, overlap in the verbal associates of the training and test stimuli. John Flavell (1961) has developed a measure of experiential contingency among the referents of words. (For example, given the occurrence of *automobile,* what is the probability of experiencing *whitewall tires,* and vice versa?) He thinks this measure is an index of denotative similarity, but I think it is an index, or predictor, of strength of association (cf. Osgood and Anderson, 1957). In any case, he finds that the prediction of judged similarity of meaning is improved by combining semantic differential D with his kind of contextual overlap measure in a multiple correlation, which implies some degree of independence between the two measures. The final word remains to be said, of course, but it is probable that we will need both types of mediational mechanisms.

Now I'd like to turn to Bousfield's interesting proposal that the word-association rationale he has developed "adequately accounts for the process of making ratings on the semantic differential." His reasoning is that a subject will rate a concept toward one end of a semantic differential scale to the extent that the concept, as a stimulus, is associated with the word defining that end of the scale, as a response. To use his own illustration, *evil* is rated at the *bad* end of the *good-bad* scale because *bad* is a fairly strong associative response to *evil*. Now this seems like a rather sensible suggestion and, better than that, one that would exorcise the concept of "meaning" even from the *n*-dimensional space of the instrument that is supposed to measure it. But what does an "adequate account" of semantic differential ratings in terms of word associations require? It requires that the direction and intensity (polarization) of the ratings be closely related, respectively, to which of the alternative scalar terms appear as associates to the concept and to the relative strengths of such associates.

Fortunately we now have available precisely the kinds of data on which to test the adequacy of Bousfield's proposal. We have the Minnesota norms for the Kent-Rosanoff Word Association Test (Russell and Jenkins, 1954), and we have, from an equivalent Minnesota student population, *An Atlas of Semantic Profiles for 360 Words* (Jenkins, Russell, and Suci, 1958), which includes most of the stimulus words on the Kent-Rosanoff test. These data permit a validation of my disbelief in Bousfield's conception.

Before giving you the results of this test, it may be useful to indicate some of the more intuitive reasons for my complete disbelief in this proposition. In the first place, the same restricted set of scalar terms can be used effectively to index the connotative meanings of a wide variety of concepts, and it is hard to believe that there would be such redundancy in word associations. Secondly, it is obvious from inspection that many of the judgments called for in typical applications of the semantic differential are quite novel, and the concepts and scales have probably seldom if ever been associated in the previous experience of the subject—e.g., *mother–cold-hot, our policy in China–high-low, mountain–masculine-feminine*—yet highly polarized reactions can be obtained. Thirdly neither the concepts nor the scales need be verbal at all. We have had abstract art and sonar signals judged against the usual verbal differentials, or usual verbal concepts such as *happy* or *man* judged against pairs of visual forms like jagged versus smooth lines, large versus small circles, or upward- versus downward-pointed arrows, and obtained entirely meaningful results. Finally, we all know that the associations given to verbal stimuli also depend upon other things than their "meanings," for example, upon frequency of usage, upon the grammatical status of the stimulus, upon trite phrases (e.g., *stop-light*, *waste-basket*, *apple-cart*, and so on).

What are the empirical facts? In the *Atlas of Semantic Profiles* 20 semantic differential scales were used, i.e., 40 words. For every Kent-Rosanoff stimulus word that had also been used as a concept in the *Atlas* (and this included about 75 per cent of them), I checked through the associates given in the Minnesota norms for any of these 40 scale terms, and where I found one, I noted both its associative frequency (per 1,000 subjects) and the mean scale position checked in the *Atlas*. I also went through the reverse procedure: for every concept in the *Atlas* which was also a Kent-Rosanoff stimulus word, I listed those scale terms for which the mean judgments were extremely polarized (means greater than +2, that is, in the extreme "1" or "7" position on the scale) and then checked to see if these terms occurred *at all* among the 1,000 associations to the stimulus word.

Let us look first at the simple occurrence versus nonoccurrence data. For the stimulus words that occur in both sets of norms, there were 145 instances where the mean judgment of a concept on a scale reaches this extreme degree of polarization. If Bousfield is right—if such extreme checking toward one end of a scale is due to strong association of that term with the concept as a stimulus—then we should certainly expect such terms at least to appear among the associative responses to the stimulus words. Such is clearly not the case. Only 38 of these 145 polarized terms in the semantic differential appear at all among the associates to the same stimulus words. In other words, for about 75 per cent of the judgments on the semantic differential which reach this high degree of polarization, the scalar term must have a general associative connection with the stimulus for less than one subject in a thousand. Here is an example: for the concept *joy*, the terms *kind, savory, successful, good, important, colorful,* and *beautiful* are the ends of the scales which reach this degree of polarization. But only *good* appears among the associations to *joy*, and this for only 9 people in 1,000.

Second, let's look at the *direction* of judgment on the semantic differential scales in relation to the words appearing as associates to the concepts being judged. Certainly, if we are to claim that where a concept is rated on a semantic differential scale depends upon which term appears as an associate, then at least the mean judgment ought to be toward that term rather than toward its opposite on the scale. There are 185 instances where a scale term appears among the word associates to the same concept. For about two-thirds of these (120), the mean scale position *is* in the right direction; but by the same token, in one-third of these instances (65 cases), the mean judgment is actually toward the opposite of the term given as an associate. For example, to the stimulus *deep* the associate *soft* is given by 38 people (which is fairly high, as such things go), yet the mean judgment of *deep* on the *hard-soft* scale is toward the *hard* side.

Now it is true that some of these instances are cases in which the direct opposite is given as the associate. There are only 6 such cases out of the 65, however. (For example, to the stimulus *beautiful* 209 subjects give *ugly* as an associate but obviously check it on the scale as extremely *beautiful*.) You might want to throw these out as special cases. But I think they represent the *reductio ad absurdum* of the proposal: here we have cases where as many as 752 out of 1,000 people (*fast* occurs 752 times to the stimulus *slow*) give the term at one end of a semantic differential scale as an associate and yet judge the same concept to be at the other extreme (2.7 toward *slow*) of the scale. In the face of such facts, how can we claim that the locations of these ratings simply reflect word-association tendencies?

Finally, we may look at the *relative-intensity* aspect of the proposition—that the greater the frequency of word association between concept and scale term, the more polarized will be the rating on the semantic differential. To get at this relation, I collected all of the word-association frequencies as functions of mean scale positions, expressed in half-unit intervals; I then transformed the raw association frequencies into $\log_{10}$ values to eliminate the extreme skewness that characterizes word-association hierarchies, and finally averaged these transformed association-frequency values for each scale interval. These mean log association frequencies, along with the equivalent average raw frequencies, are given in Table 4-2. It will be noted that there is some tendency for association

Table 4-2

Association Frequency as a Function of SD Scale Polarization

| Association frequencies | Mean judgment toward associate | | | | | |
|---|---|---|---|---|---|---|
| | 3.0–2.5 | 2.5–2.0 | 2.0–1.5 | 1.5–1.0 | 1.0–0.5 | 0.5–0.0 |
| Mean log $f$ | .87 | .70 | .69 | .38 | .24 | .30 |
| Equivalent $f$ | 7 | 5 | 5 | 2 | 2 | 2 |

| Association frequencies | Mean judgment away from associate | | | | | |
|---|---|---|---|---|---|---|
| | 0.0–0.5 | 0.5–1.0 | 1.0–1.5 | 1.5–2.0 | 2.0–2.5 | 2.5–3.0 |
| Mean log $f$ | .22 | .29 | .04 | .43 | .59 | 2.61 |
| Equivalent $f$ | 2 | 2 | 1 | 3 | 4 | 410 |

frequency to increase with polarization on the semantic differential, as Bousfield predicts, and it holds both for cases where the mean judgment is toward the associate appearing in the norms and for those where it is toward the opposite. In other words, if one of the scale terms appears at all as an associate to the concept being judged, the degree of scalar polarization does tend to be related to the association frequency. However, excluding the cases in which direct opposites account for the extreme terminal value, it can also be seen that this trend is slight; each polarization category contains association-frequency values ranging from 1/1,000 up to 25/1,000 and even 369/1,000 in one case. The correlation between log association frequency and mean scale position, for just the "toward associate" cases, is only .35. Thus only about 10 per cent of the variance in scale polarization can be accounted for by the word-association data. This, coupled with the very low absolute association frequencies (e.g., an average of only 7 responses per 1,000 subjects for the highest degree of polarization), means that we cannot accept the proposition that scale-checking behavior on the semantic differential is determined simply by word-association tendencies.

But why is there any relation at all between extremeness of judgments on the differential and frequency of association? Here I think we could profitably reread the paper by Staats and Staats (1959). Their basic notion is that the same condition of *repeated contiguity in experience of words* is simultaneously a condition for establishing both transitional relations (word association) and semantic relations (assign learning). Thus, repeated hearing and reading of *Fifth Amendment Communist* leads both to a strong associative tendency (given *Fifth Amendment,* respond *Communist*) and a shift in the meaning of *Fifth Amendment* from evaluative neutrality toward the negative meaning of *Communist.* But note carefully that there is an implicit positive assertion here: *Fifth Amendment* (users are) *Communists.* We often have experiential contingencies between words where the assertions are consistently negative, in which case we would expect high associative strength but meaningful opposition. The behavior of standard verbal opposites is a case in point. We rarely if ever (for excellent logical and semantic reasons) hear things like "John is tall *and* short" or "Black *is* white; beautiful *is* ugly" (except in Orwell's *1984*); but we repeatedly hear constructions like "John is tall, *not* short" or "It is an ugly, *not* a beautiful thing, which you desire," and so on. Finally, and perhaps most relevantly, we would expect concepts to be associated in rational speech with qualifiers similar in meaning, e.g., *honest hero, evil villain, lively jig, stately waltz,* etc., which would tend to produce both associative *and* semantic differential relations. But this is not necessary. Words may appear together rarely, and yet be meaningfully related on certain dimensions (e.g., *mountain* and *masculine*);

or words may appear in such meaningfully incompatible contingencies that associations are formed but no meaningful relations (e.g., the word *chair* is experienced contiguously with both *hard* and *soft*, so we find both terms appearing among the associates but a semantic differential rating of 4.3, which is almost exactly in the middle of the scale).

The last matter I would like to raise for discussion has more to do with language behavior generally than with Bousfield's paper per se, although it is relevant to it. This is the problem of multiple meanings of "meaning" and quantitative indices of meaning. This is another source of confusion, not only among psychologists like ourselves who study language behavior but also between us and others who study language, such as linguists and philosophers. That "meaning" would have many different meanings should not come as a surprise.

I can best demonstrate the distinction between two of the most common meanings of "meaning," *denotative meaning* and what I have called *connotative meaning*, with reference to some diagrams using psycho-

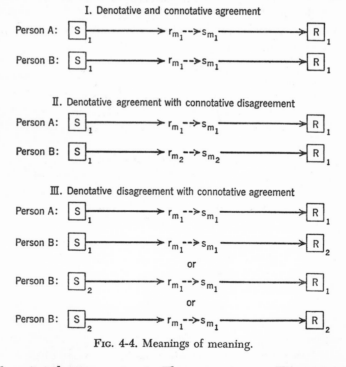

Fig. 4-4. Meanings of meaning.

logical learning-theory constructs. These are given as Figure 4-4. I define *denotive meaning* as a conventional, habitual correlation between a non-linguistic perceptual pattern, $\boxed{S}$, and some particular linguistic response, $\boxed{R}$. Two people, A and B, will be said to be in *denotative agree-*

*ment* to the extent that they display the same external correlations between nonlinguistic and linguistic events. Here we are concerned with
the arbitrary "rules of usage" which govern the vocabulary and the
grammar of a language, and this is the meaning of "meaning" that linguists and philosophers usually employ. I define *connotative meaning* as
that habitual symbolic process ($r_m \rightarrow s_m$) that occurs in a sign user when
a particular sign (perceptual or linguistic) is received or produced. Two
people, A and B, will be said to be in *connotative agreement* to the extent
that they display the same symbolic reactions to signs, as indexed by
their profiles on a semantic differential, for example. Here we are concerned with the "interpretative" process, as Charles Morris has termed it,
with the states or processes in organisms which become associated with
sign stimuli through experience, hence, with "psychological" meaning.
Linguists usually call this "affective meaning," which I think is too narrow a term.

Figure 4-4, I, presents the ideal case for effective communication, i.e.,
simultaneous denotative and connotative agreement between persons A
and B. When shown a certain rounded red object, both A and B say
"apple"; and when asked to differentiate the object or sign on a set of
semantic scales, they agree in their profiles. Figure 4-4, II, gives the
interesting case in which we have denotative agreement between A and
B but connotative disagreement. This case is interesting because it em-
phasizes the point that agreement in psychological states is not necessary
for successful communication in the usual sense—in fact, is irrelevant to it.
My favorite example is that of the normal father with a color-blind son
who is allergic to apples. Although apples neither look the same nor have
the same gratifying consequences (hence different $r_m$'s are learned) for
the father and son, both will learn the same rules of usage; the son will
bring apples when requested, say "apple" when asked what they are, and
so on. But they should have quite different semantic differential profiles.
A machine could be built to display acceptable denotative correlations
in a limited semantic area. It is this type of situation, of course, for which
the semantic differential finds its main applications, e.g., for determining
how people differ in their connotative meanings of *me*, of *Senator
McCarthy*, of *father* when we assume that the denotative correlations are
the same.

Figure 4-4, III, describes several ways in which there may be connotative agreement despite denotative disagreement. In the first case, persons
A and B use different verbal signs in the same situation. Mrs. Malaprop
is the classic example. This is also the sort of thing that goes on all the
time while a child is learning his language. Both he and his mother ap-
preciate the significance of the object *doughnut*, but for a while he calls
it "cookie." In the second case we have persons A and B using the same

linguistic sign in different stimulus situations. In many cases this is merely due to differences in denotative range; e.g., psychologists use the term "stimulus" in a different "sense" than laymen, or the neurophysiologist, for that matter. This is the paradigm on which philosophers have their controversies over the necessary conditions for synonymity and the like. The last case suggests that persons A and B may display entirely different denotative correlations on both situational and linguistic sides of the equation, and yet still be linked by connotative agreement. Take for example what is implied by the statement, "A gourmet approaches his lamb chop as a lover approaches his mistress." The only thing they have in common is their affectionate attitude. And of course this *is* the condition I mentioned earlier for metaphorical extension. We are not surprised to hear the gourmet murmur "lover" tenderly to his lamb chop or to hear the lover murmur, equally tenderly, "lamb chop" to his mistress! This is also what we have when bilingual subjects take translation-equivalent forms of the semantic differential at different times, e.g., in Japanese and then in English, and come up with identical *connotative* factors. In fact, the factors are as highly correlated as they are when obtained for Americans taking the test twice in the same language. And this, by the way, again makes me wonder about the adequacy of Bousfield's kind of representational process: his kind of representational responses certainly must be different for the Japanese and the English languages. Why, then, this near-perfect agreement in what the semantic differential measures?

I have gone through these commonsensical examples to show that these two kinds of meaning, denotative and connotative, not only refer to quite different processes but, since they do vary independently of each other, must have different indices. There is a third usage of the term "meaning" that has legitimacy in philosophical and linguistic circles, but need not concern psychologists. This is what may be called the *signification* of a term. This is the "semantic rule" for its usage, as distinct from a mere cataloguing of its uses (i.e., its denotation). The terms *father* and *me* mentioned above actually provide illustrations. The denotation of my *me* and *father* is obviously different from the denotation of your *me* and *father*, but the semantic rule or signification is the same: *me* refers to the speaker, whoever he may be, and *father* refers to the speaker's male parent (in this language-culture group, but not necessarily for others.) The reason I say signification is not particularly important to psychologists is that it is part of the metalanguage about language used by third-person observers, not part of the behavior of primary sign users.

But where does the kind of "meaning" postulated by Bousfield come in? It doesn't appear at all, to my knowledge, in the literature of semiotics, and I think for good reason. According to Bousfield, as I understand him, the meaning of a word is the associative $r_{rep}$'s it evokes, i.e.; part of the meaning of *evil* is the $r_{rep}$ for *bad*. We might call this associative meaning to distinguish it from connotation, denotation, and signification, from which it clearly differs. Now, I take it that this is different from Noble's *m*, although certainly similar to it, in that it is supposed to take into account the *nature* of the mediating associations rather than their sheer *availability*. However, since the $r_{rep}$ *bad* is simply the subvocal occurrence of the noise and its $r_{rep}$'s are merely subvocal occurrences of other arbitrary noises in lexical code, it seems to me that we have here an infinite regression that never leads back to the nonverbal bedrock of things signified. As to the similarity of Bousfield's "meaning," via $r_{rep}$'s, to Noble's *m*, I have already indicated here and elsewhere—"vehemently," as one reviewer put it—that I do not think you can equate the meaning of a sign with the associations it produces. To do so not only leads to certain absurdities ( e.g., that *beautiful* means *ugly* because this is the dominant association), but makes the term "meaning" lose its consensual validity. People simply don't use the term "meaning" to refer to a word's associations, which is the reason, I presume, that this doesn't appear in the classic philosophical literature as one of the meanings of "meaning."

I've tried to convince you—I don't know how successfully—that "meaning" is a crucially central concept in human behavior, particularly verbal behavior, and that you can neither kick it under the rug for the cleaning woman to worry about (as Skinner would do) nor translate it out of existence (as I believe Bousfield would do). I have gathered together some evidence to show, first, that there are representational processes functioning in meaningful behavior that are not of the same form as the overt verbalizations we use to express them, and second, that the reactions of subjects to a semantic differential are not predictable from knowing their word-association hierarchies. In other words, meaning exists, and it has a multidimensional nature which can be measured at least roughly.

REFERENCES

Bastian, J. R. (1957) Response chaining in verbal transfer. *Tech. Rep. No. 13*, Contract No. N8onr-66216, Office of Naval Research and University of Minnesota.

Baxter, J. C. (1959) Mediated generalization as a function of semantic differential performance. Unpublished Ph.D. dissertation, University of Texas.

Dicken, C. F. (1958) Connotative meaning as a determinant of stimulus generalization. *Tech. Rep. No. 23*, Contract No. N8onr-66216, Office of Naval Research and University of Minnesota.

Flavell, J. H. (1961) Meaning and meaning similarity: II. The semantic differential and co-occurrence as predictors of judged similarity in meaning. *J. Gen. Psychol.*, **64**, 321–335.

Jacobson, L. E. (1932) The electrophysiology of mental activities. *Amer. J. Psychol.*, 44, 677–694.

Jenkins, J. J. (Ed.) (1959) *Associative processes in verbal behavior: A report of the Minnesota Conference.* Minneapolis: University of Minnesota, Department of Psychology.

Jenkins, J. J., Russell, W. A., & Suci, G. J. (1958) An atlas of semantic profiles for 360 words. *Amer. J. Psychol.*, 71, 688–699.

Lambert, W. E., & Jakobovits, L. A. (1960) Verbal satiation and changes in the intensity of meaning. *J. Exper. Psychol.*, 60, 376–383.

Max, L. W. (1937) Experimental study of the motor theory of consciousness: IV. Action-current responses in the deaf during awakening, kinesthetic imagery and abstract thinking. *J. Comp. Psychol.*, 24, 301–344.

Mink, W. D. (1957) Semantic generalization as related to word association. *Tech. Rep. No. 17*, Contract No. N8onr-66216, Office of Naval Research and University of Minnesota.

Osgood, C. E. (1952) The nature and measurement of meaning. *Psychol. Bull.*, 49, 197–237.

Osgood, C. E., & Anderson, L. (1957) Certain relations among experienced contingencies, associative structure, and contingencies in encoded messages. *Amer. J. Psychol.*, 70, 411–420.

Razran, G. (1949) Stimulus generalization of conditioned responses. *Psychol. Bull.*, 46, 337–365.

Russell, W. A., & Jenkins, J. J. (1954) The complete Minnesota norms for responses to 100 words from the Kent-Rosanoff Word Association Test. *Tech. Rep. No. 11*, Contract No. N8onr-66216, Office of Naval Research and University of Minnesota.

Skinner, B. F. (1957) *Verbal behavior.* New York: Appleton-Century-Crofts.

Staats, A. W., & Staats, C. K. (1959) Meaning and *m*: Correlated but separate. *Psychol. Rev.*, 66, 136–144.

## SUMMARY OF CONFERENCE DISCUSSION

Some of the discussion represented an attempt to clarify the differences between Osgood and Bousfield concerning the nature of the representational responses each postulates ($r_m$ and $r_{rep}$, respectively). There were two chief points. The first was that the model of sign learning must be applicable to the preverbal child, i.e., that he can learn meanings through conditioning an association between a sign or symbol and some part of the unconditioned responses ($R_T$) made to an unconditioned stimulus before language has developed in him or before he can read or imitate a word spoken by another (Osgood). The point is that in such instances Bousfield's $r_{rep}$ would not be present. The second point was that Bousfield's $r_{rep}$ seems necessarily to have the same form as the verbal label (*bad* in the examples given), whereas this is not true of Osgood's $r_m$.[1]

[1] It seems to the editor that there was needless confusion on this point; this judgment is based on a study of Osgood's paper and of the notes of the discussion. The

Osgood stressed that the conditioned response, even in classical conditioning, may have a form different from that of the unconditioned response. However, Bousfield denied that he espouses a peripheralistic interpretation of $r_{rep}$. It seemed clear, during the discussion, that Osgood could accept Bousfield's ideas at least in the case in which verbal responses are part of $R_T$. There were suggestions that Bousfield's diagram may represent a special case of Osgood's. To Osgood's citation of Jacobson's and Max's studies against him, Bousfield replied that it is difficult, if not impossible, to distinguish emotional reactions by means of recording various visceral responses, a point directed at the differentiations required for connotative meanings in Osgood's work with the semantic differential.

There were a number of comments concerning the evidence which Osgood cited as supporting his position against Bousfield's. In the case of the Lambert study, a number of participants doubted that the repeated saying of "groni'" and "nu'ka" actually produced the same form of response as the saying of "Negro" and "canoe." Therefore, the failure to show satiation effects with the former two "words" was thought not to bear on the issue. On the other hand, the satiation experiment by Smith and Raygor (1956) was cited by Jenkins as dealing with a similar phenomenon. In this study, observation of a stimulus word for a period of time before associating to it was required of the subjects; the associations, when the subject finally gave them, were of lower commonality than would be expected.

Objection was made to Osgood's citation of studies of semantic generalization as supporting the postulation of $r_m$ as a mediating factor. The

---

nub of the discussion seems to have been concerned with the event which the sign instigates and which in turn leads to the response derivative from the painful stimulus. Osgood refers to the events following the administration of a painful stimulus by $R_T$, Bousfield by $r_{rep\ (to\ pain)}$. Osgood suggests that $r_m$ is only a part of $R_T$; although his diagram suggests otherwise, it is unlikely that Bousfield would mean that the entire reaction to the pain stimulus is recreated by the saying of a word. (He does define $r_{rep}$ as *part* of the total reaction to a stimulus.) If this is so, then both Osgood and Bousfield assert that a part of the pain reaction occurs when a word or other sign is presented; the major difference is that Bousfield argues for the *saying* of the word (explicitly or implicitly) as the critical event which the sign instigates and which in turn elicits the response to pain either directly or through the mediation of a *chain* of words. Where words are said, in the manner described, it seems that this would not offer a special problem to Osgood. His insistence is that words are not necessary to these processes. In any event, the discussion of the *form* of the response seems irrelevant to this issue, as the conditioned response in these examples is derived from the response to pain, not from events antecedent to the pain. Bousfield is asserting that the presentation of a verbal sign elicits its repetition and that the stimuli emanating from this response are conditioned to the pain response. Osgood does not include this step; the verbal response follows $r_m$ in his model as an instrumental rather than as a mediating event. (Ed.)

point made was that words which show such generalization (e.g., *glee*, *joy*) also possess considerable associative overlap. Transfer between antonymic responses also was mentioned, but Osgood interpreted this transfer as arising from response chaining. Several participants, however, were not convinced that there is no common "meaning" between antonyms. It was said that the verbal opposite of a word could be part of the $R_T$ of that word. To Osgood's suggestion that cross-modality metaphors support his position it was replied (Deese) that associations should be obtained, for example, to the color blue and to slow music in order to see whether these stimuli share associative responses. As to Baxter's study, Jenkins thought the data may only show that negatively affective words elicit larger GSRs than positively affective words. If curves are plotted on this affective scale, the two groups would be similar. The point here is that there may be a gradient of GSR reactions to the words which differ in affective rating even without conditioning. If so, the experimental data show little or no actual conditioning.[2]

Several points were made concerning Osgood's tests of Bousfield's associative interpretation of how semantic differential ratings are made. The major ones emphasized the contextual and instructional differences between conditions obtaining in the free-association situation and those obtaining under semantic differential administration. For example, repetition of the stimulus word is prohibited in free association. In addition, the task of rating differs in many ways from the task of associating to words. Ratings of degree of associative relation between two words may vary considerably from their degree of direct associative overlap, for example. Bousfield pointed out (cf. his paper, pp. 88–89) that semantic differential ratings would not have predicted the differential rates of learning the three verbal concepts he studied but that association data did. He also asked if the use of a rating procedure for ascertaining degree of association between two words (cf. p. 84) is equivalent to using the semantic differential. Osgood thought not.

Bousfield emphasized the distinctiveness and recordability of associative responses as compared to the difficulty of working with physiological responses (presumably involved in connotative $r_m$). Osgood stated that meanings can be represented as multidimensional in semantic space and

[2] Dr. Baxter has kindly provided data which clarify this point. The words used for the post-conditioning generalization test were tested prior to conditioning. In both Groups II and III the pre-conditioning GSR levels were larger for the positively evaluated words than for the negatively evaluated words. Thus, the post-training gradients plotted in Fig. 4-3 show a slope opposite to those for the same words prior to conditioning. While the entire post-conditioning GSR levels for the generalization-test words are considerably elevated over the levels before conditioning, the elevation of Group II is greater, over all, than it is for Group III. From all of these data it would appear that Dr. Jenkins's interpretation is not sustained. (Ed.)

could not see how this could be done with word associations. Noble wondered how Osgood would conceptualize the occurrence of an actual response, following an $r_m$. Osgood said that $r_m$'s are widely based on visceral reactions because the latter are highly available and readily generalized. (Several speakers pointed out the relations between his findings concerning meaning and Wundt's tridimensional theory of feeling.) Affect, being a massive affair, can be picked up on the semantic differential. He gave the following illustration. *Kind* and *bunny rabbit* may have similar $r_m$'s. On a *kind-cruel* scale, then, the word *bunny rabbit* would be rated as *kind* because of the similarity in the $r_m$'s.

A question was raised by Mandler concerning verbal response chaining. He pointed out that a given stimulus word has a number of associates in the transfer situations in question (Osgood's paper, p. 95); presumably all of these associates occur, but there are problems due to the limited time available for them to occur and also in relation to the ways in which the associative probabilities of these various responses combine. It was agreed that these processes are considered to be constructual rather than actual, although Bousfield pointed out that better results are obtained in predicting generalization when all of the common responses between two words are used than when only the primaries are used.

REFERENCE

Smith, D. E. P., & Raygor, A. L. (1956) Verbal satiation and personality. *J. Abnorm. Soc. Psychol.*, 52, 323–326.

# Chapter 5

# ASSESSMENT VERSUS EXPERIMENTAL ACQUISITION OF VERBAL HABITS

*Wallace A. Russell*

UNIVERSITY OF MINNESOTA

Concern for the effects of extra-experimental language experience upon laboratory studies of verbal learning has remained strong among researchers since Ebbinghaus (1885) offered the nonsense syllable as a solution to the problem. His effort, of course, was to minimize the effects of this factor in order to investigate more precisely the independent variables which he could manipulate within the laboratory setting.

Two lines of consideration have led to dissatisfaction with the Ebbinghaus-inspired techniques. The first has been the recognition that even with the greatest of care the natural language repertoire of human subjects cannot be eliminated as a factor in verbal learning experiments, and very probably cannot even be reduced to a reasonably low level of influence. The second has contended that it is not desirable in many instances to try to do without the effects of natural language experience. These effects, it is held, are themselves important variables for study, and, indeed, the effects of other laboratory manipulations may be most significantly studied in interaction with them. Implicit in this position is the notion that it is probably not possible to find laboratory operations which can satisfactorily reproduce the effects of the natural language repertoire.

As a consequence of these considerations, it has become common practice in verbal learning research to take account of extra-experimental language experience by evaluating or assessing the relevant aspects of this complex variable through the use of a variety of tests. Responses made to these tests are used as the basis for inferring such things as familiarity (Haagen, 1949), meaningfulness (Noble, 1952; Jenkins, Russell, and Suci, 1958), association strength (Russell and Jenkins, 1954), etc. Such response-inferred concepts may then be used either as independent or control variables depending upon the nature of the studies in progress.

The investigation of verbal habits provides a specific illustration of both the direct experimental and the assessment approaches. A habit, on the one hand, may be acquired in the laboratory under appropriately controlled learning conditions and in the strict Ebbinghaus tradition. On the other hand, the strength of a habit may be estimated by observations of responses presumed to reflect the results of past learning in everyday circumstances. In the latter instance, the methods of assessment are essentially psychometric, but in either case, the ensuing effects of the habits involved may be determined by relevant experiments.

Each of these procedures is relatively straightforward empirically. A number of problems arise, however, when they are considered jointly as alternative techniques for establishing the state of a single concept such as habit, and when they are viewed, as it were, strategically, in terms of their potential contribution to the understanding of linguistic processes.

Two questions which have often been posed by investigators in this area, albeit in a nontechnical way, provide pegs around which a discussion of these problems may be organized. The first, having reference to test-inferred versus experimentally acquired verbal habits, asks, "Are we in both cases dealing with the same theoretical concept?" The second, reflecting some suspicion of the potency of laboratory manipulation of verbal habits, wonders, "Can experimentally acquired habits be made to demonstrate all the functions of natural language habits?"

*Do Test-inferred Habits and Experimentally Acquired Habits Refer to the Same Concept?*

There can be little question that in the usual case test-inferred verbal habits are assumed to be measuring a concept that might, at least in principle, be directly varied by manipulation of appropriate antecedent conditions. Word-association strengths derived from normative data are commonly presumed to be resultants of learning processes which could under other circumstances be directly controlled to produce variation in measured strength. Other examples in closely related areas are not difficult to find. When familiarity is gauged by subjects' ratings, it has been assumed that differential numbers of exposures to experimental stimuli could also have been used to produce varying familiarity levels. Measured meaning, however defined, is conceived of as having the same conceptual referent as would a procedure which provided experiences designed to produce different meanings. In general, the responses of the subject to the items of the test are seen as bearing a relationship to some construct which is also related to a particular set of more or less specifiable antecedent conditions.

This common situation is schematically represented in Figure 5-1. There the concept verbal habit is located in the "construct level" between the two vertical lines separating "observable antecedent conditions," on

the left, from "overt behavior," on the right. The arrows indicate statements relating the units involved. The obvious feature of the figure is
that the statements relating the conditions eventuating in habit formation to verbal habit refer to the same construct as the statement having
reference to test performance. That is, a verbal habit inferred by virtue
of a knowledge of certain specified antecedent conditions and the set of
relational statements labeled (a) in Figure 5-1 is identical with one which
could be inferred from a knowledge of test performance and the relational statement (b).

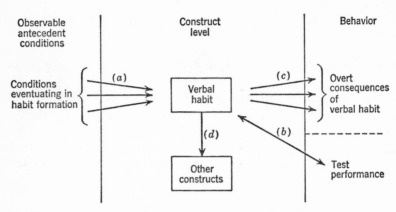

Fig. 5-1. Some relationships involved in the coordination of the concept of verbal
habit as inferred from test performance and that inferred on the basis of observable
antecedent conditions.

Of course it is not logically necessary to attempt the theoretical integration that Figure 5-1 implies. Given a knowledge of test performance,
there is no necessity to be concerned with possible relationships of the
scores to any theoretical notion. Rather, one could be quite atheoretical
in uncovering response-response laws between test scores and other aspects of behavior. Such a course would involve only the right-hand side
of Figure 5-1 and deal only with raw empirical contingencies. Or it
would be equally possible to introduce test-inferred concepts which were
not to be identified with any concept having specified antecedents. In
this case, statements comparable to that diagrammatically labeled (b)
would be formulated, but the concept referred to would be conceived of
as a different one from the verbal habit shown. This would leave the
matter of coordinating constructs inferred from tests and those inferred
from manipulated antecedent conditions entirely untouched.

In the case of test-inferred verbal habits, however, these alternatives
are difficult, since the very term habit has come to be used predominantly
as a name for a strictly theoretical construct, and more particularly, for

a construct whose relationship to antecedent conditions has been a central focus of investigation by learning theorists for a great many years. Terminological considerations alone would demand the use of some other term if test-inferred concepts in this area were not to be identified with a construct having such antecedents.

## Some Factors That Make for Imperfect Coordination of Test-inferred and Experimentally Acquired Habits

Ideally, given the situation sketched in Figure 5-1, it should be possible to infer the strength of a given verbal habit in two equivalent ways. The inference made on the basis of knowledge or control of antecedent conditions should be the same as that made from test-derived information.

On a practical basis, however, there are a number of factors which could lead to imperfect agreement between estimates of habit strength obtained from these two sources. Those to be considered first are not factors which would weigh seriously against the basic identity of the concepts referred to in each case, but are variables which would introduce a certain amount of error into the estimations and thus lead to imperfect empirical coordination. Some of the considerations would apply equally well to estimates made by either technique, but for simplicity's sake they will be dealt with only in relation to habits assessed by means of a test.

*The Inference of Habit Strengths from Norms for a Population.* Verbal habits in relation to certain materials are frequently inferred on the basis of population norms. For example, the frequency of a particular word as a free association to another word is determined over a large group, and this figure is used to provide an estimate of the strength of this association in the verbal repertoire of an individual experimental subject. The legitimacy of this application of a normative result to an individual is logically questionable on a number of grounds. In the terms of Figure 5-1, the "test performance" from which the state of the verbal habit is inferred becomes the behavior of the norm group rather than an actual sampling of the responses of the particular experimental subject about whom the inference is made. This hazardous procedure implies a series of tenuous assumptions concerning the relationship of group norms to individual response repertoires within the norm group as well as the requirement that the subject be a representative of the population sampled in the norms. Imperfect assessment of habit strength attributable to failure to meet any of these conditions would only add to the errors that are inherent in predicting the individual case from averages of a variable population. In view of these possibilities for imprecision, it is easy to see how estimates of this sort might coordinate with estimates based on antecedent conditions in only the roughest fashion. Indeed, in view of the logical difficulties, it is surprising that the empirical findings with this method have proved as useful as they have. Apparently there are very solid relationships between individual verbal habit strengths and normative results (Thumb and Marbe, 1901; Rosen and Russell, 1957) which allow the latter to operate as far more powerful tools than a consideration of their formal characteristics might suggest.

*The Reliability of Individual Tests.* In many instances it is possible to avoid the difficulties of using population norms by administering appropriate tests to the individuals actually under experimental observation. The meaningfulness of certain words, for example, may be rated by the experimental subjects themselves, and differences in these ratings may be used as the basis for prediction of differential performances. Simple unreliability of the ratings, of course, must in this and related cases be acknowledged as a possible source of error.

*The Validity of Tests of Verbal Habits.* Careful consideration of what constitutes validity when tests are used to assess theoretical constructs has led in recent years to a considerable increase in our understanding of the complexity of the issues involved (Cronbach and Meehl, 1955). These issues have been most extensively elaborated in connection with the general problem of the measurement of drives and motives, and often with reference to the Taylor anxiety scale as a measure of drive. Initial work with the Taylor scale sought simply to show that differences in the behavior during conditioning of subjects who scored high and low on the Anxiety scale were what would be predicted on the basis of assumed differences in the level of Hull's construct "D." The rationale was that the scale would be a valid measure of "D" to the extent that scale differences produced the same consequences for behavior as those attributed to "D." This position may be clarified with reference to Figure 5-1, if what is there called "verbal habit" is recognized to have conceptual status comparable to "D." The argument would hold that the relationship (b) was unidirectional, allowing one to infer the state of the construct from test performance but not necessarily the converse as the two-headed arrow shown in the figure would indicate. Further, the validity of the test would depend upon the demonstration that the consequences of differential test scores were isomorphic with the statements labeled (c) and presumably those labeled (d). The former represent, of course, the overt behavioral consequences of the construct, and the latter the relationships between the construct and other theoretical states. More simply, the test would be considered valid if the consequences related to different test scores were the same as those attributed to the construct.

The flood of empirical and theoretical work which has been inspired by this early view of the Taylor scale and the problem of its validity is by no means over. Nevertheless, a number of issues have risen in connection with this formulation, and they are of such general significance for this discussion of test-assessed verbal habits that a review of them should be profitable.

1. Should the items in the test be derivable as necessary consequences of the state being measured? Jessor and Hammond (1957) have criticized the Taylor scale because there is no unambiguous statement to be found relating the theoretical construct involved to the performance on the test items and leading clearly from the former to the latter. They state (p. 163):

"In what way are the form of the scale, the item selection procedure, the item content, and the nature of the responses elicited by the scale coordinated to or derived from the Hullian framework as indicants of drive? Nowhere, to our knowledge, is this made explicit or is a suitable answer to be found; yet this is precisely what our point of view would demand."

Their suggestion would seem to be that the relationship (b) in Figure 5-1 must be bidirectional, as the two-headed arrow would indicate. That is, not only should test performance allow an inference about the state of the construct, but from a knowledge of the state of the construct it should be possible to derive the test performance as a necessary consequent. Such a requirement would lead to the inclusion of statement (b) as part of the general consequences (c) in Figure 5-1.

If test performance is derivable from the properties of the construct, then, as Jessor and Hammond (1957) point out, failure to confirm predictions made on the basis of theory could clearly tell against the theory rather than leave confusion as to whether the theory, the test, or both were invalid. Certainly this is an advantage, but, particularly in cases where the theory is well established on other grounds, it would seem far too stringent to require this relationship in all cases. While it would ensure relatively clearer tests of a theory, it might very well restrict the search for test items unduly. In the particular matter of this discussion, it would mean that tests for verbal habit strengths could only be composed of items reflecting the direct consequences of the construct, and any fortunate correlation of a nonlogical but, say, culturally determined sort could not be capitalized upon in the search for test items. In traditional test-construction situations, items with empirical but nonderivable relations with a criterion have made up a large portion of the most useful items, and there would seem to be no reason to forbid this variety in the construction of tests assessing the value of a construct. Granted that the relationships (c) in the figure can guide a search for valid items, such a search need not be restricted to them.

2. In how much detail must the nomological net surrounding a construct be specified? The ideal, of course, would be for the construct to be

the nexus for a large number of relational statements. The more of these there are and the more specific they are, the more unambiguously can the validity of the test be determined. This is particularly true of the (c) statements in Figure 5-1. When these are numerous and clear, the validation procedure is the relatively straightforward one of demonstrating that the pattern of consequences to different test scores corresponds to that postulated to follow from the construct. To the extent that correspondence is found and to the degree that the same pattern of consequences cannot rationally be thought to result from the influence of other variables, confidence in the validity of the test increases. When the postulated consequences of a construct are few in number or vague in content, the probability that the same pattern could be generated in some other way increases and the validity of the test becomes questionable. For example, the Taylor scale studies have emphasized the correspondence between scale scores and consequences revealing the energizing function of "D." It has been suggested that analogous consequences could be expected if the scale measured various facilitating or disrupting habits rather than "D." If the consequences of differential test scores can be rationally attributed to concomitantly assessed variables other than the one supposedly measured, even though the correspondence to construct-relevant effects is high, the validity of the test remains in doubt. By increasing the richness of the formal network around the construct, the likelihood that this situation will obtain diminishes.

3. How necessary is it to demonstrate that, for a particular task, test-score differences can be used to produce group differences comparable to those obtained when the concept is experimentally induced in the same situation? Kausler and Trapp (1959) have raised this question in connection with the validation of drive-oriented scales such as the Taylor scale. Because of the probable interaction between the level of "D" and the amount of intra-task competition, the question of task comparability for high and low "D" groups is in their case a serious one. It may well be less serious in the case of other constructs where no such interaction effects are likely to be present, as is the situation with respect to verbal habits. Only in those instances where the effect of an experimentally acquired habit upon a laboratory task is in doubt would it seem to be necessary for purposes of validation to vary both test-assessed and experimentally acquired habits within the same experiment.

Obviously, the issues arising from the question of the validity of construct-oriented tests are complex and worthy of more consideration in their own right. Even if the criteria for validity of a test of this sort were well understood, however, there would remain the consideration that validity is always a matter of degree, and that, in any case when it is less than perfect, there will be some incomplete meshing of test assessment and laboratory induction of theoretical states.

### Some Possible Critical Differences in the Antecedents of Test-inferred Natural Language Habits and Experimentally Acquired Habits

More serious than the difficulties thus far discussed are the possibilities that in addition to the technical problems involved in establishing the equivalence of test and laboratory approaches to verbal habits there may be substantive differences in the antecedents of natural language habits which give them properties which are quite different from those normally produced in laboratory settings. This, at base, is the empirical proposition that test-assessed natural language habits as they are now measured are not the same theoretical "animal" as the usual experimentally acquired habits. It is probably the suspicion that this may be so that leads many experimenters to avoid test techniques whenever possible. There are, as a matter of fact, a number of reasons to justify this suspicion.

In the first place, the exact antecedents of natural language habits are unknown. In most instances this must always remain the case. Hence, equivalence of response-inferred habits of this kind to experimentally acquired habits can best be demonstrated only for consequences, not for antecedents. Furthermore, what little can be guessed at concerning the antecedents of natural language habits does not on the surface support their claim to comparability to experimentally acquired habits.

It is obvious that they differ with respect to the length of learning history. Real language habits typically involve years of spaced learning in contrast to minutes of massed learning for laboratory habits. It is not encouraging to imagine the ways in which equivalences between such different histories might be established.

The best guess as to the reinforcement contingencies of natural language habits is that they have been immensely complicated over a long period. The per cent of reinforcement, the per cent of non-reinforcement, of possibilities for correction or noncorrection have varied so much over a long period as to give a statistical learning theorist a nightmare if he is asked to produce a rational prediction about the future manifestations of the habit.

There is also the known fact that natural language habits have been learned as a part of a large network of associations which offers a vast potential for complex transfer effects which may variously help or hinder extinction or new learning related to particular habits.

A less historical and more contemporary consideration has to do with the fact that the learning effects upon natural language habits are continuing all the time, not only during experimental sessions. Reinforcements or punishments continue to operate as the subject lives in his community, or even as he thinks linguistically to himself. Natural language habits may be in a perpetual state of change.

Finally, there is the possibility that real language habits may have special properties gained through interaction with personality structures. This is a difficult point to elaborate in the absence of an advanced theory of personality structures, but it is certainly conceivable that organizing traits or stable general dispositions could provide influences on the manifestation of simple natural-language verbal habits in a way that would be difficult to imagine for the relatively isolated associations produced in the laboratory.

All of these possibilities suggest that the antecedents, and potentially the consequences, of test-inferred natural language habits are not easily seen as comparable to those of experimentally acquired habits. If a case is to be made for the identification of habits thus inferred with habits produced through controlled learning procedures, there is still a great deal of work ahead.

## Some Research Possibilities

A serious concern for establishing the equivalence of test-assessed and experimentally acquired verbal habits could lead to systematic research of considerable scope. While there is some evidence in the literature pertaining to some aspects of these problems, there is very little in the way of thoroughgoing evaluation of any one measurement technique along the lines necessary to establish convincingly the desired coordinations.

One profitable line of research might be to work first, not with the measurement of natural language habits, but with the simpler problem of determining the response indices of the strength of experimentally acquired habits. When antecedent control of the habit strength is possible, then the exact relationship between known manipulations of antecedent conditions and changes in the responses to test items can be empirically established. In addition, subjects selected as having equal habit strengths on the basis of the test or on the basis of known learning experience could be employed to demonstrate the comparability of the consequences of the states thus assessed. In this latter case, it would seem very desirable to establish this comparability over a large number, ideally all, of the consequences of the theoretical state in question. In the case of habit strength, these consequences might involve such things as response latency, probability, resistance to extinction, influence on transfer or continued learning, etc. Such broad comparability of consequences would be perhaps the best argument for the identity of the theoretical state assessed by the two methods. Indeed, research along these lines could explore all of the possibilities for joint variation suggested by the indicated relations in Figure 5-1 and could provide the groundwork for the development of tests of verbal habit strength which could meet all of the possible criteria for validity mentioned earlier in this discussion.

In the case of natural language habits in subjects selected after the language has been well learned, the joint variation of antecedents and test responses is, of course, not possible. If the test-assessed habit can be shown to have multiple consequences equivalent to those of other experimentally acquired habits, confidence in the identity of the concepts involved could nevertheless become very great.

Finally, the possible empirical value of research based on test assessment, even where the equivalence to constructs with specified antecedents is not established or even assumed, deserves mention. Response-response regularities obtained in such studies can prove highly useful not only in the practical sense but also in the sense that they can establish facts about phenomena which otherwise might go unstudied. Particularly in the study of verbal learning and performance, it is likely that there are certain linguistic effects which, until much more is known about the antecedents of natural language learning, can only be studied, as it were, in nature and by means of test assessment of some of the variables involved.

In summary, then, it would appear that the question of the conceptual identity of test-inferred habits and experimentally acquired habits is one that cannot be easily answered in the affirmative. There are, however, techniques by which confidence in such a coordination could be increased, and reason to hold that independent research with each approach may be fruitful.

## Can Experimentally Acquired Habits Demonstrate All the Functions of Natural Language Habits?

To the psycholinguistically oriented investigator the task of "building in" by experimental techniques verbal habits which have all the functions of natural language habits seems as formidable, say, as the production in the laboratory of the characteristics of a full-blown personality trait. Nevertheless, the alternative to this staggering task is to assume that there are some characteristics of verbal habits which can only be produced in natural, nonlaboratory settings. This is a repugnant assumption because it suggests that, at best, there is an unfortunate limitation to the use of experimental manipulation in language study or, at worst, that there are unanalyzable forces at work in natural settings, the exact nature of which must always remain a mystery. The second major question around which the problems of assessment versus experimental acquisition of verbal habits may be organized, then, is in the nature of a challenge to the ingenuity of experimentalists. Can experimentally acquired habits demonstrate all the functions of natural language habits?

Surely, the stability, the apparently complex interrelationships, and the organization that characterize natural language habits seem to defy efforts at laboratory analogues. And this is true even when it is recognized that to be scientifically fruitful it is not necessary or in many cases desirable to reproduce at one time in the laboratory the entire complexity or the intensity of the phenomena that are observed in a naturalistic setting. It is the essence of scientific technique to isolate variables and to study their effects in situations which are often highly "unnatural" but which have the advantage of being free of the uncalculated influence of irrelevant factors.

The effort in the laboratory is not to recreate events originally occurring in uncontrolled situations but to produce for systematic study the individual variables which *in toto* have the characteristics which could account for occurrences observed in everyday life. But this is scant comfort if, as is the case with verbal habits, there is the impression that the individual variables involved have not yet been wholly identified or that, even if they had been, it might be exceedingly difficult or impossible to bring some of them into the laboratory.

No one seriously doubts, of course, that part of the job has been done. The "classical" variables of experimental verbal learning, such as repetition, meaningfulness, spacing, etc., contribute significantly to an understanding of the functioning of natural language habits. But skepticism as to whether the traditional variables are enough no doubt lies behind the frequent decision of researchers to work with the natural language repertoire which their subjects bring with them to the laboratory. At least those linguistic tendencies are ones to which the relevant variables must have contributed. This "advantage," however, turns into the opposite as soon as the investigator becomes concerned with explanation, or as soon as he asks the genetic question how his response-inferred tendency got to be the way it was. Then he realizes how much more comfortable he would be if he had positive knowledge of all of the antecedents of the state he is working with, and he is forced to consider the possibility of introducing new experimental variables to increase the explanatory power of his formulations.

A look at some recent findings might suggest that it is too early to be a confirmed skeptic concerning the possibility of bringing such further relevant variables into the laboratory for study. For many years the verbal learning methods described in introductory texts had seemed on the way to becoming so standardized that there seemed little room for variation. Currently, though, there have been signs of new interest in the possible ways in which verbal habits might be "built in" in the laboratory. Certainly, as soon as it is recognized that the varieties of conditions under which habits may be learned may be an important determiner of their further influence upon behavior, there is no dearth of suggestions as to ways in which these conditions might be profitably varied.

Peterson (1956), for example, has demonstrated the feasibility of using the paired-associates technique to establish, not single associations, but multiple verbal response hierarchies. This is a complication which allows "built-in" habits to approximate one characteristic of natural language habits.

Lenneberg (1957), in his "A Probabilistic Approach to Language Learning," has explored how increasing or decreasing the determinacy of "nonsense" color names influences the difficulty of a learning task. This is another isolatable variable which must influence natural language learning and yet which until recently might have seemed an unlikely prospect for inclusion as a variable in laboratory learning.

Departures of this sort from traditional techniques of laboratory learning suggest the possibilities that lie in the controlled introduction of still other variables. This direction could lead more and more toward laboratory learning of artificial languages. It should be expected that such artificial languages would at first be extremely simple (Lenneberg refers to the learning of four color words as a nonsense language), but there is no reason to believe that the effects of grammatical restraints and "context effects" could not be introduced with profit.

It has already been mentioned that the reinforcement history of verbal habits might provide one of the critical differences between natural language and experimentally acquired habits. There seems to be no compelling reason why much more complex reinforcement schedules than those usually used cannot be utilized in laboratory studies. The remarkable stability of apparently low strength natural language habits, where strength is inferred from word-association norms, has often been informally noted. Little seems to be known in detail about resistance to extinction and "reinforcement-matching" problems, but the hypothesis that certain schedules of reinforcement could produce habits which would result in low levels of response probability plus high resistance to extinction would seem worthy of investigation. Such a finding would lead to the questioning of frequency of occurrence as an adequate response index of habit strength and perhaps to the discovery of ways of producing laboratory habits as resistant to change as natural language habits.

Once variations in conditions of laboratory learning were shown to be important, factors once deemed too difficult to manipulate might be explored. There is no theoretical reason, for example, why the length of the training period in laboratory learning needs to be as short as it usually is. If the very long-standing training applied to natural language habits gives them qualities to differentiate them from experimentally acquired habits, this factor can at least be better handled than it usually is. It may prove desirable in some studies to "build in" habits for a period of time extending over months and running into many experimental sessions. Naturally, there are technical difficulties in such research but the pay-off in broadened possibilities for laboratory-controlled learning might be great.

One further possibility for increasing our knowledge of the antecedent conditions of habits comparable to natural language tendencies may lie in controlled longitudinal studies of first- or second-language learning. In the case of first-language learning it would be difficult, probably impossible, to obtain complete control over the language experiences of the subject. But control is always a matter of degree, and a blend of experimental and naturalistic observation could prove feasible. Second-language learning in schools, or in the laboratory, could even more easily be controlled and utilized in experimental studies. Foley and Mathews (1943) have made some efforts in this direction, without actually modifying the second-language learning procedure.

All of these suggestions do not prove that experimentally acquired habits can be made to demonstrate all significant language functions. On the other hand, they do indicate that there is little reason for pessimism. The application of new ingenuity in the "building in" of verbal habits seems likely to go a long way in taking into account variables which have been suspected as important in natural language learning but which have found no place for study in the standard laboratory learning procedures.

In conclusion, one may ask whether success in re-creating language functions in the laboratory would remove the necessity for using test-inferred verbal habits in language research. Only a little reflection would indicate a clearly negative answer. Once the possibility of manipulating the relevant antecedent conditions for verbal habits was at hand, it would open the door for a definitive integration of response-inferred and experimentally induced states or concepts. With this accomplished, there would undoubtedly be times when it would be more practical to use test assessment than to rely on more time-consuming and laborious experimental manipulations to produce the desired state. At present, one can only advocate the industrious exploration of both avenues of investigation and dream of the utopian days when one can be confident that the two lead to the same destination.

REFERENCES

Cronbach, L. J., & Meehl, P. E. (1955) Construct validity in psychological tests. *Psychol. Bull.*, **52**, 281–302.

Ebbinghaus, H. (1885) *Über das Gedächtnis.* Leipzig: Duncker & Humblot. (1913) H. Ruger & C. Bussenius (Trans.) New York: Teachers College.

Foley, J. P., & Mathews, M. A. (1943) Mediated generalization and the interpretation of verbal behavior: IV. Experimental study of the development of inter-lingusitic synonym gradients. *J. Exp. Psychol.*, **33**, 188–200.

Haagen, C. H. (1949) Synonymity, vividness, familiarity and association value ratings of 400 pairs of common adjectives. *J. Psychol.*, **27**, 453–463.

Jenkins, J. J., Russell, W. A., & Suci, G. J. (1958) An atlas of semantic profiles for 360 words. *Amer. J. Psychol.*, **71**, 688–699.

Jessor, R., & Hammond, K. R. (1957) Construct validity and the Taylor anxiety scale. *Psychol. Bull.*, **54**, 161–170.

Lenneberg, E. H. (1957) A probabilistic approach to language learning. *Behav. Sci.*, **2**, 1–12.

Kausler, D. H., & Trapp, E. P. (1959) Methodological considerations in the construct validation of drive-oriented scales. *Psychol. Bull.*, **56**, 152–157.

Noble, C. E. (1952) An analysis of meaning. *Psychol. Rev.*, **59**, 421–430.

Peterson, L. R. (1956) Prediction of response in verbal habit hierarchies. *J. Exp. Psychol.*, **51**, 249–252.

Rosen, E., & Russell, W. A. (1957) Frequency characteristics of successive word-association. *Amer. J. Psychol.*, **70**, 120–122.

Russell, W. A., & Jenkins, J. J. (1954) The complete Minnesota norms for responses to 100 words from the Kent-Rosanoff Word Association Test. *Tech. Rep. No. 11*, Contract No. N8onr-66216, Office of Naval Research and University of Minnesota.

Thumb, A., & Marbe, K. (1901) *Experimentelle Untersuchungen über die psychologischen Grundlagen der sprachlichen Analogiebildung.* Leipzig: W. Englemann.

# COMMENTS ON PROFESSOR RUSSELL'S PAPER

## George Mandler

UNIVERSITY OF TORONTO

Dr. Russell's paper has raised several questions about the experimental investigation of verbal behavior. I have no major arguments with him about the issues raised; all of them are central to the problem of erecting a satisfactory explanatory system for verbal behavior. Moreover, I share Dr. Russell's caution about going from response-response correlations to the inference of antecedent processes; if anything, I am somewhat more hesitant and dubious about their relevance. I would like to emphasize what appear to me the most important issues raised and to add some general questions about the future of experimental techniques in the study of verbal behavior.

I would like to speak, if possible, in a theoretically more neutral language than Dr. Russell did. Thus, it is often necessary not to speak of verbal *habits* with, as he points out, the implied condition of number of preceding learning trials, but rather of verbal behavior in general; not to speak of meaningfulness, but rather of associative frequency; not of strength of associations, but rather of empirical probability.

Let me turn first to the issue of the theoretical equivalence of test-inferred and experimentally acquired habits.

## The Inference of Habit Strengths from Norms for a Population

Dr. Russell raises the question whether we can legitimately apply to a particular individual the norms obtained from a sample of subjects. I believe there are three questions involved here: Can we ever go from the sample means to the individual? Can we legitimately and safely infer the processes which are used to explain normative hierarchies of response probabilities? And finally, are our assessment techniques always the relevant methods to assess response hierarchies?

As far as the first question is concerned, we can give, in one sense, an unequivocally negative answer. We may not assume that the assessment of behavior which varies among subjects and among stimuli permits any inference about the behavior of a single subject in response to a single stimulus. We can argue from some recent findings that differences in response characteristics among individuals are a different theoretical animal from differences in response characteristics of a group of individuals to a sample of stimuli. For example, we presented 32 subjects with 20 stimuli and instructed the subjects to give all the continuing associations which each stimulus evoked in a 30-second period. We then computed for each subject and for each stimulus the mean frequency across all stimuli and subjects respectively. We also determined the percentage of all associations (given by each person and elicited by each stimulus) which were given to a particular stimulus by one and no other subject. Thus for each subject we obtained a frequency measure ($f$) and an idiosyncrasy measure (I%). Two similar measures were obtained for each stimulus. When these two variables are correlated for the population of 32 subjects, $r = +.440$, and for the population of 20 stimuli, $r = -.692$ (Mandler, 1959). We conclude that our frequency and idiosyncrasy measures are two different theoretical constructs depending on whether they are characteristic of stimuli or of subjects.

This discussion does not involve the empirical question whether the response of a group of people to an array of stimuli may be used to infer the response of a single person to the same array. Presumably the population characteristics represent some cumulative effect of the characteristics of the individuals who make up the population. The question of variation among the individuals who make up this population is empirical in character, but will be determined by theoretical considerations such as oscillation problems and the relation between associative hierarchies within subjects and within populations.

Our second question concerned the inference of the antecedent processes when we are presented with assessment variables. Implicit in the theoretical discussion of the population norms is the assumption that all the items have similar histories. Specifically, we assume that when a particular associative response has a high frequency to a particular stimulus in a sample of subjects, then all persons who gave that response gave it, so to say, for the same reason. In other words, we assume that the antecedent history of the response "chair" to "table" is the same for different subjects. Or, even more radically, that the acquisition process which produces "chair" in a subject is the *same type of process* which produces "round" as a response to "table" in that subject. In psychological parlance, we rarely make distinctions such as those between nonverbal and intraverbal conditions of elicitation, to follow Skinner's terminology. In a more general sense, I am reminded of Saporta's comments at the 1955 Minnesota Conference (Jenkins, 1959) that psychologists seem to know, or act as if they know, what words are and consequently treat all words alike. The linguist seems to be rather appalled at this psychological pretension, and would urge us to make some finer distinctions when measuring associative verbal behavior. It may be the case that these finer distinctions won't make any difference in the kind of relationships which interest us, but shouldn't we look first?

The third point to be made about the correspondence between the assessment techniques we use and the response hierarchies we postulate is a simple reminder that even in response-response research we often measure one thing and assume that we are measuring another. Thus, for example, the hierarchy of associations derived from the Minnesota norms, where single associations were used, is not necessarily the same as the hierarchy of continued associative sampling. The evidence points to a high correlation, but can one be reasonably inferred from the other?

## Experimentally Acquired Habits and Significant Language Function

The second set of questions I would like to raise concerns the different antecedents of assessed verbal behavior and of experimentally acquired behavior, as well as the general problem of the lacunae in the experimental investigation of language functions.

Implicit in much of the research on verbal learning is not only the remnant of the Ebbinghaus attempt to construct "nonsense" words, which Russell discussed, but also the notion that in verbal learning we are dealing with an organism who is structurally as naive as a rat pressing a bar. By "structurally naive" I refer to the assumption that no organizational or structural effects are carried over to the new behavior. I would suggest, to the contrary, that verbal learning is superimposed upon a structure of behavior, i.e., verbal behavior, which is much more powerful a determiner of that behavior than any structure which we may build into the organism, no matter how long we train him. Adjectives will fit into the kind of syntactical structures in which adjectives have for years been used by the subjects, and groups of two or three or more words will also elicit organizations which years of learning have prepared for such groups. In part we often overlook these factors because we have developed from a field which might best be described as "learning with words" rather than "verbal learning"; our primary interest has been *learning* rather than *language*. I believe this is the reason why the Rock (1957) experiment and the Berko (1958) experiment had to come from a tradition other than that of the stimulus-response laboratories. Similarly, it can be argued that the associative acquisition of *single* pairs of well-integrated verbal units is a one-trial phenomenon as a rule rather than as the exception. But our way of thinking in terms of habits and learning trials has prevented us from considering these systematically. Rather than look at the linguists and the structural psychologists either wistfully or suspiciously, we might profitably follow Russell's suggestion and introduce the effects of grammatical restraints into the laboratory. I am not suggesting that we move out of the laboratory but rather that we bring knowledge of syntax and structure and their effects into the laboratory to find out what they are all about.

Let me suggest some of the directions in which such research might go. Take for example, the Mowrer-Bousfield-Staats models for the acquisition of meaning. Mowrer (1954) argues that sentences of the form "*Tom* (is a) *thief*" occasion the conditioning of meaning from *thief* to *Tom*. Now Mowrer has some misgivings about this in later parts of his paper, but I would suggest that misgivings are not enough; it just will not do to ignore the function of the copula as Mowrer suggests. What about the sentence "*Tom* (is not a) *thief*"? Does the word "not" simply abrogate the laws of classical conditioning? And if so, how? Or will conditioning still take place? How about families of sentences such as

"*Tom* is *well*"
"*Tom* is a *well*"
"*Tom* is not *well*"
"*Tom* is not a *well*"?

What laws of conditioning apply here? And is the process unidirectional? Or does some other process, as Mowrer seems to suggest, change the meaning of *thief* (as well as of *Tom*) in the "*Tom* is a *thief*" paradigm?

In a more general form it can be argued that syntactic structure determines both the position and the form of a verbal unit. For example, if a subject is given the two sentences

*"Joe saw a man"*
and
*"I fleg a wuz"*

and instructed to substitute the word *fleg* anywhere in the first sentence, his most likely substitution is

*"Joe* flegged *a man."*

In this case both the position and form of a *new* word are determined by structural considerations. Further questions may then be asked about the interaction of associative, syntactic, and phonemic variables in this paradigm.

Only a small part of the possible questions about the effects of structure have been investigated experimentally; many more remain to be brought into the laboratory. For example: What are the conditions for the development of structure? Perhaps some structural laws may be derived from associative phenomena, as we tried to do at Harvard in the case of overlearning. How well does a subject learn permissible and nonpermissible sentences? And as a corollary, what are the effects, both facilitating and interfering, of syntax? Do they follow some known associative laws? What happens to the conditioning paradigm under various syntactical constraints?

It must be remembered, of course, that research on syntactic structures will generally be limited to transfer effects. The effects of well-established structural modes on new problems or tasks can be evaluated, but the acquisition of new syntactic habits can only be viewed in interaction with the strongly established syntactic behavior of the adult subject.

If we want to look at the *development* of syntactic structures, we probably will have to go to another area of research—to early verbal learning and the development of language in the first four years of life.

If we had paid more attention to these areas, we probably would have found out earlier about the independence of response learning and associative learning. (At least I would have found it out prior to 1954 if I had watched newly verbal children.) And we may also get some clues from children about the development of "meaning responses," the action-eliciting and action-following functions of language, the relative roles of the speaker and the listener, the acquisition of labeling and of intraverbal behavior, and so forth. The use of psychological methods and knowledge will do much to undo criticisms by the linguists, who, by the way, have given us very few insights about language acquisition in exchange for their general critique. Contemporary verbal learning theory has done an excellent job on a limited range of problems; but only if we try to extend it to the important problems of structure, response learning, and so forth, will it prove viable in the psychological community.

### REFERENCES

Berko, J. (1958) The child's learning of English morphology. *Word,* **14,** 150–177.

Jenkins, J. J. (Ed.) (1959) *Associative processes in verbal behavior: A report of the Minnesota Conference.* Minneapolis: University of Minnesota, Department of Psychology.

Mandler, G. (1959) Stimulus variables and subject variables: A caution. *Psychol. Rev.,* **66,** 145–149.

Mowrer, O. H. (1954) The psychologist looks at language. *Amer. Psychologist,* **9,** 660–694.

Rock, I. (1957) The role of repetition in associative learning. *Amer. J. Psychol.* **70,** 186–193.

## SUMMARY OF CONFERENCE DISCUSSION

Mandler's finding that the correlation between the number of associations and the idiosyncrasy of associations was +.440 when calculated across subjects and −.692 when calculated across stimuli occasioned a good deal of discussion. While it appears that these findings mean that one cannot readily derive stimulus characteristics from subject characteristics and conversely,[1] there was still concern for the case in which the subject's response-strength hierarchy is or may be inferred from the response hierarchy generated from the responses of a normative sample to the given stimulus. Mandler seemed to feel that this inference is a difficult one to justify, but Jenkins emphasized the need for a measure of associative strength, and Osgood indicated that the best prediction for a subject about whom nothing is known is afforded by the norms. Mandler raised the following example. Suppose a subject responds to the word *chair* by saying *utensil* as his first response. If he continues to associate, will he eventually give *table* (the high-frequency associate)? The occurrence of *table* late in the associative series, Mandler said, would suggest a great deal of "oscillation" in the associative hierarchies. Jenkins stated that

[1] Mandler (1959, p. 148) interpreted these relations as suggesting that "individuals who give many associations tend to exhaust the common vocabulary and become idiosyncratic, while stimulus objects which elicit many associations are probably more familiar and elicit few idiosyncratic associations." (Ed.)

persons who give a high proportion of relatively infrequent responses on their first run through an association test tend to give different responses on later administrations of the test. Mandler added that when subjects give continuous associations for 30 seconds to various kinds of stimuli, the percentage of idiosyncratic responses increases as a function of the ordinal position of the response (Mandler and Parnes, 1957, p. 63, fig. 1); the function is negatively accelerated and reaches an asymptote at about the fifth or sixth response. Presumably this would mean that a high commonality response has a better chance of being emitted earlier in a sequence than it has later in the sequence. Jenkins suggested that the response-frequency hierarchies of at least some people may have very steep slopes, and Osgood pointed out that context or set might produce such idiosyncratic responses. Further use of the method of continued association was urged.

In another connection, Bousfield raised the question of how best to measure fluency. He pointed out that if one cumulates verbal responses given to a stimulus over time, the resulting curves for different subjects will be negatively accelerated and approach asymptotes. However, the curves may vary in both total output and in the rate at which they approach asymptotes. After a given time interval two subjects may have given the same number of responses to the stimulus, but their output functions both before and after this temporal juncture may differ considerably. His point concerned the way in which verbal fluency should be measured and how comparisons on this variable among people should be made. Others (Mandler, Jenkins, Osgood) stated that with instructions to give continuous associations with no stimulus the output curve continues for long periods at a steady or even an increasing rate. Noble emphasized the importance of using a constant time interval and noncumulative plot to bring out individual differences. Number of associations and rate at which associations are given are different measures (Mandler, Noble), and their predictive relation to other variables differs (Postman, Noble).

In discussing the Mowrer paradigm for the conditioning of meaning, Mandler raised a number of questions in his paper. Osgood, in the discussion, indicated that sheer contiguity is not an adequate factor for conditioning to occur, using as an example the sentence, "Tom who lives around the corner is an angel; Paul who lives somewhere else is a devil." The word Paul is more contiguous to angel than Tom is, but Tom is the word that goes with angel (cf. Osgood, Suci, and Tannenbaum, 1957, p. 201). Relations of this example to Thorndike's conception of belongingness were pointed out by Deese (Thorndike, 1932). Osgood with his example emphasized the importance that linguistic structure as a variable may have on whatever conditioning may take place, and Mandler that in the case "Tom is a thief" the meaning of thief, as well as that of Tom, may change, a point not consistent with classical theory because it involves backward conditioning. Mandler argued that the *is not* sentence may be no different from the other ("Tom is not a thief" versus "Tom is a thief") but that data are needed on this point. Bousfield suggested that perhaps an antonymic response is occasioned by the *not*.

Osgood mentioned his and Tannenbaum's work with assertions which associate or dissociate pairs of concepts, like Eisenhower and the steel strike. (For example, "Eisenhower is for the steel strike"; "Eisenhower is against the steel strike.") He pointed out that evaluations of the concepts after such associative or dissociative assertions shift in lawful ways according to the congruity principle (Osgood and Tannenbaum, 1955; Osgood, Suci, and Tannenbaum, 1957, pp. 201 ff.), and that the results for dissociative assertions do not fit a conditioning paradigm.

Questions were raised about what can be done with the Mowrer and other paradigms experimentally. Should time intervals be inserted between subject and predicate to determine if the results change as they should in terms of what we know about conditioning (Mandler)? Can semantic generalization be reduced by means of pairing concepts in dissociative assertions (Musgrave)? Can such systems be built in (Deese)? Do we go to the natural language looking for variables suggested by the model (Deese)? Russell thought that perhaps we must begin in the natural language with R-R (response-response) laws.

Normative study of children's verbalization was suggested as a way of evaluating paradigms (Jenkins), but Postman felt that further study is needed of the process of association before attention is devoted to more complex factors. He said that he is unable to give an associative explanation of the learning of a serial list and would like to solve this problem before going on. Others argued that more complex processes, like syntactic ones, may be involved in apparently simple associative situations (Russell, Mandler). Mandler appeared to argue that this must be so in list learning; such learning requires many trials, whereas a single pair of well-encoded words, he asserted, can be learned in a single trial and be retained indefinitely. Peterson's (1956) experiment was raised as an objection to this statement (Goss, Postman), but this citation was rejected on the ground that there was insufficient response encoding (Deese). There was further argument about the possibility of one-trial learning, some seeming to believe its general occurrence (Deese, Osgood, Mandler) and others doubting its generality (Underwood, Postman). Goss cited findings (Sugarman and Goss, 1959) contrary to Mandler's implication that frequency of occurrence does not build up response strength. Each stimulus was paired with two responses and the responses occurred in different ratios (50:50, 60:40, 70:30, 80:20, 90:10, 100:0). Above a 50:50

ratio the more frequently presented response begins to gain in dominance.

Postman pointed out the role of language habits in verbal learning is increasingly being recognized.

## REFERENCES

Mandler, G. (1959) Stimulus variables and subject variables: A caution. *Psychol. Rev.*, 66, 145–149.

Mandler, G., & Parnes, E. W. (1957) Frequency and idiosyncracy of associative responses. *J. Abnorm. Soc. Psychol.*, 55, 58–65.

Osgood, C. E., Suci, G. J., & Tannenbaum, P. H. (1957) *The measurement of meaning*. Urbana, Ill.: University of Illinois Press.

Osgood, C. E., & Tannenbaum, P. H. (1955) The principle of congruity in the prediction of attitude change. *Psychol. Rev.*, 62, 42–55.

Peterson, L. R. (1956) Prediction of response in verbal habit hierarchies. *J. Exp. Psychol.*, 51, 249–252.

Sugarman, M. E., & Goss, A. E. (1959) Paired-associates learning with varying relative percentages of occurrences of alternative response members. *Tech. Rep. No. 2*, Contract No. Nonr-2691(00), Office of Naval Research and University of Massachusetts.

Thorndike, E. L., *et al.* (1932) *The fundamentals of learning*. New York: Teachers College.

# Chapter 6

# VERBAL LEARNING AND INDIVIDUAL DIFFERENCES

## Clyde E. Noble

MONTANA STATE UNIVERSITY

The purpose of this essay is twofold: (1) to assess the current state of our knowledge about individual differences in the domain of verbal learning, and (2) to present the outline of a research program which would integrate these specialties by means of a functional analysis of acquisition curves in standard verbal learning situations where human factors appear as major parameters.

One of the principal areas of research on human behavior is concerned with the learning of verbal responses as a function of such experimental variables as amount of practice, length of list, and the meaningfulness of the material. An equally important field of investigation is that of individual differences, wherein verbal ability is measured and placed in correlation with other psychometric indices derived from numerical, spatial, and reasoning tests. Until recently, the experimental (S-R) and correlational (R-R) approaches to behavior science were separate endeavors. Indeed, many still regard them as rival "schools" of psychology. Related to this is another historical schism in our science: that of particular (idiographic) versus general (nomothetic) modes of description. Ever since the Titchener-Baldwin debate (Boring, 1950), it has been popularly believed that an understanding of concrete individual cases is somehow incompatible with the quest for abstract uniformities characteristic of groups (e.g., Allport, 1937; Snygg and Combs, 1949). My own viewpoint is that these two sets of techniques are not antithetical but are actually complementary and should be employed jointly. By providing statistical control over variables which are not amenable to experimental manipulation, in addition to serving as indispensable tools in hypothesis testing and in the measurement of goodness of fit, correlational methods are extremely helpful in establishing and evaluating generalized laws. Similarly, all nomothetic laws have to be supplemented by idiographic data about the initial or boundary conditions (e.g., state of the organism, apparatus characteristics) when predictions of singular events are made (Nagel, 1952).

Thirty years ago Woodworth (1929) explicitly brought organismic (O) factors into the context of experimental research by substituting the S-O-R formula for the oversimplified S-R formula. Although others (e.g., Thorndike) were aware of the importance of O-factors, they did not advertise the point. Shortly afterwards, Tolman (1932) recommended a fusion of "individual" and "normative" psychologies into a "complete" psychology. Little was done to implement such a program, however, until the next decade when Hull (1945) proposed that differences among subjects might affect only the numerical constants of a behavior equation, not its mathematical form; i.e., general laws obtained inductively from statistical samples ought to include the entire range of traits and abilities.

As I interpret Hull's (1952) final postulate of the learning process, the excitatory tendencies $(E = H \times D)$ of stimuli to elicit responses of a given class $(R_p)$ grow exponentially with the number of reinforced trials $(N)$, but by a particular rate $(r)$ and to a particular asymptote $(a)$ which are contingent respectively upon correlational (e.g., ability) and experimental (e.g., drive) factors. From the additional assumptions of a subtractive reaction threshold and a cumulative normal (oscillatory) relationship between $R_p$ and $E$, it can be deduced that empirical learning curves fitting the paradigm $R_p = f(N, a, r)$ should be skewed, sigmoidal, and nonparallel in form under systematic variation of the parameters $a$ and $r$. Highlighting Woodworth's organismic variables while also taking Tolman literally, Hull's hypothesis thus leads to an emphasis on finding composition (e.g., interaction) laws of the type $R_p = f(S \times O)$.

A possible misinterpretation should be extinguished here before we proceed to a consideration of empirical evidence for or against the existence of interactions between learning and individual differences. As pointed out elsewhere (C. E. Noble, J. L. Noble, and Alcock, 1958), interaction laws are not a *necessary* consequence of Hull's notion. Degree of nonparallelism is at least contingent upon the response measure, task characteristics, and the selection technique used. I would restrict the statement made above to relative frequency scores in selective learning tasks where ability stratification is based on over-all proficiency. For example, perceptual-motor skill curves are inconsistent for several reasons (Noble, 1959), one of the most critical being distribution of practice (Zeaman and Kaufman, 1955).

## SOME DATA AND PROBLEMS

Illustrative human data bearing upon Hull's proposal have been reported for the following tasks: rotary pursuit (Reynolds and Adams, 1954), complex coordination (Fleishman, 1957), two-hand coordination

(Cieutat and Noble, 1958), alphabet printing (Zeaman and Kaufman, 1955), discrimination reaction (Adams, 1957), eyelid conditioning (Spence, 1956), trial-and-error learning (C. E. Noble, J. L. Noble, and Alcock, 1958), serial verbal learning (Noble, 1952; Noble and Fuchs, 1959; Barnett, Ellis, and Pryer, 1960; Ellis, M. W. Pryer, Distefano, and R. S. Pryer, 1960), and paired-associates verbal learning (Mandler and Huttenlocher, 1956; Noble and McNeely, 1957; Cieutat, Stockwell, and Noble, 1958; Cieutat, 1959; Noble, 1959). In general, the *selective learning* evidence is consistent with our deduction: rate of acquisition is a positive function of initial level of ability. Specifically for *verbal learning*, the last nine studies cited found interactions between individual differences in ability, on the one hand, and number of practice trials, serial position difficulty, and stimulus or response meaningfulness, on the other. Data of this type suggest that verbal learning is a fertile field for research on learning and individual differences.

From the standpoint of an experimental psychologist, acquisition and retention curves are geometric descriptions of the functional relationships empirically found to connect certain selected central tendencies of dependent behavior samples (response classes) to primary independent variables (experimental or stimulus factors) like the number of practice trials. Occasionally, secondary independent variables (correlational or organismic factors) appear as parameters in our graphs, but it is more common for an investigator simply to assume that his average sample scores are tolerable estimates of the population values and to eschew stratification or other control procedures. If he gives the matter much thought, he may compute—and even plot in the results section—the magnitude of the vertical dispersions around his means, medians, or proportions. Yet when he comes to the discussion section, does he not typically regard this scatter as "natural" or "expected" variance due to "error" arising from presumably multiple but unknown, and maybe unknowable, sources? I believe this is a tacit assumption held by many behavior scientists, particularly by those who have not drunk very deeply at the Pierian spring of statistics. Concepts like probability, chance, and randomness require more than tasting to be understood. Perhaps the idea that we "can't fight" error variance is another of those gloomy aphorisms we have inherited from the indeterminists, the emergentists, the teleologists, the classical rationalists, the antimechanists, and the free-willers—from all those who are steadfastly opposed to what they interpret as unholy encroachments of deterministic science upon the domain of personal freedom. That their fears are groundless, deriving as they do from an erroneous conception of the modern philosophy of science, is by now well known (Russell, 1929; Grünbaum, 1952; Bergmann, 1957). But traditional dogmas continue to affect current practices, and a confused para-statistical or quasi-deterministic view of human nature can be a very twisted crutch, ill designed for even clever psychologists safely to lean upon. Whatever the reasons may be, I doubt that any vigorous systematic effort is being directed at the present time to finding out such elementary things as the following: (1) what the sources of error variance in verbal learning curves are, and (2) to what extent they can be controlled. Experimental psychology will not have made its peace with differential psychology until more answers to these two questions are available.

It is common knowledge (Anastasi, 1958) that significant gains in performance on (verbal) intelligence tests result from practice, coaching, and the development of "test wiseness" by the subjects. But whether individual differences increase or decrease with practice depends upon stage of practice, training method, response-scoring technique, and on whether absolute or relative measures of variability are employed. For half a century this issue of the effects of training on individual differences has been argued pro and con with little realization of the need for a systematic conception of the full range of behavior possible when practice is extended to large values. This entails a discovery of the mathematical family of curves in closest agreement with the data so that factors like initial proficiency, rate of change, and asymptotic limit could be specified and their controlling variables identified. My present guess is that, in a constant-trials design where all subjects are trained to about the same high proficiency level, the first third or so of practice will produce divergence (increasing $\sigma$) in $R_p$ scores, whereas the last two-thirds will produce convergence (decreasing $\sigma$) among the stratified subgroups.

For reasons presented above, the generalized curve form should be slightly sigmoidal and definitely positively skewed. Considering verbal learning as an instance of selective learning (Spence, 1956), it may be possible to apply an existing mathematical model to the data in an effort to rationalize these ability × learning interactions. Thus, if a technique could be found to produce determinate guessing probabilities at the outset, and if the inflection point of the curve is contingent upon subjects' ability level, an acquistion equation of the type

$$R_p = a(i)^{r^N} \tag{1}$$

might be suitable, where $R_p$ is the probability of a correct response, $a$ is the asymptote, $i$ is the initial probability, $r$ is the rate of acquisition, and $N$ is the number of practice trials. A possible method for eliciting randomly correct verbalizations on trial 1 would be to utilize the principle of *familiarization* (Noble, 1955; Noble, 1960) to build in a repertoire of equiprobable yet independent response tendencies. This modified memory-drum task would then constitute a verbal analogue of the nonverbal selective learning situation to which equation 1 has been successfully applied in the analysis of ability × learning interactions in the field of multiple-choice phenomena (C. E. Noble, J. L. Noble, and Alcock, 1958).

Much work remains to be done before Hull's proposal can be fully evaluated, as several writers (Koch, 1954; Hilgard, 1956; Cronbach, 1957) have pointed out. One problem concerns the theoretical difficulty of integrating historical (learning) and ahistorical (psychometric) explanatory models. Presumably, the laws would be of the "historical-process" variety (Bergmann, 1957, p. 129)—a fusion of the principles of "mnemic" and "efficient" causation (Johnson, 1939). To understand what might be involved in pairing these two notions, let us recall the familiar paradigm of *process* laws exemplified by celestial mechanics. Here the empirical description of a physical system (masses, positions, velocities) is combined with specifications of the initial conditions (state at time $t_1$) to yield a calculation of the configuration at another moment (state at time $t_2$). A physicist's ability to perform such operations (prediction, postdiction) depends on his having access to certain differential equations (Newtonian process formulas) which contain rate-of-change variables, together with the necessary operational definitions. Explicitly or not, he proceeds on four basic assumptions: (1) that he is dealing with a closed system (meaning no other relevant variables) or that the boundary conditions are known (e.g., the gravitational constant at that place); (2) that his use of continuous functions does not violate the logic of applying real numbers to natural phenomena; (3) that time itself has no causal efficacy, only the events which fill it; and (4) that even if his boundary conditions are not completely specified (e.g., disturbances of measurement or the unexpected arrival of an asteroid), he may expect to encounter limited predictability but no necessary "philosophical" failure of determinism.

What I have said for a physical macro-system goes, in principle, for any biological macro-system, not excluding man. The logic is the same; only the locus of application differs. In verbal learning experiments closure is partially achieved by isolating subjects individually in a soundproof chamber, neutralizing visual distractions via fixation procedures, insuring receptor orientation to the relevant stimuli, and administering standardized procedural instructions. Remaining organismic boundary conditions (ability, age, sex, prior associations, etc.), not being susceptible to manipulative control at present, must of course be kept constant, randomized, or at least carefully recorded so that successful predictions can be made. (In the context of a different experimental design, incidentally, some of the above-mentioned factors might be regarded as *initial* conditions of the system.) Coming now to *historical* laws, I refer to those functional dependencies which fit a slightly different schema, one which adds repetitional or temporal variables to the classical process structure. By means of such mnemic factors we can accomplish "stretch-point" computations, as contrasted with the "point-to-point" computations of the process schema. A paradigm representing action-over-distance-in-time, then, gives us "laws that predict the 'future' not from the 'present' alone but from the present in conjunction with some information about the 'past'" (Bergmann, 1957, p. 126). Finally, the form of *historical-process* laws would be some novel composite of the two schemata presented above, and would in time doubtless become infested with complex integrodifferential equations. One blessing might accrue, however; the advent of historical-process laws would presage the end of psychologists' polemical wrangling over factual issues like field versus nonfield theories, contemporaneity versus historicity, peripheralism versus centralism, and continuity versus noncontinuity learning principles.

A second problem arises from the complicating effects of behavioral oscillation (Hull, 1943a). Hull thought that although predictions for individual organisms might not be completely error-free, they should hold for central tendencies within the limits of normal variability. Controversy over this issue is keen. Aware of the ubiquitous variability within and among organisms, dissenters (e.g., Brunswik, 1943) speak confusingly of "laws" which allow prediction with certainty versus "statistics (correlations)" which permit only probability statements. Their pessimistic conclusion: psychology must give up its quest for nomothetic laws and be content with correlation coefficients. One sensible rejoinder to Brunswik (Hull, 1943b) is that part of our uncertainty may be due to imperfect control and errors of measurement rather than to a capricious subject matter. Even in physics, we are reminded, "The contingency of the initial conditions is in marked contrast with the permanency of the laws" (D'Abro, 1951, p. 46). The oscillation concept enters Hull's theory as a statistical postulate (1943a; 1952), yet his system is deterministic in form. What would the Brunswikians have us do, renounce experimentation and degenerate to a point where the chances are the same of obtaining a *casual* as a *causal* relationship? Part of the blur in "probabilistic functionalism" seems to come from misinterpretations of what the Heisenberg indeterminacy principle implies for predictability in the behavioral sciences. Briefly, it is no more relevant to people than to planets (London, 1945; Grünbaum, 1952). As far as physicists are concerned (D'Abro, 1951), "No inconsistency is involved between the vagueness of the uncertainty relations and the extreme accuracy with which rigorous causal relations may be represented in space-time on the macroscopic level" (p. 961); furthermore, "Where statistical processes are involved, the new quantum philosophy retains the classical belief in strict causal relations accompanying the possibility of an accurate space-time description" (p.

954). So much for specious "quantum" arguments. The underlying fallacy is not hard to detect: equivocation when using the term "individual."

Now everyone will agree, by the semantical rules of the probability calculus, that laws of relative chance convey no information about individual events. With a slight modification of our foregoing paradigm, however, primary *statistical* laws (in Hull's, not Brunswik's sense) can be linked to a secondary historical-process schema in which some of the postulates and definitions of the basic theory are statistical in nature. Spence's analysis of human conditioning curves (1956) shows how Hull's oscillation function can be construed as a manipulable quantity (dependent variable) responsive to experimental control. In the course of this analysis he also removes some of the superficial inconsistencies between continuity (Hull and Spence) and noncontinuity (Guthrie and Estes) theories, as in his discussion of the Voeks experiment. Similar strategies have been tried in the kinetic and quantum theories without forsaking a deterministic frame of reference (Bergmann, 1957). To be a determinist, in other words, does not require that one subscribe to an atomistic (reductionistic) world view purged of statistical concepts, not even in physiological psychology. Nor does this brand of determinism make any foolish *a priori* claim that the universe is or must be causally organized, nor even that scientists are smart enough to discover all the laws that are in nature to be discovered. Rather, I think of a statistical determinist as one who, accepting the *practical* limitations of both observation and induction, entertains the hypothesis (based on steadily mounting empirical evidence) that for any dependent variable class he can, *in principle*, find the class of independent variables of which it is a function. At any rate, to return once more to the Hull-Brunswik argument, experimentalists who prefer "systematic" rather than "representative" design will undoubtedly base their research upon nomothetically derived hypotheses (Postman, 1955), realizing that the inductive foundation is secure for generalizations not only about main effects but about interactions as well.

A third difficulty in attempting to realize the goal Hull has set for psychologists concerns the rationalization of the constants in the prediction equations. This will require multivariate experimental designs to determine the numerical values, errors of measurement, interdependence, and interchangeability of the human-factor constants. A fourth problem is that group curves often contain artifacts due to pooling different individual functions (Estes, 1956). If the rank of the data matrix is greater than two, distortions result (Gulliksen, 1959) necessitating the technique of stratification into homogeneous subgroups (Spence, 1956; C. E. Noble, J. L. Noble, and Alcock, 1958). In this case, nomothesis approaches idiography with the single organism as a limit, the nonstatistical convergence

Skinner (1957) has long advocated. When to these four issues is added the question of composition laws suggested by the experiments cited above, one realizes the need for comprehensive, theory-oriented research on human verbal learning which combines the experimental-correlational and nomothetic-idiographic methodologies.

## METHODOLOGY

In view of the psychometric information available on human O-variables (e.g., verbal ability), together with the experimental data on their interactions with S-variables (e.g., practice) and R-variables (e.g., learning scores), it appears timely for psychologists to attempt an integration of the fields of learning and individual differences in the area of verbal behavior. As one incentive, there is the possibility of wider generality attaching to the findings than if some nonverbal activity were chosen. I believe it is generally accepted that man is a verbal animal and that the manipulation of symbols (thinking, reasoning) in science as in everyday life depends largely on verbal processes (Skinner, 1957). Hence it follows that a fuller understanding of the role of individual differences in verbal learning will have both theoretical and practical implications. But, as Underwood said recently, "We have as yet no methodical plan for exploring the limits or generalities of relationships" (1957, p. 168). His conclusion serves to define the aim of the present chapter: to encourage the establishment of such a plan by experimental learning psychologists.

Effective research on verbal learning continues to be strongly influenced by the associationistic tradition (Irion, 1959). The reasons for this are well known. They include an emphasis on objectivity, control, experimentation, quantification, and causal (deterministic) analysis. Although regarded occasionally as "limited," "artificial," or "unrepresentative," the experimental procedures typified by the serial and paired-associates learning methods have actually advanced our scientific knowledge of verbal processes farther than any non-associationistic procedures. Therefore, it is only sensible to proceed in a field which is already well developed to the search for more inclusive concepts, laws, and theories. In this way gains of a combinatorial type may be realized as we move from the consideration of relatively simple phenomena to those fraught with greater complexity.

If one is committed to predicting future behavior by means of statistico-historical-process laws, however, one must know both past and present events. An illustrative schema is shown in Figure 6-1. Of the two independent bases of prediction, the past (antecedent) conditions include learning, inhibition, and motivational variables, while the present (initial) conditions include perceptual factors, psychometric data, and task descriptions. It is in the latter category that so many psychologists have failed to maintain procedural conformity (Melton, 1950; Ammons, 1955; Hilgard, 1956; Irion, 1958). Yet rigid adherence to convention is not enough. We must also encourage originality and critical acumen in the choice of variables and techniques. The trick is to combine standardization with some flexibility and a bit of rationale.

The specification of *association value* is a case in point. For over a quarter of a century now, psychologists have cited Glaze's (1928) inaccurate, dated, and unreliable norms instead of Krueger's (1934) superior values. Allowing due credit to a pioneer, there is no comparison

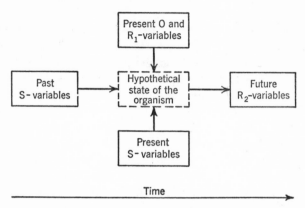

FIG. 6-1. Schema illustrating a prediction process in psychology which utilizes both antecedent-condition (historical) and initial-condition (contemporary) variables. In abstract terms $R_2 = f(S, O, R_1)$.

between an $n$ of 15 and one of 200, even though Krueger used different subsamples of raters to reduce the labor per man. In 1957 we reported new measurements (Noble, Stockwell, and Pryer, 1957) obtained from 200 unselected subjects at Louisiana State University for a sample of 100 consonant-vowel-consonant (CVC) combinations drawn randomly from a corrected set of 1,665 Glaze-type CVCs (eliminating Y as a vowel). Our values had high reliability but only 81.0 per cent of the variance in common with Krueger and 65.6 per cent with Glaze. More alarming than this unreliability of the older norms, however, were two other facts: (1) evidence of curvilinear regression wherever the Glaze values were used, and (2) dependency of association value upon $n$, leading to serious underestimates of low association values when the number of raters is small. Neither Krueger nor we found any truly *nonsense* syllables; i.e., stimuli whose response-evocation powers were zero in the sense that no subject reported having any associations to them. Hence our reason for recommending the neutral term "CVC" (Noble, Stockwell, and Pryer, 1957) to specify the stimulus population without ambiguity.

It may be of interest to know that the Montana laboratory has just completed the rather formidable task of measuring the *association values, rated associations,* and *scaled meaningfulness* ($m'$) of all $21 \times 5 \times 20 = 2,100$ CVCs (including 437 real words), employing 200 subjects each of whom responded to the entire set of stimuli. We used the same five-point rating schedule of number of associations ("none" to "very many") as in the Louisiana study, but the Montana procedure was paced rather than self-paced. Analyses of rated associations indicate close agreement with the Louisiana norms, as shown by a correlation of .965. This coefficient means that the two sets of norms have 93.12 per cent of their variance in common. An intergroup reliability coefficient, obtained by correlating the 100 CVC means of a random half of the subject sample with the other half, is .995 (adjusted for attenuation). The internal consistency test for the equal-interval $m'$ scale had an average error of only 1.9 per cent. I believe that this project will give students of verbal behavior current, accurate, and reliable norms which do not confound association value with individual differences as in Krueger's work.

But another caution is in order; this concerns the operational distinction between *association value* (percentage of ratings greater than "none") and *scaled meaningfulness* (standard-score transformations of the five-category distributions). Because of fundamental scale differences, these two variables are nonlinearly related to each other. In fact, when association value is plotted as a function of scaled meaningfulness ($m'$) for 21 representative stimuli, as shown in Figure 6-2, it is evident that the ordinate is a probability function of the abscissa. That is, the curve represents how the per cent (or relative frequency) of dichotomized "yes-no" responses is distributed with respect to increases in an essentially continuous variable. Note particularly how insensitive to changes in scaled meaningfulness are the upper levels of association value. The trouble with the vertical scale is the absence of a (constant) unit of measurement. For methodological reasons, therefore, I think psychologists should give up primitive association-value norms of the Glaze type and try to develop more sophisticated measurements which have a rational basis in psychological theory. If, for instance, we wish to understand a positive test of the hypothesis that "meaningfulness facilitates learning," then let us be more specific about the theoretical factors underlying *meaningfulness,* e.g., frequency of associations (Noble, 1952; Noble and Parker, 1960; Parker and Noble, 1960). Obviously, theory will be better served by empirical operations which get at the relevant variables as directly as possible and with minimum error.

My position on standardization is simple: let us adopt standards, but let us first be sure that the standards are scientifically worth adopting. Based on such considerations, a uniform experimental procedure is clearly indicated, so that quantitative human-factor data can be directly assimilated into the existing network of empirical laws governing the learning process. If we fail to achieve standardization, our laws will have only limited generality and system will be unattainable. To quote

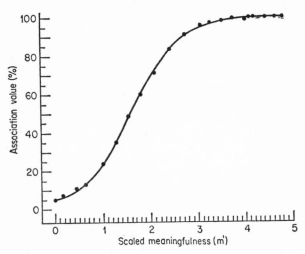

FIG. 6-2. Relationship between association value and scaled meaningfulness ($m'$) for 21 CVCs selected from the total population of 2,100. Each point is based on the responses of 200 subjects. The $m'$ scale values are $x/\sigma$ transformations calculated by the method of successive intervals.

Irion: "There can be no doubt that this is one of the most pressing problems of contemporary research in the area of rote learning" (1959, p. 549).

In addition to standardization of methods and materials (e.g., stimulus duration, instructions, distribution of practice, amount of material, meaningfulness), more aptitude testing and taxonomic evaluation of the various motivational and personality characteristics related to verbal behavior (e.g., origin, rate, asymptote) may be necessary. Related problems are concerned with defining the response units and explaining changes in correlations and beta weights of predictor tests as practice increases on the criterion task. One interpretation (Fleishman,

1957) has suggested the possibility of progressive alterations in factorial structure, while another hypothesis is that the ability requirements "are the same at any stage of training but that training changes the strength of certain component responses" (Adams, 1957, p. 129). Attempts to resolve these issues should be combined with multivariate explorations of the human factors which modify experimental treatment effects.

A good example of the joint use of nomothetic and idiographic methods in this area is contained in a report from the Minnesota laboratory (Peterson and Jenkins, 1957). Group phenomena were found quite applicable to individual cases; e.g., subjects selected for diversity on the trait of associative commonality (Russell and Jenkins, 1954). To illustrate the fusion of correlational and experimental methods, recent research in the Montana laboratory (C. E. Noble, J. L. Noble, and Alcock, 1958) gave validity coefficients ranging between .28 and .37 for predicting serial verbal learning from brief printed tests of verbal meaning, word fluency, and reasoning. The maximum multiple correlation was .43 for the latter two predictors ($n = 103$). Initial measures during early trials, on the other hand, correlated about .50 with the same criterion. Presence of specific factors, absence of a general learning factor, high test intercorrelations, and restriction of range are among the reasons why these coefficients leave a disappointingly large proportion of variance unaccounted for. Perhaps a "residual gain" measure (Du Bois, 1958) would be useful if tests related to final proficiency could be found. "The development of selection devices for various types of learning situations which would permit the characteristics of the sample studied to be specified in a quantitative fashion would represent an enormous methodological advance" (McGeoch and Irion, 1952, p. 564). In other words, we must find out how to standardize organisms as well as stimuli. Following the successful completion of this stage, the investigation of interaction laws could begin. Finally, as more extensive deductive connections among the definitions and laws begin to mature, theoretical formulations of general applicability would be expected to appear.

In summary, the specific phases of the proposed research would be (1) standardization of methods and materials, (2) development of verbal aptitude tests of origin, rate, and asymptote differences, (3) multivariate exploration of selected human factors and identification of the major experimental variables relevant to individual differences, (4) analyses of interactions between the experimental and psychometric variables by means of repeated-measurement (learning) designs, (5) systematic attempts to integrate such empirical findings into an articulate theory possessing considerable scope.

## SUMMARY

This essay has presented a brief review and evaluation of the available data on verbal learning and individual differences. A need was expressed for comprehensive, theory-oriented research in this area which would combine the experimental-correlational and nomothetic-idiographic techniques. Following a treatment of certain methodological and theoretical problems involved in the processes of standardization, prediction, and interaction analysis, a five-point research program was outlined.

### REFERENCES

Adams, J. A. (1957) The relationship between certain measures of ability and the acquisition of a psychomotor criterion response. *J. Gen. Psychol.*, 56, 121–134.

Allport, G. W. (1937) *Personality.* New York: Holt, Rinehart & Winston.

Ammons, R. B. (1955) Rotary pursuit apparatus: I. Survey of variables. *Psychol. Bull.*, 52, 69–76.

Anastasi, A. (1958) *Differential psychology.* (3rd ed.) New York: Macmillan.

Barnett, C. D., Ellis, N. R., & Pryer, M. W. (1960) Serial position effects in superior and retarded subjects. *Psychol. Rep.*, 7, 111–113.

Bergmann, G. (1957) *Philosophy of science.* Madison, Wis.: University of Wisconsin Press.

Boring, E. G. (1950) *A history of experimental psychology.* (2nd ed.) New York: Appleton-Century-Crofts.

Brunswik, E. (1943) Organismic achievement and environmental probability. *Psychol. Rev.*, 50, 255–272.

Cieutat, V. J. (1959) Supplementary report: Stimulus and response meaningfulness ($m'$) in paired-associate learning by hospitalized mental patients. *J. Exp. Psychol.*, 58, 490.

Cieutat, V. J., & Noble, C. E. (1958) Ability vs. practice in two-hand coordination. *Percept. Mot. Skills*, 8, 226.

Cieutat, V. J., Stockwell, F. E., & Noble, C. E. (1958) The interaction of ability and amount of practice with stimulus and response meaningfulness ($m, m'$) in paired-associate learning. *J. Exp. Psychol.*, 56, 193–202.

Cronbach, L. J. (1957) The two disciplines of scientific psychology. *Amer. Psychologist*, 12, 671–684.

D'Abro, A. (1951) *The rise of the new physics.* New York: Dover.

Du Bois, P. H. (1958) Introductory remarks. In P. H. Du Bois & W. H. Manning (Eds.), The measurement of learning. *Tech. Rep. No. 6*, Contract No. Nonr-816, Office of Naval Research and Washington University. Pp. 1–3.

Ellis, N. R., Pryer, M. W., Distefano, M. K., Jr., & Pryer, R. S. (1960) Learning in mentally defective, normal, and superior subjects. *Amer. J. Ment. Defic.*, 64, 725–734.

Estes, W. K. (1956) The problem of inference from curves based on group data. *Psychol. Bull.*, **53**, 134–140.

Fleishman, E. A. (1957) A comparative study of aptitude patterns in unskilled and skilled psychomotor performances. *J. Appl. Psychol.*, **41**, 263–272.

Glaze, J. A. (1928) The association value of non-sense syllables. *J. Genet. Psychol.*, **35**, 255–267.

Grünbaum, A. (1952) Causality and the science of human behavior. *Amer. Scient.*, **40**, 665–676.

Gulliksen, H. (1959) Mathematical solutions for psychological problems. *Amer. Scient.*, **47**, 178–201.

Hilgard, E. R. (1956) *Theories of learning.* (2nd ed.) New York: Appleton-Century-Crofts.

Hull, C. L. (1943a) *Principles of behavior.* New York: Appleton-Century-Crofts.

Hull, C. L. (1943b) The problem of intervening variables in molar behavior theory. *Psychol. Rev.*, **50**, 273–291.

Hull, C. L. (1945) The place of innate individual and species differences in a natural-science theory of behavior. *Psychol. Rev.*, **52**, 55–60.

Hull, C. L. (1952) *A behavior system.* New Haven, Conn.: Yale University Press.

Irion, A. L. (1959) Rote learning. In S. Koch (Ed.), *Psychology: A study of a science.* Vol. II. New York: McGraw-Hill. Pp. 538–560.

Johnson, H. M. (1939) Rival principles of causal explanation in psychology. *Psychol. Rev.*, **46**, 493–516.

Koch, S. (1954) Clark L. Hull. In W. K. Estes *et al.*, *Modern learning theory.* New York: Appleton-Century-Crofts. Pp. 1–176.

Krueger, W. C. F. (1934) The relative difficulty of non-sense syllables. *J. Exp. Psychol.*, **17**, 145–153.

London, I. D. (1945) Psychology and Heisenberg's principle of indeterminacy. *Psychol. Rev.*, **52**, 162–168.

McGeoch, J. A., & Irion, A. L. (1952) *The psychology of human learning.* (2nd ed.) New York: Longmans.

Mandler, G., & Huttenlocher, J. (1956) The relationship between associative frequency, associative ability, and paired-associate learning. *Amer. J. Psychol.*, **69**, 424–428.

Melton, A. W. (1950) Learning. In W. S. Monroe (Ed.), *Encyclopedia of educational research.* (Rev. ed.) New York: Macmillan. Pp. 668–690.

Nagel, E. (1952) The logic of historical analysis. *Scient. Mon.*, **74**, 162–169.

Noble, C. E. (1952) The role of stimulus meaning ($m$) in serial verbal learning. *J. Exp. Psychol.*, **43**, 437–446; **44**, 465.

Noble, C. E. (1955) The effect of familiarization upon serial verbal learning. *J. Exp. Psychol.*, **49**, 333–338.

Noble, C. E. (1959) Ability vs. practice in paired-associate learning. *J. Psychol.*, **47**, 331–335.

Noble, C. E. (1960) Supplementary report: Familiarity and frequency. *J. Exp. Psychol.*, **59**, 432–433; **60**, 418.

Noble, C. E., & Fuchs, J. E. (1959) Serial errors in human learning: a test of the McCrary-Hunter hypothesis. *Science*, 129, 570–571.

Noble, C. E., & McNeely, D. A. (1957) The role of meaningfulness (*m*) in paired-associate verbal learning. *J. Exp. Psychol.*, 53, 16–22.

Noble, C. E., Noble, J. L., & Alcock, W. T. (1958) Prediction of individual differences in human trial-and-error learning. *Percept. Mot. Skills*, 8, 151–172.

Noble, C. E., & Parker, G. V. C. (1960) The Montana scale of meaningfulness (*m*). *Psychol. Rep.*, 7, 325–331.

Noble, C. E., Stockwell, F. E., & Pryer, M. W. (1957) Meaningfulness (*m'*) and association value (*a*) in paired-associate syllable learning. *Psychol. Rep.*, 3, 441–452.

Parker, G. V. C., & Noble, C. E. (1960) Effects of experimentally-produced meaningfulness (*m*) on paired-associate learning. *Amer. Psychologist*, 15, 451. (Abstract)

Peterson, M. S., & Jenkins, J. J. (1957) Word association phenomena at the individual level: A pair of case studies. *Tech. Rep. No. 16*, Contract No. N8onr-66216, Office of Naval Research and University of Minnesota.

Postman, L. (1955) The probability approach and nomothetic theory. *Psychol. Rev.*, 62, 218–225.

Reynolds, B., & Adams, J. A. (1954) Psychomotor performance as a function of initial level of ability. *Amer. J. Psychol.*, 67, 268–277.

Russell, B. (1929) *Our knowledge of the external world*. New York: Norton.

Russell, W. A., & Jenkins, J. J. (1954) The complete Minnesota norms for responses to 100 words from the Kent-Rosanoff Word Association Test. *Tech. Rep. No. 11*, Contract No. N8onr-66216, Office of Naval Research and University of Minnesota.

Skinner, B. F. (1957) *Verbal behavior*. New York: Appleton-Century-Crofts.

Snygg, D., & Combs, A. W. (1949) *Individual behavior*. New York: Harper.

Spence, K. W. (1956) *Behavior theory and conditioning*. New Haven, Conn.: Yale University Press.

Tolman, E. C. (1932) *Purposive behavior in animals and men*. New York: Appleton-Century-Crofts.

Underwood, B. J. (1957) *Psychological research*. New York: Appleton-Century-Crofts.

Woodworth, R. S. (1929) *Psychology*. (Rev. ed.) New York: Holt, Rinehart & Winston.

Zeaman, D., & Kaufman, H. (1955) Individual differences and theory in a motor learning task. *Psychol. Monogr.*, 69, No. 6 (Whole No. 391).

# COMMENTS ON PROFESSOR NOBLE'S PAPER
## James J. Jenkins
### UNIVERSITY OF MINNESOTA

Let me begin my remarks by asserting that I endorse Noble's point of view strongly and that I am very happy that we have a paper on individual differences at this conference. I think that a decade ago this would not have happened. Lykken and I (1957) in our *Annual Review* chapter "Individual Differences" urged very strongly that experimentalists and psychometricians try to move more closely together. We pointed there to Robert L. Thorndike's (1954) rather shocking study which showed that the interests of "clinicians," "experimentalists," and "psychometricians" were all negatively correlated. Lest you think this is a contrast between "hardheads" and "softheads," I hasten to point out that two very hardheaded groups—the laboratory-oriented, statistical-design–conscious experimentalists and the scale-building, factor-analytic, computing-machine psychometrists have interests which correlate −.80! More recently Cronbach (1957), in his presidential address to the American Psychological Association, drew attention to this same unfortunate gulf which separates "correlational psychology" from "experimental psychology" and deplored its undesirable consequences. My feeling is that if we permit this condition to continue (or even encourage it!), we run the serious risk of having two half-developed half-fields in psychology.

In the learning area especially, I believe we neglect individual differences. We have given a great deal of attention to the conditions and contents of learning experiments but very little to the attributes of subjects. We know a lot about what I would call "process laws" but very little about "subject laws." In many laboratories it is the practice to give prelearning trials and throw out heterogeneous subjects in order to decrease experimental variance and interference effects. All of us, I am sure, are guilty of discarding at least "slow learners" and throwing out potentially interesting data. In brief, I believe that anyone at this conference could write a set of rules for selecting materials and procedures which would make rote learning difficult or easy, but I doubt that anyone here can give even a partial listing of the attributes or abilities which would enable us to select in advance either good or poor rote learners.

If we are tempted to study some individual-differences parameter, we are likely to make a few tests looking for individual differences and, finding no decisive relations between these tests and anything else, discover that differential variables are tough and messy conceptually and leave the field. The classic attempt was the set of studies by Woodrow (1946) which seems to have discouraged succeeding psychological generations from such lines of investigation.

There are current examples which appear promising, but we need to concern ourselves that they be followed up. One of the most fascinating, I think, is the Plenderleith and Postman (1956; 1957) study of individual differences in incidental learning. Here the investigators generated a very clever construct which they called the ability to take "multiple sets." They devised a test situation to measure the hypothesized ability independently and then verified that, in fact, people scoring high on the test performances were superior incidental learners. It is a beautiful piece of work which ties an associative theory of learning to an associative behavior tendency of individuals, but it has not been pursued further.

Another good example is the study by Zeaman and Kaufman that Noble refers to. These investigators were following a program like that of Noble's. They took the Hullian system and drove it to the limit to force it to yield up an individual-differences parameter. That the system is clumsy seems clear, but that it worked should be an occasion of rejoicing on all sides.

Over all, it is plain that *programs* of research are called for. Occasional advances will be lost or their meanings remain obscure unless systematic programs with both "manipulated" variables and "status" variables are pursued.

Now in pursuing these programs, there are some difficult problems in store. The first and most salient of these is that we do not know what "verbal ability" is with reference to our standard learning procedures. It may very well be that different verbal learning tasks (learning prose, serial learning, paired-associates learning, etc.) draw on different abilities or utilize some set of abilities with different weights. In addition, it is likely that the skills involved in learning nonsense syllables may be different from those employed when familiar words are to be learned. And finally, it is almost certain that the relative weights of individual-differences factors involved in learning change as the subjects increase in experience in a given learning task.

Within paired-associates learning itself, we may have three kinds of learning going on simultaneously or sequentially. As shown in the diagram, one must learn to encode the stimulus only in its presence; the response word, first in its presence and then in its absence; and finally one must relate the appropriate response to the stimulus.

It is conceivable that different skills are employed in each of these tasks and that the ease or difficulty of learning any of these may be independent of the other kinds of learning and more or less important in over-all performance depending on the particular point at which the learning task is studied.

I believe that it would be valuable to start with a factor analysis of verbal abilities (such as Carroll's, 1941) and work forward from there toward various learning tasks. On the other hand, since most of us are deeply involved in paired-associates learning, an alternative I would also argue for would be that of centering the attack on the components of this task. This approach would probably have the greatest immediate pay-off for us. Obviously, we do not want to choose *between* these courses of action but rather combine them in the most fruitful way we can. The full understanding of the human-being-engaged-in-verbal-learning and the incorporation of this understanding in the body of general psychology requires the experimentalist's understanding of the process and the differential psychologist's understanding of the subject.

I think much of the work of the differential psychologist in the past has been relatively sterile (though it will be useful to us methodologically). It has in the main settled for description and intercorrelation and, when no "general learning factor" emerged, the description was too tedious and fragmentary for a busy experimentalist to bother with. The experimentalist who is close to the learning situation and who has honed his theoretical tools for a long time is in a better position to generate hypotheses which would provide the starting points for such research—let me cite again the generation of a hypothetical construct by Postman and Plenderleith—but in the past he has rarely pursued this aim. I think we certainly want to put our bets on theory construction as opposed to "blind descriptive analysis," even though we may have little agreement as to which theory we want to try.

Noble proposes that we take the Hullian formulation and systematically pursue it. Is it really possible to get numbers to fill in the slots where the parameters are supposed to go? I hope so and I think we all want to encourage this line of attack though we may personally prefer others. My personal bets are elsewhere, but I am happy that Noble puts his here. It is certainly high time that Hull was taken that seriously.

With regard to methodology, I am sure we will have some debate. As Noble points out, "The trick is to combine standardization with some flexibility and a bit of rationale." But this is difficult. Noble chooses for his example the specification of association values of "nonsense syllables" or "CVCs." It is indeed difficult to understand why the Glaze norms persist in popularity, but it is equally difficult to see why psychologists ignore linguists who tell us that some of these are not syllables and some are not even CVCs [e.g., GEX is actually (in pronunciation) CVCC]. When we rate these materials on association value, are we deceiving ourselves that we are adding to objectivity? In the first place, are *ratings* to be desired more than the associations themselves? Secondly, is association value a derived measure of something more basic like "pronounceability" or the "nearness to English" of the letter cluster? Last year Joseph Greenberg, a linguist at Columbia, guessed at the subject's pronunciation of the entries of Noble's list of 100 syllables and worked out the number of English monosyllables he could generate from each by single-place phoneme substitutions. At his desk (with no subjects to test at all) he generated a "meaningfulness" count of this sort that correlated +.70 with the scale values assigned by 200 subjects. I would not yet be sure that we are prepared to standardize this operation as Noble proposes.

I think it might be fruitful for us to work on standardizing instructions, etc., in some manner so as to minimize variance in subjects or experimenters or to agree on what constitutes sufficient pretraining of subjects, but I suspect that these in themselves may be important variables in task sets and strategies that we may want to manipulate for some time before we fix on a standard for everyone.

I am certain at any rate that, regardless of proposed standardization, there will be deviates who will disregard the standards and come up with interesting findings.

In conclusion let me repeat that I am glad that this paper has been included and that I hope it has some effect on our field. Perhaps a decade hence a conference like this one will include major substantive papers which will bear out the optimism with which both Noble and I view this topic.

### REFERENCES

Carroll, J. B. (1941) A factor analysis of verbal abilities. *Psychometrika,* **6,** 279–307.

Cronbach, L. J. (1957) The two disciplines of scientific psychology. *Amer. Psychologist,* **12,** 671–684.

Jenkins, J. J., & Lykken, D. T. (1957) Individual differences. *Ann. Rev. Psychol.,* **8,** 79–112.

Plenderleith, Mavis, & Postman, L. (1956) Discriminative and verbal habits in incidental learning. *Amer. J. Psychol.,* **69,** 236–243.

Plenderleith, Mavis, & Postman, L. (1957) Individual differences in intentional and incidental learning. *Brit. J. Psychol.,* **48,** 241–248.

Thorndike, R. L. (1954) The psychological value systems of psychologists. *Amer. Psychologist,* **9,** 787–789.

Woodrow, H. (1946) The ability to learn. *Psychol. Rev.,* **53,** 147–158.

## SUMMARY OF CONFERENCE DISCUSSION

In the course of the discussion concerning individual differences, it was pointed out that questionnaires like the Taylor Scale of Manifest Anxiety may often be useful when employed in experiments but that there is a tendency for research workers to use such scales in ways probably not justified by their original purposes and construction. This comment, made by several discussants, was directed to the point that the Taylor scale has been used in a variety of studies which have led to the accumulation of widely diverse results. Some participants expressed the view that this scale may be as meaningful a measure of drive as hours of food deprivation (Melton), even though experimentalists would usually prefer the latter.

The encoding process received further discussion in this session, and there was a split in the group as to whether it could possibly be conceived as involving an associative process (Deese) or not (Bousfield).

Considerable concern was evidenced over the problem of how the individual-difference variables with which experimentalists might begin to work could be selected. There are many such variables, and concern centered on how to select those which might be most profitably studied in relation to verbal learning. Postman pointed out that there are individual differences in various measures internal to the learning task itself. He expressed interest in such differences as possibly leading to information concerning the learning process. Psychometrically measured individual differences are another matter, and Postman finds it not very interesting to attend to such differences merely to reduce variability. Underwood pointed out that performances on successive lists are highly correlated. Individual differences produce a great deal of the variance in the data of verbal learning, but he has been unable, despite intensive search, to find interactions between such individual differences and the variables measured in learning experiments. It was suggested that perhaps the conditions of his experiments in some way minimize such interactions (Osgood). Bousfield pointed out that associative output curves for different individuals could reach identical asymptotes but approach them at different rates; thus, depending upon the temporal point at which the output is assessed, the subjects could be described as the same or as different. This would obviously make a difference in the relationship of the output measure with variables of the learning task. Noble indicated that he has obtained interactions between individual differences and learning variables.

Other problems which arose in this discussion concerned Jenkins's point as to the linguistic features of the "nonsense syllable." There appeared to be agreement that Jenkins's point is well taken. The distinction between S-R laws and R-R laws was argued at length, and the group found the distinction a difficult one to make for a number of situations. Underwood expressed vigorous opposition to Noble's emphasis on standardization of method in experiments in verbal learning (cf. Noble's paper, p. 142).

# Chapter 7

# THE PRESENT STATUS
# OF INTERFERENCE THEORY

*Leo Postman*

UNIVERSITY OF CALIFORNIA

Interference theory occupies an unchallenged position as the major significant analysis of the process of forgetting. The only serious opposition has come from the trace theory of the Gestalt psychologists, but that point of view has thus far proved experimentally sterile and resistant to rigorous test. As a result, the recent years have seen little debate about the basic assumptions of interference theory. Developments in the study of forgetting have consisted largely of extensions and refinements of interference theory and of methodological advances in the measurement of retention. The present paper will address itself to these developments. The discussion will be divided into two main sections: (a) a consideration of formal experiments on retroactive and proactive inhibition, and (b) an analysis of extra-experimental sources of interference.

## RETROACTIVE AND PROACTIVE INHIBITION

The competition-of-response theory as formulated by McGeoch (1942) provides a convenient point of departure for a review of recent developments and current problems. According to this theory, two response systems acquired in succession both remain available to the subject at the time of recall. If two responses are attached to similar or identical stimuli, competition occurs and the stronger response is given; responses of equal strength may block each other. Similarity of experimental context as well as similarity of the stimuli in the two lists favors competition.

For analytic purposes, it is important to make a clear distinction between two components of this theoretical position. The first is what Barnes and Underwood (1959) call the independence hypothesis. The second is the hypothesis of response dominance at recall. The independence hypothesis asserts that the associative strength of the responses in the first list is not changed by the interpolation of a second list. The two response systems remain independent and intact. The hypothesis of response dominance specifies the mechanism responsible for the observed retention loss, viz., the displacement of the correct response in one list by a stronger incorrect response from the other list. The two hypotheses are not necessarily linked. Thus, it would be possible to reject the independence hypothesis but to regard reproductive inhibition as the mechanism entirely responsible for effective interference at recall.

With this distinction in mind, we shall consider in turn the status of the independence hypothesis and of reproductive inhibition as the mechanism of interference at recall and in relearning. The independence hypothesis will be shown to be untenable in light of the experimental evidence. Important modifications have been made, and additional ones will be suggested, in the interpretation of the mechanism of competition.

## The Unlearning Hypothesis

The failure of the independence hypothesis will be considered first for situations in which intertask transfer is negative and then for situations in which intertask transfer is positive. The evidence will show that in the former case the strength of the first-list associations decreases as a function of interpolated learning, while in the second case their strength increases.

*Two-factor Theory.* The first important challenge to the independence hypothesis came, of course, from the two-factor theory of Melton and Irwin (1940). It is useful to recall the reasons which led these investigators to advance the unlearning hypothesis. First, there was no consistent relationship between the number of overt interlist intrusions and the amount of retroactive inhibition (RI) at recall. The proportion of RI attributable to such intrusions rose to a maximum and then declined as a function of the degree of interpolated learning (IL). Since RI at recall increased steadily, a factor other than reproductive inhibition had to be largely responsible for the observed interference at the highest level of IL. Second, RI was most persistent at intermediate levels of IL and dissipated rapidly when the degree of IL was high. Hence, the detrimental effects of the second factor must be more transitory than those of reproductive inhibition. These findings fell into place when the second factor was identified as the unlearning of the first list during the acquisition of the second list. Responses from the first list which occur during IL are "extinguished" and are not available on the recall trial. Such responses can, however, be relearned with considerable saving, and the effects of unlearning on retention are, therefore, extremely transitory.

The fact which is of critical importance for the unlearning hypothesis is the lack of correlation between amount of RI and overt interlist intrusions. Such a lack of agreement between the two indices of interference has been confirmed repeatedly in later investigations and may be considered an established fact. The high proportion of failures at the highest levels of IL suggests that some responses remain unavailable to the subject even when the discrepancy between the strengths of the two lists virtually eliminates overt competition between specific responses. If a substantial proportion of the failures can, indeed, be attributed to the unavailability of first-list responses, unlearning must be assumed to have occurred. The inversion in the relationship between degree of IL and the persistence of RI is consistent with the assumption of unlearning but less critical to the hypothesis since it is possible to conceive of extinction effects which are as persistent as those of response competition.

The lack of correlation between amount of RI and number of overt intrusions does not in itself compel the assumption of unlearning and is capable of alternative interpretations. Thus, we can attribute the decline in intrusions at high levels of IL to increasing differentiation between the two lists (Thune and Underwood, 1943; Underwood, 1945). Differentiation, i.e., discrimination of list membership, is assumed to be a positively accelerated function of the degree of IL and to vary inversely with the time interval between the end of IL and the relearning (RL). At the highest levels of IL, therefore, intrusions are readily discriminated as incorrect responses and rejected. In short, the ratio of implicit to explicit intrusions increases with differentiation. The concept of differentiation receives strong independent support from studies of proactive inhibition (PI) in which the frequency of overt intrusions (a) reaches a maximum at intermediate degrees of prior learning (PL) and (b) increases as a function of the time interval between learning and recall, especially at the highest levels of PL where initial differentiation is high (Underwood, 1949). The fact that there is a lack of correlation between the total amount of retention loss and the number of overt intrusions in PI is important since in this case the rise in the proportion of failures cannot be attributed to unlearning. The explanatory power of the concept of differentiation is also brought out by comparisons between the effects of varying degrees of IL on a single list and of comparable numbers of interpolated trials on multiple lists. In contrast to the results obtained with a single list, the frequency of overt interlist intrusions did not vary with the number of interpolated lists. Since each of the successive lists received a constant number of trials, there was little opportunity for differentiation to develop (Underwood, 1945). In the case of multiple interpolated lists, as in the case of a single list, the frequency of intrusions does not vary in a one-to-one fashion with the total amount of interference, but the lack of correlation occurs for different reasons. The results become consistent only when we consider the opportunities for differentiation in the two experimental situations.

The specific manifestations of interference thus vary with the degree of differentiation between the two lists. In the conventional RI experiment the observable consequences of unlearning and differentiation are not easy to separate. Acceptance of the differentiation hypothesis does not, however, in any sense contradict the assumption of unlearning. Unlearning may serve to change the relative strengths of competing items and thus influence the probability of explicit and implicit intrusions. These considerations make it clear that conclusive evidence for or against unlearning had to come from procedures which made it possible to measure the availability of responses from the two lists independently of differentiation. A first important step in that direction was taken by the introduction of the method of modified free recall, or MFR (Underwood, 1948; Briggs, 1954; Briggs, Thompson and Brogden, 1954).

*The Measurement of Response Availability.* In an MFR test, the subject is presented with the common stimulus term (A) of the two lists and required to give a response either from the first list (B) or from the second list (C). Thus, the relative strength of the two response systems is determined when the subject does not attempt to discriminate list membership. As IL is continued, the frequency of responses from the first list declines and that of responses from the second list increases. Responses from the second list begin to be dominant when the two lists have been learned to approximately the same degree. It is precisely at the point of approximate equality between the two lists that interlist intrusions reach their maximum when retention is measured by the conventional method of paced anticipation. These results are fully consistent with the unlearning hypothesis, and indeed, with two-factor theory. Responses from the first list are increasingly displaced by responses from the second list in the course of interpolated learning even when the subject is free to respond from either series. Juxtaposition of the results of MFR and conventional anticipation tests shows that the decline in interlist intrusions coincides with the progressive weakening of responses from the first list. These results still fall short, however, of providing crucial evidence for the unlearning hypothesis. Since the subject is required to give a response *either* from the first *or* from the second list, MFR measures response dominance. A response from the first list which is displaced by one from the second list may still be available to the subject. The fact that conventional anticipation tests yield less RI than do MFR tests (Briggs, 1957) supports this assumption.

The relationships between response dominance in MFR and overt inter-list intrusions again can be interpreted in terms of differentiation as well as unlearning.

More direct support for the hypothesis of unlearning comes from the temporal changes in response dominance as measured by MFR. Underwood (1948) was the first to show that the relative frequency of responses from the first list increases during a 24-hour retention interval, whereas responses from the second list decline. He suggested that responses from the first list were unlearned (extinguished) during interpolated learning and then showed what is analogous to spontaneous recovery during the retention interval. This conclusion was supported by the increase in extra-experimental associations which had presumably been unlearned during original learning (OL) and IL. Underwood's results and conclusions received substantial support from the studies of Briggs (1954). Considerable significance must be attached to these systematic changes in response dominance over time. Since differentiation is not a factor in MFR, the shifts in list dominance point to a change in the relative availability of the two response systems. The usefulness of conceiving of unlearning as a process analogous to the extinction of conditioned responses is clearly supported.

As we have tried to show, a critical test of the unlearning hypothesis requires an unequivocal measure of the availability of first-list responses after IL. A crucial experiment satisfying this requirement was recently carried out by Barnes and Underwood (1959). The results of this study appear to give conclusive support to the unlearning hypothesis. Using the A-B, A-C paradigm with nonsense syllables as stimuli and adjectives as responses, Barnes and Underwood held degree of OL constant and systematically varied the number of interpolated trials. At the end of IL, the subjects were provided with the stimulus terms (A) and instructed to write down both the responses from the first list (B) and the responses from the second list (C). Later they were required to identify the list membership of the responses. By this procedure Barnes and Underwood eliminated the effects of both response competition and differentiation on the subjects' recall and obtained what amounts to a pure measure of response availability at the end of IL. The results are quite clear-cut. As degree of IL increased, there was a progressive decline in the number of responses from the first list and a steady rise in the number of responses from the second list. When both responses were available, items from the second list tended to be recalled before items from the first list. List membership was identified with a high degree of accuracy; i.e., there was little loss of differentiation immediately after the end of IL. Barnes and Underwood conclude that "the present results would strongly suggest that nearly all RI could be accounted for by unlearning or extinction if unlimited recall time is given immediately after interpolated learning" (p. 103). Lack of differentiation would develop after an interval of time and add response competition as a further source of interference. If and when the responses extinguished during IL recover fully, response competition would remain as the only source of interference. This argument constitutes a restatement of two-factor theory, with the important additional assumption that the contribution of the two components varies systematically with the length of the retention interval. Thus, the known experimental facts about temporal changes in the amount and manifestations of interference are incorporated into the theory.

With the reduction in availability of first-list responses firmly established, it is fair to conclude that unlearning is an indispensable concept in the analysis of retroactive interference. An obvious next step is to measure the recovery of extinguished first-list responses under conditions which eliminate the effects of response competition. This purpose can be accomplished by use of the technique of Barnes and Underwood after different intervals following IL. Such an investigation is at present being carried out at Berkeley by Miss Suzanne Adams. The experiment conforms to the A-B, A-C paradigm, with consonant syllables as stimuli and nonsense syllables of medium association value as responses. Retention for responses from both lists is measured immediately after the end of IL, after 48 hours, and after one week. Although the study is still in progress, it can be stated that the results thus far (a) have fully confirmed the findings of Barnes and Underwood on extinction of first-list responses, and (b) give clear evidence for the recovery of first-list responses over time. There is every reason to believe that the extension of two-factor theory proposed by Barnes and Underwood will adequately account for the course of interference when intertask transfer is negative.

## Response Generalization and Mediation

*Response Generalization.* The weight of the evidence is also against the independence hypothesis when we consider situations in which intertask transfer is positive. The relevant experimental data come from studies of interlist interference (or facilitation) as a function of response similarity. At a given level of stimulus similarity, associative transfer from the first to the second list becomes increasingly positive as response similarity is increased (e.g., Underwood, 1951). Assuming that associative transfer and retroaction vary together, Osgood (1949) predicted that amount of RI should vary inversely with the degree of response similarity, reaching its maximum when successive responses are opposed in meaning. The available experimental results do, in general, show an inverse relationship between response similarity and RI (Osgood, 1946; Osgood, 1948; Young, 1955; Gladis and Braun, 1958). The only exception is found in the results of Bugelski and Cadwallader (1956) who report more RI with similar than with neutral or opposed responses. The reason for this deviant finding is not immediately apparent. It is true that Osgood used mixed lists, whereas Bugelski and Cadwallader used homogeneous lists. An inverse relationship between response similarity and RI was, however, found in other studies employing homogeneous lists (Young; Gladis and Braun). Moreover, as Twedt and Underwood (1959) have recently shown, there is little difference between the transfer effects obtained with the two kinds of lists.

Decreases in RI with increasing response similarity are inconsistent with the independence hypothesis. Overt intrusions during IL and in recall and relearning increase as a function of response similarity. Thus, response similarity favors competition, but the total amount of RI is less than with dissimilar responses (Osgood, 1953, p. 546). The negative relationship between overt competition and RI can be explained on the assumption that, given a critical amount of response similarity, the strength of the first list increases during IL; the higher the degree of response similarity, the larger are the increments to the strength of first-list responses. A mechanism which may well account for such positive transfer effects is that of response generalization (Osgood, 1946; Underwood, 1951; Young, 1955). The implications of this hypothesis for the relationship between response similarity and RI were spelled out fully in Young's (1955) paper. The essence of the argument is that (a) direct reinforcement of stimulus-response associations in the first list (A-B) spreads to the associations in the second list (generalized reinforcement of A-B'), and (b) direct reinforcement of responses in the second list similarly spreads to the responses in the first list. When the two lists are learned to the same criterion, the net associative strength of the first list is greater than that of the second. This difference follows from the fact that the first list receives generalized reinforcement after attainment of the criterion, whereas in the second list generalized reinforcement precedes attainment of the criterion. If there is retroactive inhibition rather than facilitation under these conditions, the decrements must be attributed to competition between similar responses.

*Response Mediation.* An alternative explanation of the mechanism of positive transfer with identical stimuli and similar responses was recently proposed by Barnes and Underwood (1959), who applied their revised method of MFR (recall for responses from both lists) to lists conforming to the A-B, A-B' as well as to the A-B, A-C paradigm. With response competition eliminated, they found (a) no decline in responses from the first list and (b) nearly perfect recall for responses from the second list. The authors suggest that the direct mediation of second-list responses by first-

list responses, i.e., acquisition of the chain A-B-B', provides the most par-
simonious interpretation of these results. If the second list is learned
through mediation, responses from the first list are practiced and strengthened during IL. Except for response competition, retroactive facilitation
should result. Responses which are highly similar are also likely to be
strongly associated. Thus, the direct relationship between response similarity, on the one hand, and associative transfer and resistance to RI, on
the other, is encompassed by the mediation hypothesis. Barnes and Underwood suggest that direct mediation is a more plausible mechanism
than response generalization since it provides a better explanation of the
almost perfect transfer from the first to the second list. The majority of
subjects, moreover, state that mediation occurs during the acquisition of
the second list.

There are some very interesting implications of this analysis which
invite experimental test. Since the availability of first-list responses does
not decline during IL, all of the RI measured in conventional anticipation tests of recall must be attributed to loss of differentiation leading to
confusion between the mediating and mediated response. Since differentiation declines with the length of the interval between IL and recall, RI
should increase as a function of time when the A-B, A-B' paradigm is
used, in contrast to the slight decline in RI found with the A-B, A-C
paradigm (Underwood, 1948). It will also be of considerable interest to
measure the retention of A-B and A-B' by the Barnes and Underwood
technique after different intervals of time (as in the experiment of Adams
for the A-B, A-C case). Since no recovery of extinguished experimental
associations is to be assumed, any observed retention losses would have
to be attributed to extra-experimental interferences. Pre-experimental
associations which were presumably extinguished during OL and IL
would be expected to recover during the retention interval. MFR tests
suggest that the recovery of such associations is slow but shows positive
acceleration after 24 hours. Other things being equal, extra-experimental
interference should be of equal magnitude in the A-B, A-C and the A-B,
A-B' case. Allowance for the possible effects of extra-experimental interference does not, therefore, change the prediction that RI should increase
more in the latter than in the former case.

The assumption of direct mediation may help to account for the failure
to find rises in PI with increasing response similarity, as would be expected on the basis of the response-generalization hypothesis (Morgan
and Underwood, 1950; Young, 1955). When response similarity is high
direct mediation not only provides additional practice on the first list
during IL but also maintains the second-list responses at high strength.
It is interesting to note that in Young's study the number of interlist

intrusions during the recall of the second list increased as a function of response similarity, even though total PI did not. It is plausible that response similarity favors confusion between mediators and mediated responses. Such confusions do not appear sufficient, however, to offset the high positive transfer effects produced by direct mediation.

*Relationship between Unlearning and Response Mediation.* The relationship between the two mechanisms of transfer, unlearning and mediation, deserves consideration. When response similarity is low, e.g., when the responses in the two lists bear no apparent relationship to each other, there is clear evidence for extinction of first-list responses during IL. When response similarity is high, the evidence of Barnes and Underwood strongly points to forward (i.e., list 1–list 2) mediation. It is difficult to assume mediation in the A-B, A-C case since decreasing strength of B is correlated with increasing strength of C. Extinction of first-list responses, on the other hand, is implausible in the A-B, A-B' case unless backward mediation (A-B'-B) is assumed, for which there is no evidence. Thus, we appear to be dealing with two distinct mechanisms of transfer, each of which applies to a different range of response similarity. Assumption of a basic discontinuity of transfer mechanisms would probably lead to theoretical difficulties since response similarity is a continuous variable, although it may be possible to think of a "threshold region" along the continuum marking the transition from unlearning to mediation. It is possible, on the other hand, to speculate about an alternative conception which would consider the mechanism of mediation primary and consider unlearning a derived effect which becomes more and more probable as response similarity decreases. Let us assume that mediation invariably occurs at the beginning of practice on the second list: the subject attempts to learn A-B-C as well as A-B-B'. Since the association between B and C is weak, mediation will result in frequent errors; i.e., C will often be displaced by other responses strongly associated with B, e.g., B'. As a result, the mediator as well as the erroneous mediated responses are extinguished. By the same token, the chain A-B-B' will result in correct performance and be strengthened. This account gains some plausibility from the fact that overt intrusions of first-list responses are rare during acquisition of the second list. At that time the subject is able to distinguish between mediator and mediated response, and it is the unsuccessful mediator which is extinguished. One empirical implication of the present interpretation which might be worth checking would be the occurrence of errors mediated by B, i.e., responses of the class B', during the early stages of the acquisition of A-C. In any event, the relationship between unlearning and mediation awaits further theoretical and experimental analysis.

*The Manifestations of Response Competition*

*Specific and Generalized Response Competition.* We have concluded that the independence hypothesis is untenable and that the availability of first-list responses changes during IL. In conventional anticipation tests of recall, the subject's performance is, of course, determined not only by the availability of responses but also by the competition between available responses. The degree and form of such competition are, in turn, a function of differentiation. In discussions of competition, analysis has focused primarily on competition between specific responses associated with identical or similar stimuli, and differentiation has referred to the subject's ability to discriminate the list membership of these responses. This account of the process of competition may not be complete. Evidence will now be presented in support of a distinction between *specific* response competition and *generalized* response competition. The introduction of this distinction may be useful in resolving some apparent inconsistencies in available experimental results, particularly as regards the relationship between overt intrusions and retention loss, and differences between RI and PI.

By specific response competition we shall mean the displacement of a given correct response by a momentarily dominant response from the interfering list. By generalized response competition we shall mean the subject's tendency ("set") to continue responding from the list which he practiced last. Like specific response competition, generalized competition varies directly with the strength of IL relative to that of OL. In contrast to specific response competition, it is assumed to decrease with the length of the interval between the end of IL and RL. Generalized competition serves to enhance retention loss when an RI design is used, and to reduce retention loss when a PI design is used.

*Evidence for Generalized Response Competition.* The distinction between generalized and specific response competition was invoked by Newton and Wickens (1956) in their analysis of some significant new findings on the relationship between RI and the temporal point of the interpolated activity. With an A-B, C-D design they found RI to increase progressively with the interval between OL and IL, so that interference was maximized when IL occurred immediately before RL. Since the degree of IL *decreased* with the length of the interval between OL and IL, and in view of the dissimilarity of the stimulus terms, it is difficult to attribute the rise in RI to increasing competition between specific responses from the two lists. Such competition should, in fact, be minimized when RL occurs immediately after IL since differentiation between the lists is high under such conditions. The fact that no overt intrusions occurred at recall supports the view that there was little specific response competition. It is plausible, therefore, to attribute the observed rise in RI to generalized response competition which varies inversely with the length of the interval between IL and RL.

Another finding lending direct support to the concept of generalized response competition was recently reported by Postman and Riley (1959). In their study, serial lists of nonsense syllables were used to measure RI and PI as a function of the degree of original and interfering learning. One of the clearest and most consistent differences between RI and PI was brought to light by a comparison between the serial position curves of the work groups on successive trials of RL. A typical set of results is

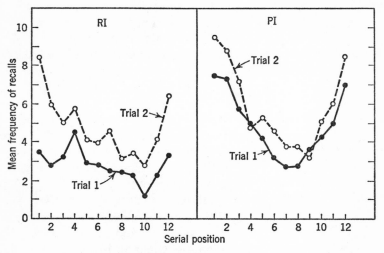

FIG. 7-1. Average serial position curves of RI and PI work groups at recall. There were 20 trials of OL. (*Postman and Riley,* 1959.)

shown in Figure 7-1. On the first trial of RL, the serial position curves of the RI work groups are substantially flatter than those of the PI work groups. (The curve for the rest group, which is not shown, is bow-shaped and similar to that of the PI groups.) The flattening of the curve is most pronounced at the beginning of the list; i.e., the usual primacy effect is completely absent. On the second trial of RL, the curve of the RI groups recovers its typical bow-shaped appearance and is comparable to that of the PI groups. The massive, and extremely transitory, RI for the initial section of the list may be attributed to generalized competition, which is reduced or eliminated once the context of the original list is reestablished.

When the retention interval is short and interlist differentiation is high, generalized competition should result in a large number of failures to respond during recall of the first list since the subject would recognize responses from the second list as incorrect and reject them. The number of such failures should be high even when the two lists have been learned to an approximately equal degree and the conditions are thus favorable to overt competition between specific responses. Figure 7-2 shows, for the experiment just mentioned, the mean numbers of failures and overt errors (including intra-list errors and overt intrusions) given by the work groups which received equal numbers of trials on the first and second

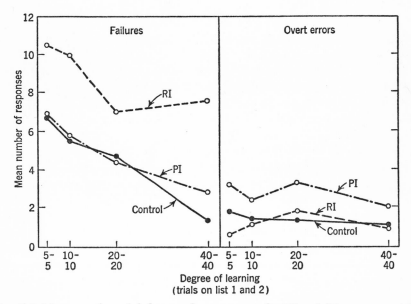

Fig. 7-2. Mean number of failures and overt errors for RI and PI groups receiving equal numbers of trials on the first and second list. (*Postman and Riley,* 1959.)

list. The results for the appropriate control groups are included. It is clear that practically all of the observed RI can be accounted for by failures to respond. There are only small differences between the RI work groups and the control groups in the number of overt errors. In the case of the PI groups, on the other hand, a very substantial portion of the observed interference is attributable to increases in overt errors. Thus, the RI groups consistently give many more failures than the PI groups. The relationship between the two kinds of work groups is clearly reversed for overt errors.

At least some of the failures of the RI groups may be attributed to the effects of unlearning. As Figure 7-1 indicates, however, a large proportion of the failures occurs in the early part of the list where OL responses are strong and should be relatively resistant to unlearning. The argument admittedly lacks precision at this point since both unlearning and generalized response competition should be conducive to failures at recall. A sharper analytic separation between the two assumed effects will be required.

It is interesting to note that the relative frequency of failures is higher in the present study than in earlier experiments (at least at the lower degrees of OL where direct comparisons are possible). This difference may be due to the fact that the present study used naïve subjects, whereas most of the earlier studies used experienced subjects in counterbalanced designs. One of the skills which an experienced subject may acquire is to change readily from list to list; i.e., he learns to change his set quickly and effectively.

Experiments showing that differences between OL and IL with respect to external environment and postural adjustment reduce the amount of RI (Bilodeau and Schlosberg, 1951; Greenspoon and Renyard, 1957) also point to the effectiveness of generalized competition at recall. Such changes in context weaken the subject's tendency to continue responding with items from the IL list at the time of recall. Manipulations of instructions and testing procedures designed to produce a change in set between OL and IL, and again between IL and RL, have also proved effective in decreasing RI (Gibson and Gibson, 1934; Jenkins and Postman, 1949; Waters and Peel, 1935). Finally, a recent study by Thune (1958) should be mentioned which showed that a warm-up activity specific to OL reduced RI by a significant amount. In all such cases it is possible, of course, that the experimental manipulation of associative context decreased specific as well as generalized competition. With the exception of Thune's study, however, the results were obtained with short retention intervals, i.e., under conditions favorable to the discrimination of the list membership of individual responses.

The distinction between generalized and specific response competition is not sharp, and its ultimate theoretical justification may well be open to question. In both cases we deal with the evocation of second-list responses during the attempted recall of the first list, and both must be assumed to be a function of interlist similarity. At the present the distinction has, however, considerable pragmatic usefulness. It calls attention to the fact that massive competition may occur even when there is no similarity between specific stimulus items in the two lists (as in the A-B, C-D design of Newton and Wickens, 1956). Reference to generalized response competition also helps to account for heavy amounts of RI observed when IL is learned to a lower degree than OL (McGeoch, 1932; McGeoch, 1936; Postman and Riley, 1959).

## COMPARISON OF RETROACTIVE AND PROACTIVE INHIBITION

We have examined the present status of some of the theoretical concepts designed to account for the amount and manifestations of interference in experiments on retroactive and proactive inhibition. It may be useful to summarize our conclusions at this point and at the same time apply them to a systematic comparison between RI and PI. It is clear that the assumptions one makes about the conditions of effective interference have a number of testable implications for expected differences in the amount and characteristics of RI and PI.

1. The independence hypothesis is considered untenable. When intertask transfer is negative, first-list responses are unlearned during IL. Unlearning should make RI greater than PI. The data uniformly support this conclusion (e.g., Melton and Von Lackum, 1941; Underwood, 1945; Postman and Riley, 1959). When intertask transfer is positive (e.g., with high response similarity), first-list responses mediate the acquisition of second-list responses. Thus, the first list receives additional practice during IL, and RI should be less than PI. There is some limited support for the prediction (Young, 1955).

2. The amount and characteristics of response competition vary not only with the relative strengths of the two response systems but also with the degree of differentiation between the two lists. Degree of differentiation, in turn, decreases with the length of the time interval between the end of practice and RL. With a constant retention interval, there is necessarily a longer time period between the end of PL and recall than between the end of IL and recall. As a result, loss of differentiation should be greater under PI than RI conditions. The temporal arrangement of the two experimental designs may thus serve to reduce the difference between RI and PI.

3. Generalized as well as specific response competition is assumed to influence the subject's performance on the test of recall. Generalized response competition lowers the performance of RI work groups as compared with PI work groups. Such competition can be studied most directly in experiments in which there is little or no formal similarity between the stimulus items in the two lists. When the retention interval is short and the subject's ability to identify the list membership of responses is presumed to be high, generalized response competition should lead to a high frequency of failures in RI, especially in the early sections of the list. As was shown above, these expectations are borne out.

4. The relative temporal changes in RI and PI should vary with the nature of the experimental paradigm. When intertask transfer is negative (A-B, A-C), recovery of extinguished first-list responses should lead to a decline in RI and corresponding increases in PI. When intertask transfer

is positive (A-B, A-B′), no difference in the temporal development of the two types of interference is predicted.

One conclusion worthy of especial emphasis is that RI should not be expected to be invariably greater than PI. Unlearning and generalized competition favor such a difference. Loss of differentiation should, on the other hand, be greater under PI conditions, and this difference may become important with relatively short retention intervals. Recovery of extinguished first-list associations should, with long retention intervals, reverse the difference when intertask transfer is negative.

## EXTRA-EXPERIMENTAL SOURCES OF INTERFERENCE

Perhaps the single most important recent development in interference theory is the increasing recognition of proactive inhibition as a mechanism of interference. The major value of this development lies in the fact that it has provided us with a new purchase on the analysis of long-term forgetting outside the laboratory. The arguments pointing to the significance of proaction were marshaled by Underwood in his important paper "Interference and Forgetting" (1957). The evidence presented by Underwood shows that in the large majority of experimental studies of long-term retention the amount of forgetting was greatly overestimated because of the use of practiced subjects whose performance was depressed by considerable amounts of PI accumulated in the course of the experiments. Recent studies using naïve subjects have, indeed, shown substantially smaller losses than had been reported under comparable conditions (e.g., Underwood and Richardson, 1956; Postman and Rau, 1957). Since the amount forgotten by naïve subjects turns out to be relatively small, it becomes plausible to attribute the observed losses to interferences outside the laboratory. Underwood points out that most of the extra-experimental interference is likely to be proactive rather than retroactive since the opportunities for acquiring competing verbal habits are clearly greater prior to the experiment than during the relatively short time intervals typically used in investigations of retention.

A major theoretical and experimental problem which faces us is the application of the concepts of interference theory, which were developed in formal studies of RI and PI, to the analysis of long-term forgetting outside the laboratory. The basic assumption is that forgetting outside the laboratory is a function of the same variables and represents the same processes as are observed in formal studies of interserial interference. Thus far, there is little empirical evidence in support of this assumption. A systematic attack on this problem calls for (a) a detailed specification of the implications of interference theory for the retention of different kinds of materials, including the expected growth of error tendencies, and (b) the development of experimental designs which permit critical tests of these implications.

The following extension of interference theory to the analysis of extra-experimental forgetting is based largely on a paper by Underwood and Postman (1960) which also reports an experiment in which some of the propositions derived from the theory were put to experimental test.

*Gradients of Interference in Long-term Retention.* When a single list of verbal items is learned in the laboratory, retention losses measured after an interval of time are assumed to result from interference by verbal habits practiced before or after the experimental session. Although both proactive and retroactive inhibition undoubtedly occur, forgetting must be attributed primarily to interference from stable language habits with which the subject entered the experimental situation, i.e., to proactive inhibition. The assumed process of interference may be represented most conveniently in terms of the A-B, A-C paradigm, where A is a stimulus term in the experimental list, B is a response associated with A through linguistic usage, and C is the response to A prescribed in the experiment. Acquisition of the prescribed association requires the un-learning or extinction of the pre-experimental association, A-B, and its replacement by A-C. The evidence reviewed earlier makes it reasonable to assume that the extinguished habit, A-B, will gradually recover as a function of time and compete with A-C at the time of recall. If A-B is a stable language habit, its pre-experimental strength was undoubtedly much greater than that imparted to A-C during the experiment. Thus, A-B will readily recover sufficient strength to compete effectively with A-C. Of course, if A-B is practiced after the end of the experiment, the process of recovery is speeded up and the probability of effective competition is increased.[1]

Experimental tests of this hypothesis require, first of all, the specification of the linguistic habits (A-B) with which the subject enters the experimental situation and which become sources of interference at recall. Two major sources of interference which contribute to the forgetting of rote series may be distinguished, viz., letter-sequence interference and unit-sequence interference.

Letter-sequence interference will occur to the extent that the sequences of letters prescribed in the experiment do not conform to those characteristic of the language. For any given sequence of letters making up a nonsense syllable, a consonant syllable, or a word, there are certain tran-

---

[1] It may be possible to construct lists for which the relationship between the subject's language habits and the associations prescribed in the experiment conforms to the A-B, A-B' paradigm. Under these conditions, retention losses would result from a confusion between mediators and mediated responses. The A-B, A-C case is, however, much more likely to apply to the retention of arbitrary rote series.

sitional probabilities in the language. During the acquisition of such items, letter-sequence habits characteristic of normal linguistic patterns must be temporarily broken in order for the prescribed sequence to be acquired. These habits recover in time and interfere with the retention of the arbitrary units. The higher the probability of occurrence of the prescribed sequence in the language, the smaller should be the amount of letter-sequence interference at recall. Thus, it is possible to specify a gradient of letter-sequence interference which drops progressively as the items to be learned approach the sequences which occur most frequently in the language. When the items to be learned are words with high frequencies of occurrence, the amount of letter-sequence interference is assumed to have decreased to zero.

Sequential associations between units constitute another source of interference. The discrete responses which the subject is required to emit, e.g., nonsense syllables, consonant syllables, or words, are the units with which we are concerned here. Linguistic usage establishes a hierarchy of associations between such units, just as it does in the case of letter sequences. In the typical rote-learning situation the A-B, A-C paradigm again applies; i.e., the pre-experimental associations must be unlearned or extinguished and the prescribed associations substituted for them. The extinguished associations recover over time and compete with the prescribed units at the time of recall. The amount of unit-sequence interference will be expected to vary directly with the frequency of occurrence of the unit qua unit in the language. The more frequently a unit is used, the more likely it is to acquire strong associates which will compete with those prescribed in the experimental series. The gradient of unit-sequence interference thus increases as a function of the frequency of occurrence of the unit in the language. If the items to be learned are ranged along a continuum extending from the most improbable letter-sequences to the most frequent words, two intersecting gradients of interference can be plotted against this continuum. The gradient of letter-sequence interference is at its maximum at the low end of the continuum where the association between successive letters is weak, and declines as common linguistic units are approached. The gradient of unit-sequence interference first comes into play when the sequences of letters begin to constitute syllables or words with some probability of occurrence in the language, and increases thereafter, reaching its maximum for high-frequency words. If the arrangement of the items is thought to reflect the dimension of meaningfulness, maxima of interference are expected to occur for items at the low and high extremes of the dimension, the former attributable predominantly to letter-sequence interference and the latter to unit-sequence interference. Interference should be minimal for items falling toward the center of the continuum. Such items would represent frequent combinations of letters without being verbal units to which strong associations are likely to accrue in the course of daily usage.

*Implications for Learning and Retention.* The implications of the hypothesis for learning and retention will now be discussed in some detail. Turning to acquisition first, it is useful for purposes of this discussion to adopt an analytic distinction between two successive stages of learning, viz., an integrative and an associative stage (Underwood, Runquist, and Schulz, 1959). During the first stage the items in the list become available to the subject as responses. If the required units are not already in the subject's repertoire, they must be integrated during that stage; i.e., associations must be formed between the successive letters making up the sequence. During the second stage the responses are connected with the appropriate stimuli, e.g., the preceding items in a serial list or the prescribed stimulus terms in a list of paired associates. Although the two stages undoubtedly overlap, the distinction has proved useful for analytic purposes. It is clear that letter-sequence interference should slow down the integrative stage. It is difficult to make precise predictions concerning the effects of unit-sequence interference on the associative stage. It is a fact that speed of learning has been found to be positively correlated with $m$ value, i.e., with the number of different associations evoked by the learning items (Noble, 1952; Noble and McNeely, 1957; Cieutat, Stockwell, and Noble, 1958). The availability of multiple associations appears to facilitate the establishment of the prescribed linkages among the items in the list. Our analysis makes it plausible, on the other hand, that the extinction of pre-experimental associations should delay acquisition. Much will probably depend on the extent to which units are included in the list among which there are pre-experimental associations. Importations of units from outside the list during learning are typically few and far between; i.e., identification of list membership is rapid and accurate. The data obtained in our recent study do, indeed, show that pre-experimental associations among the units within a list give rise to frequent and persistent intra-list errors. In any event, it is essential that account be taken of differences in associative strength at the end of learning in assessing the amount of forgetting for different kinds of materials. Appropriate corrections for differences in associative strength can be made by means of successive-probability analysis (Underwood, 1954) or by adding control groups whose retention is measured immediately after the end of learning.

For retention, the hypothesis predicts that losses due to letter-sequence interference should be accompanied by overt errors reflecting the subject's letter-sequence habits. Thus, letter-sequence interference necessarily makes the correct responses *less available* at recall. As for unit-sequence interference, recovery of pre-experimental associations may reduce the subject's ability to reproduce the items in the prescribed order without necessarily reducing their availability as responses. In fact, as Deese (1959) has shown, strong interitem associations may, under certain conditions, facilitate retention when the items do not have to be reproduced in sequential order. In assessing unit-sequence interference, the effects on response availability and on the reproduction of serial order must, therefore, be distinguished. The problem here is reminiscent of that encountered in the discussion of unlearning.

*Experimental Evidence.* We shall now briefly summarize some experimental results which bear on our analysis of extra-experimental sources of interference in long-term forgetting. The first study to be mentioned is that by Underwood and Postman (1960). Four lists of three-letter units were chosen with a view to obtaining evidence on the operation of the letter-sequence and unit-sequence gradients of interference: high-frequency words (Hi-W); high-frequency trigrams (Hi-T); low-frequency words (Lo-W); and low-frequency trigrams (Lo-T). At each of the two levels of frequency, the probabilities of the letter sequences in words and trigrams were closely equated. It was assumed that letter-sequence interference for the high-frequency lists would be virtually nil; unit-sequence interference should be greater for high-frequency words than for high-frequency trigrams. Retention should, therefore, be better for the latter. The prediction for the two low-frequency lists was less certain since the extent of the two gradients is not known. Both of the low-frequency lists should be subject to letter-sequence interferences, although the words might represent a selection of easily integrated units. Nor was it clear whether a substantial difference in unit-sequence interference should be expected between the two low-frequency lists. These lists were included, however, for purposes of sampling the two assumed gradients. The lists were learned by the method of serial anticipation to a criterion of one perfect recitation, and retention was tested by recall and relearning after 30 seconds and after one week. These are the main findings:

1. Words were learned faster than trigrams. In the case of trigrams, but not of words, frequency favored speed of learning, but the difference was not significant. The largest number of intra-list errors occurred during the learning of List Hi-W, presumably reflecting interference from pre-experimental associations. It is probable that these errors retarded the speed of acquisition of List Hi-W. A stage analysis showed the high-frequency words to be more available than the low-frequency words, but this difference in availability was not reflected in the speed of learning to criterion.

2. The results of the recall tests are presented in Figure 7-3. The total recall scores show only small differences in the amount of forgetting. At the very least, then, the traditional assumption that meaningfulness favors

retention has been refuted. A more detailed analysis showed, moreover, that in the initial and middle sections of the list high-frequency trigrams were, indeed, retained better than high-frequency words.[2]

3. As measured by the speed of relearning to criterion, high-frequency trigrams are retained better than any of the other materials. This finding fully supports the assumption of a gradient of unit-sequence interference.

4. The pattern of errors in relearning is consistent with the theoretical

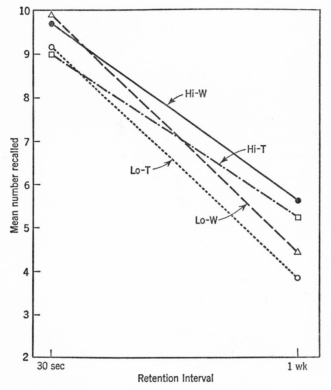

FIG. 7-3. Mean recall scores for different kinds of three-letter units. (*Underwood and Postman, 1960, p. 83.*)

expectations. Figure 7-4 shows the mean number of intra-list errors per trial in relearning to criterion. The recovery of such errors, reflecting unit-sequence interference, is clearly greater for words than for trigrams, and maximal for List Hi-W. As Figure 7-5 shows, on the other hand, the

---

[2] This difference is reversed in the final section of the list. Internal evidence in the data suggests that a list of words is characterized by less sequential dependency than a list of nonsense items; i.e., the loss of weak items in the middle of the list detracts less from the recall of strong terminal items in a list of words than in a list of trigrams. The problem of sequential dependency in recall deserves further study.

increase in letter-sequence errors is considerably greater for the low-frequency lists than for the high-frequency lists. Since few letters were imported from outside the list, the possibility cannot be ruled out that the results in Figure 7-5 reflect an interaction of low meaningfulness and intra-list similarity. The fact that many of the errors form letter sequences of higher frequency than those they replace supports an interpretation in terms of letter-sequence interference.

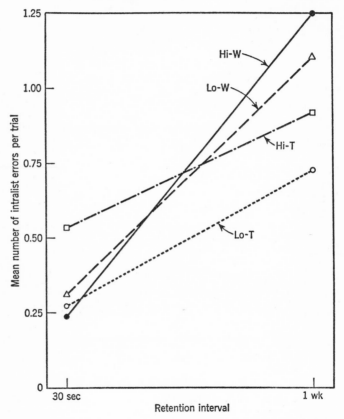

FIG. 7-4. Mean numbers of intra-list errors per trial in relearning different kinds of three-letter units. (*Underwood and Postman*, 1960, *p.* 89.)

While not all the predictions were borne out and some problems of interpretation remain, the results give encouragement to our conception of the sources of extra-experimental interference. Further evidence consistent with the results of this study was obtained in two experiments (Postman, 1961).[3]

These experiments focused on the operation of the gradient of unit-

[3] This research was supported by a grant from the National Science Foundation.

sequence interference in the retention of meaningful words. In the study just described, the two lists of words differed not only with respect to their frequency of occurrence in the language but also with respect to the probability of their letter sequences. In the present experiments, two-syllable nouns of high and low frequency of occurrence were used. There were, however, no consistent differences in the frequency of the successive letter sequences of which they were composed. Thus, differences in retention could be attributed directly to the effects of unit-sequence interference. The lists were learned by the method of serial anticipation to

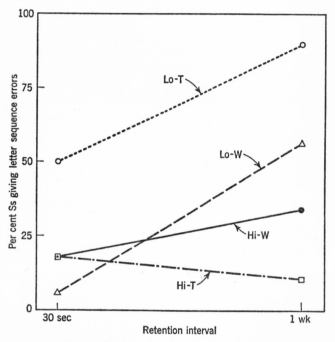

Fig. 7-5. Percentages of Ss giving letter-sequence errors during relearning of different kinds of three-letter units. Percentages of Ss are plotted because of high frequency of scores of zero at 30 seconds. (*Underwood and Postman*, 1960, *p.* 93.)

a criterion of one perfect repetition. In the first of the two experiments, the lists were relearned to criterion after intervals of 30 seconds, two days, and seven days. Here are the major findings of the first study.

1. High-frequency lists were learned significantly faster than low-frequency lists. The difference in the length of the words and the fact that the items were pronounced rather than spelled may account for the discrepancy between this study and the earlier one with respect to speed of learning. As before, the number of intra-list errors was considerably greater for the high-frequency lists than for the low-frequency lists. The

intra-list errors made during the learning of the high-frequency lists were of a higher average degree of remoteness than those made during the acquisition of the low-frequency list.

2. The forgetting curves for the two kinds of lists are presented in Figure 7-6. There is a tendency for the low-frequency lists to be forgotten more slowly—note that the curves cross at the seven-day interval—but the difference is not significant. The failure to find a significant difference in favor of the high-frequency list is, however, noteworthy in view of the difference in speed of learning. Again, there is no evidence whatsoever for superior retention of materials of high meaningfulness. The re-

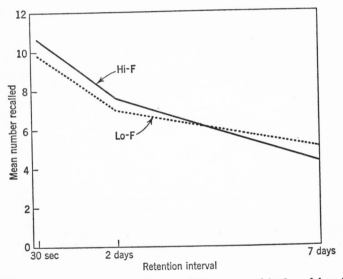

FIG. 7-6. Retention curves for lists of two-syllable nouns of high and low frequency of usage. (*Postman*, 1961.)

sults of a sectional analysis are consistent with those of the earlier experiment in showing substantially better retention of the low-frequency items in the initial section of the list.

3. Analysis of the errors at recall and in relearning indicates that unit-sequence interferences recover at differential rates for the two kinds of lists. Figure 7-7 shows the frequency of intra-list errors at recall for the three retention intervals. The errors have been divided into two groups, viz., those of first degree of remoteness and those of higher degrees of remoteness. The latter are assumed to provide an especially sensitive index of extra-experimental associations. Both types of errors recover at a faster rate for the high-frequency lists, and the differential rate of recovery is more pronounced for errors of the higher degree of remote-

ness. As Figure 7-8 shows, the trends for errors in relearning are consistent with the results found at recall.

As we pointed out earlier, unit-sequence interference may disturb the reproduction of items in the prescribed serial order without reducing the availability of correct responses. The question arises, therefore, as to whether a paced anticipation test masks a greater availability of the high-frequency responses. In order to determine whether such was, indeed, the case, a second experiment was performed in which the same lists were used but retention was tested by the method of free recall after

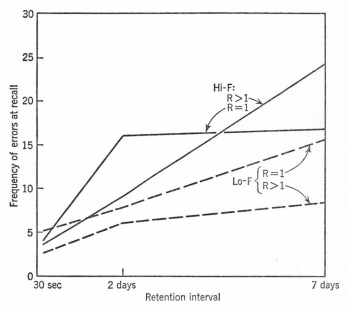

FIG. 7-7. Frequency of intra-list errors given during recall of lists of high and low frequency. $R = 1$ refers to errors of first degree remoteness; $R > 1$ refers to errors of higher degree of remoteness. (*Postman*, 1961.)

30 seconds and after seven days. During the tests of recall the rate at which responses were emitted was recorded. The basic results are shown in Figure 7-9. Three main findings should be noted: (a) total amount recalled is considerably higher than that obtained by the conventional method of anticipation; (b) rate of recall is considerably slower after one week than at the end of learning; (c) there is little difference between the lists of high and low frequency. Thus, the difference between the two tests is of the same order of magnitude for the two kinds of lists. Although the data are not shown, it can be added that the reproduction of the original serial order is significantly poorer for the high-frequency lists than for the low-frequency lists. Thus, the results of the test of free recall

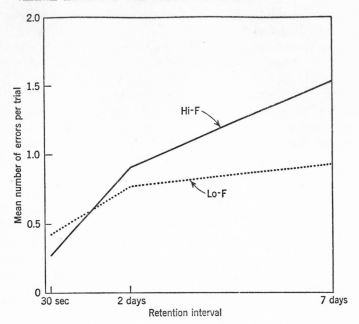

FIG. 7-8. Mean number of errors per trial in relearning words of high and low frequency to criterion. (*Postman*, 1961.)

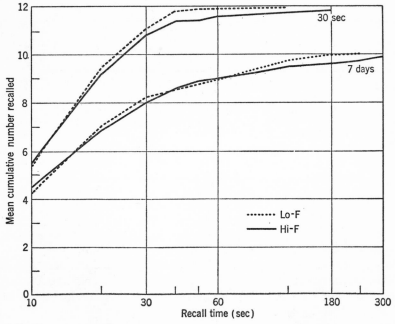

FIG. 7-9. Mean cumulative numbers of items correctly reproduced on test of free recall for words of high and low frequency. (*Postman*, 1961.)

are entirely consistent with those of the anticipation test in showing little difference in the total amount recalled and a greater disturbance of serial order for the high-frequency list. In short, high-frequency words are not more available than low-frequency words one week after the end of learning.

Our conclusions concerning the effects of unit-sequence interference must remain conservative at this time. The failure to find better recall for the high-frequency lists, which were acquired faster than the low-frequency lists, and the error functions are consistent with the hypothesis. A significant difference in favor of the low-frequency items would, of course, make the argument considerably more compelling. It is possible that the rate at which pre-experimental associations recover is sufficiently slow to require much longer retention intervals for conclusive demonstration of the differences in the amount of unit-sequence interference. The important point to emphasize at this time is that an analytic approach to the problem of extra-experimental interference appears possible and calls for a sustained experimental effort. This may well be the area which requires our most urgent attention for the development of the interference theory of forgetting.

## REFERENCES

Barnes, J. M., & Underwood, B. J. (1959) Fate of first-list associations in transfer theory. *J. Exp. Psychol.*, **58**, 97–105.

Bilodeau, I. McD., & Schlosberg, H. (1951) Similarity in stimulating conditions as a variable in retroactive inhibition. *J. Exp. Psychol.*, **41**, 199–204.

Briggs, G. E. (1954) Acquisition, extinction and recovery functions in retroactive inhibition. *J. Exp. Psychol.*, **47**, 285–293.

Briggs, G. E. (1957) Retroactive inhibition as a function of degree of original and interpolated learning. *J. Exp. Psychol.*, **53**, 60–67.

Briggs, G. E., Thompson, R. F., & Brogden, W. J. (1954) Retention functions in reproductive inhibition. *J. Exp. Psychol.*, **48**, 419–428.

Bugelski, B. R., & Cadwallader, T. C. (1956) A reappraisal of the transfer and retroaction surface. *J. Exp. Psychol.*, **52**, 360–366.

Cieutat, V. J., Stockwell, F. E., & Noble, C. E. (1958) The interaction of ability and amount of practice with stimulus and response meaningfulness (*m*, *m'*) in paired-associate learning. *J. Exp. Psychol.*, **56**, 193–202.

Deese, J. (1959) Influence of inter-item associative strength upon immediate free recall. *Psychol. Rep.*, **5**, 305–312.

Gibson, Eleanor J., & Gibson, J. J. (1934) Retention and the interpolated task. *Amer. J. Psychol.*, **46**, 603–610.

Gladis, M., & Braun, H. W. (1958) Age differences and retroaction as a function of intertask response similarity. *J. Exp. Psychol.*, **55**, 25–30.

Greenspoon, J., & Renyard, R. (1957) Stimulus conditions and retroactive inhibition. *J. Exp. Psychol.*, **53**, 55–59.

Jenkins, W. O., & Postman, L. (1949) An experimental analysis of set in rote learning: Retroactive inhibition as a function of changing set. *J. Exp. Psychol.*, **39**, 69–73.

McGeoch, J. A. (1932) The influence of degree of interpolated learning upon retroactive inhibition. *Amer. J. Psychol.*, **44**, 695–708.

McGeoch, J. A. (1936) Studies in retroactive inhibition: VII. Retroactive inhibition as a function of the length and frequency of presentation of the interpolated lists. *J. Exp. Psychol.*, **19**, 674–693.

McGeoch, J. A. (1942) *The psychology of human learning: An introduction.* New York: Longmans.

Melton, A. W., & Irwin, J. McQ. (1940) The influence of degree of interpolated learning on retroactive inhibition and the overt transfer of specific responses. *Amer. J. Psychol.*, **53**, 173–203.

Melton, A. W., & Von Lackum, W. J. (1941) Retroactive and proactive inhibition in retention: Evidence for a two-factor theory of retroactive inhibition. *Amer. J. Psychol.*, **54**, 157–173.

Morgan, R. L., & Underwood, B. J. (1950) Proactive inhibition as a function of response similarity. *J. Exp. Psychol.*, **40**, 592–603.

Newton, J. M., & Wickens, D. D. (1956) Retroactive inhibition as a function of the temporal position of interpolated learning. *J. Exp. Psychol.*, **51**, 149–154.

Noble, C. E. (1952) The role of meaningfulness ($m$) in serial verbal learning. *J. Exp. Psychol.*, **43**, 437–446.

Noble, C. E., & McNeely, D. A. (1957) The role of meaningfulness ($m$) in paired-associate verbal learning. *J. Exp. Psychol.*, **53**, 16–22.

Osgood, C. E. (1946) Meaningful similarity and interference in learning. *J. Exp. Psychol.*, **36**, 277–301.

Osgood, C. E. (1948) An investigation into the causes of retroactive inhibition. *J. Exp. Psychol.*, **38**, 132–154.

Osgood, C. E. (1949) The similarity paradox in human learning: A resolution. *Psychol. Rev.* **56**, 132–143.

Osgood, C. E. (1953) *Method and theory in experimental psychology.* New York: Oxford.

Postman, L. (1961) Extra-experimental interference and the retention of words. *J. Exp. Psychol.*, **61**, 97–110.

Postman, L., & Rau, Lucy (1957) Retention as a function of the method of measurement. *Univer. Calif. Publ. Psychol.*, **8**, 217–270.

Postman, L., & Riley, D. A. (1959) Degree of learning and interserial interference in retention. *Univer. Calif. Publ. Psychol.*, **8**, 271–396.

Thune, L. E. (1958) Reproductive interference following "appropriate" and "inappropriate" warm-up activities. *J. Exp. Psychol.*, **55**, 535–542.

Thune, L. E., & Underwood, B. J. (1943) Retroactive inhibition as a function of degree of interpolated learning. *J. Exp. Psychol.*, **32**, 185–200.

Twedt, Helen M., & Underwood, B. J. (1959) Mixed vs. unmixed lists in transfer studies. *J. Exp. Psychol.*, **58**, 111–116.

Underwood, B. J. (1945) The effect of successive interpolations on retroactive and proactive inhibition. *Psychol. Monogr.*, **59**, No. 3.

Underwood, B. J. (1948) Proactive and retroactive inhibition after five and forty-eight hours. *J. Exp. Psychol.*, 38, 29–38.

Underwood, B. J. (1948) "Spontaneous" recovery of verbal associations. *J. Exp. Psychol.*, 38, 429–439.

Underwood, B. J. (1949) Proactive inhibition as a function of time and degree of prior learning. *J. Exp. Psychol.*, 39, 24–34.

Underwood, B. J. (1951) Associative transfer in verbal learning as a function of response similarity and degree of first-list learning. *J. Exp. Psychol.*, 42, 44–53.

Underwood, B. J. (1954) Speed of learning and amount retained: A consideration of methodology. *Psychol. Bull.*, 51, 276–282.

Underwood, B. J. (1957) Interference and forgetting. *Psychol. Rev.* 64, 49–60.

Underwood, B. J., & Postman, L. (1960) Extra-experimental sources of interference in forgetting. *Psychol. Rev.*, 67, 73–95.

Underwood, B. J., & Richardson, J. (1956) The influence of meaningfulness, intralist similarity, and serial position on retention. *J. Exp. Psychol.*, 52, 119–126.

Underwood, B. J., Runquist, W. N., & Schulz, R. W. (1959) Response learning in paired-associate lists as a function of intralist similarity. *J. Exp. Psychol.*, 58, 70–78.

Waters, R. H., & Peel, Z. E. (1935) Similarity in the form of original and interpolated learning and retroactive inhibition. *Amer. J. Psychol.*, 47, 477–481.

Young, R. K. (1955) Retroactive and proactive effects under varying conditions of response similarity. *J. Exp. Psychol.* 50, 113–119.

# COMMENTS ON PROFESSOR POSTMAN'S PAPER

## Arthur W. Melton

UNIVERSITY OF MICHIGAN

Postman has given us an integrative summary of the issues and experiments associated with interference theories of forgetting which will certainly take its proper place as a classic alongside McGeoch's "Forgetting and the Law of Disuse" (1932) and Underwood's "Interference and Forgetting" (1957). This is not to imply that his paper is a complete survey and integration of data from all types of learning or even for all of the variables known to have a substantial influence on the amount of interference in the retention of verbal materials, for such was clearly not his intention. But it does represent a comprehensive, if not exhaustive, and insightful assembly of the state of knowledge with respect to interference effects in the recall and relearning of verbal materials that have been put in the "long-term" memory store through repetition under the conditions of rote learning. The emphasis is upon recall and relearning, rather than recognition memory; upon variations in the degrees of learning of the habits, rather than similarity factors; upon verbal learning, rather than perceptual or perceptual-motor learning; upon rote learning, rather than forms of learning that require discovery of the required "correct" response.

In view of the history of interference theories of forgetting, it seems fitting and proper that the analysis should be limited to this restricted set of experimental operations. Data produced by those operations gave rise to all of the principal concepts involved in these theories: the concept of retroactive inhibition, or RI (Müller and Pilzecker, 1900), the perseveration concept (Müller and Pilzecker, 1900), the reproductive inhibition theory of RI (McGeoch, 1932), the unlearning concept and the two-factor theory of RI (Melton and Irwin, 1940), the list-differentiation concept (Thune and Underwood, 1943), the generalized response-set concept (Newton and Wickens, 1956), and the concept of proactive inhibition (PI) in retention (Whitely and Blankenship, 1936). Those operations likewise produced the data that led to recognition of the theoretical significance of comparative studies of PI and RI (Melton and Von Lackum, 1941), and finally to the overwhelming importance of PI (Underwood, 1957).

These comments about the general excellence and scope of Postman's analysis would be misleading by omission if I said nothing about the way in which he brings the focus of all this scientific experience onto a new and exciting direction in experimental work on the forgetting of verbal materials. Even those myriad experimental psychologists who have heretofore failed to become excited about the conflicting interference theories of forgetting will surely—at least some of them—see the methodological and theoretical breakthrough that is encompassed in the notion that new learning restructures old habit systems and that the principal source of interference in retention of the new is the recovery of the older and better-established systems. Will this revitalize once again this truly *elder* but sporadically pursued problem of experimental-theoretical psychology? I think so, but that remains to be seen. More will be said about this later.

My further discussion of this important paper will be divided into three parts: (1) commentary on some specifics of the paper as they relate to the present status of the interference theory of forgetting; (2) commentary on the new direction for research on forgetting which is formulated as the climax of the argument; and (3) commentary on the limitations of the paper and of the experimental approach that it reflects when one chooses to define the problem of memory and forgetting as fundamental to all behavior theory.

## THE STATUS OF INTERFERENCE THEORY

My first comment about the status of interference theories, as summarized by Postman, is metapsychological. In these days when one sometimes is led to believe that he is a poor scientist—or at least a very old-fashioned scientist—unless he has an explicit theoretical model, preferably a mathematical model, to guide his research, it is noteworthy that Postman did not need to use the word *model* at all. This is for the very good reason that data, not models, have been the grist for progress in the understanding of forgetting. The insights and refinements of concepts about forgetting have been generated, sometimes even forced, by data resulting from the plotting of *functions* that relate dependent variables, such as correct recalls, interlist and intra-list intrusions, and relearning measures, to rather obvious independent variables. Examples of the latter are (a) the degree of original learning (OL), prior learning (PL), and interpolated learning (IL); (b) the similarity of OL, PL, and IL either together or separately for stimulus and response elements; and (c) the time intervals between OL, PL, and IL, and between each of these and the test for retention.

The only notable exceptions to this attribution of theoretical advances to systematic quantitative data are the equally significant instances in which the data plus the theory made it quite clear that new methods of experimental observation were required. The outstanding instances of this were, first, the observation and recording of errors of commission (interlist intrusions) in written recalls (McKinney and McGeoch, 1935) and in anticipation learning (Melton and Irwin, 1940) in order to test an explicit inference from the reproductive inhibition theory of RI. Since then, no competent investigation of interference in forgetting has failed to record such intrusions, and the benefits for theory are attested by the frequent use of such intrusion data by Postman as critical evidence in the evaluation of alternative interpretations, e.g., the "unlearning" hypothesis and the generalized-interference hypothesis. A second instance of importance is, of course, the invention of the modified free recall (MFR) technique (Underwood, 1948) and refinements of it (Briggs, 1954, Briggs, 1957; Briggs, Thompson, and Brogden, 1954; Barnes and Underwood, 1959), which now permit the firm assertion that first-list responses are, in fact, made unavailable to the subject by second-list learning, but "spontaneously recover" after an interval of 48 hours. On the surface, the method provides information that favors the "unlearning" hypothesis, but of greater importance is the fact that it specifies a non-monotonic forgetting curve for first-list responses. The third and perhaps most dramatic instance of the influence of method on theory is the case of the counterbalanced-conditions experiment, to which Under-wood (1957) successfully attributes our erroneous emphasis on RI in forgetting. Almost all generalizations (prior to 1957) about RI and PI, as well as "normal" forgetting, were contaminated by large effects due to cumulative PI from list to list; when these intra-experiment PI effects are eliminated by a one-condition-per-subject design, the rate of "normal" forgetting is seen to be much slower than previously supposed, the rela-tive amounts of RI and PI become highly specific to certain factors in the experiment (Postman and Riley, 1959), and PI from pre-experimental verbal habits becomes a consideration of major significance for the inter-pretation of forgetting.

My other comments about the status of interference theory will briefly consider the theoretical concepts that have been introduced during the last 20 years. As I see it, these concepts belong in three categories. There are, first, and perhaps most important for general behavior theory, those that have to do with specific response competition and its direct effects on the recall and relearning of specific responses to specific stimuli. These are the concepts of response blocking (which is certainly not specific to forgetting theory), unlearning, and differentiation. Secondly, there is the concept of generalized response competition, as this term is used and defended by Postman; and, thirdly, there is the concept of disruption of associative context, as extensively discussed by Postman and Riley (1959) but only briefly mentioned by Postman here. This concept refers to a secondary effect of response competition, either specific or general-ized, which causes forgetting of otherwise available responses when the associative context (i.e., intra-list associative context) is disrupted by the occurrence of an overt or covert intrusion (error). The evidence mar-shaled to support the necessity of partitioning interference effects into at least these three categories is impressive; likewise impressive is the evi-dence for the notions of differentiation and unlearning within the cate-gory of specific response competition. But each concept needs much more critical examination in experiment and theory, as Postman regu-larly indicates in his own way. I will attempt to make the same point in my own way.

First, with respect to the concept of response blocking, my comment can be brief because Postman has made abundantly clear that the block-ing of response A by the occurrence of response B, when both are verbal responses, is extraordinarily sensitive to the measurement operations em-ployed. He also makes quite clear that we will continue to have difficulty (and fallibility) in making inferences about the sequences of responses, both blocking and blocked, when all we observe and record in behavior is the occurrence of an overt response ("intrusion" or "correct") in an arbitrarily defined recall period. Here it is obvious that we need much more widespread employment of latency measures in tests for recall in order to gain some information about the occurrence of mediating responses which should be correlated with latency changes. Also, it seems obvious that we need to exploit the ingenious free-recall techniques previously referred to as MFR and MMFR. But even with these methodological improvements, it is suggested to me that our next methodological breakthrough may well be in the invention of even more ingenious methods for improving the certainty of our inferences about what is happening in that brief span of time between the presentation of the stimulus term and the occurrence of the overt response in attempted recall. Perhaps the combination of different instructional sets and the MFR or MMFR techniques will do the trick; or perhaps we can gain important information through the application of physiological indices whose possible relevance to the recall process has been demonstrated by Berry and Davis (1958; 1960).

Secondly, with respect to the unlearning hypothesis. It seems clear that Melton and Irwin (1940) were right, but for the wrong reasons. The original argument was that the high RI at high levels of IL which produced low frequencies of intrusions should be attributed to unlearning, rather than to competition of responses. While we were properly tentative about the unlearning hypothesis, as evidenced by our calling it "Factor X" (the other-than-competition factor), and we were even more tentative about suggesting that it was an analogue of experimental extinction in classical conditioning, the logic of our original argument took a very proper and thorough beating from Thune and Underwood (1943), and our dallying with the concepts of classical conditioning was declared absurd by Gibson (1941). But the notion of unlearning persisted in modified form, perhaps because all of us know that we do learn *not* to make responses in certain situations even though they may be rewarded in others, and the occurrence of unreinforced (punished?) intrusions from OL during the learning of IL satisfied the conditions for such unlearning to occur.

When modified (by Thune and Underwood, 1943) to account for only a portion of the discrepancy between the RI attributable to intrusions and the total RI, the hypothesis made sense out of otherwise incompletely sensible results. And then, of course, Barnes and Underwood (1959) gave us the seemingly definitive evidence that some responses from OL are actually not available under their modification of MFR (MMFR) which permits the subject to give the OL response, the IL response, or both. However, I still think there is much to be known before we can put the factor of unlearning firmly in our empirically generated model of the forgetting process. For one thing, within the context of the Barnes and Underwood experiment, I would like to have evidence that there is some correlation between the specific responses that were unavailable in specific subjects and the specific non-reinforced intrusions of these same responses during IL. A correlation, even a $\chi^2$ at the .05 level, would increase my confidence in the unlearning hypothesis to the .01 level. Another kind of evidence that would be persuasive would be the demonstration that after learning A-B and then learning A-C, A-B', and C-D in a mixed list, the items given the A-C treatment in IL were significantly less available by the MMFR test than the items given the C-D treatment (i.e., not represented in IL at all). My worry here is that during IL subjects learn not to respond with any OL response and that it takes a while to unlearn this set. Such a notion has clear ties with the concept of differentiation of list membership, so that an independent index of differentiation should show an interaction with the nonavailability of OL responses in MMFR. Also, the notion has much in common with the concept of generalized competition, in that both appeal to the concept of response set, and there may be a negative as well as a positive component of the set established during IL.

Perhaps the most persuasive argument for specific response unlearning during IL is the evidence for "spontaneous recovery" of those responses over time. Certainly, we will await with great interest the full report of the study by Miss Suzanne Adams, as briefly described by Postman. Nevertheless, it seems to me that the same kinds of questions must be asked about these recovered nonavailable responses as about the nonavailable responses at any point in time. The problem deserves a major emphasis in our experimental efforts.

In the discussion above I have invoked the concept of list differentiation, but I hope that this did not imply wholehearted acceptance of it. Of all the concepts that have been appealed to in the interference theories of forgetting, this one gives me the most difficulty. For one thing, I am never quite sure what is being referred to. Gibson (1940) long ago introduced a notion of differentiation, but this referred primarily to the relative degrees of learning of two responses to the same or similar stimuli, or to the differentiation of stimuli by attaching different responses to them. When one stimulus ($S_a$) is highly similar to another ($S_{ax}$), but not identical, I can understand the process of differentiation. But when the different responses are attached to the identical stimulus (as in A-B, A-C paired-associates learning), I have difficulty with the concept of differentiation because the cues for the discriminative responses are not under the control of the investigator. This is, of course, the situation in which Thune and Underwood (1943) originated their concept of differentiation. For them it became synonymous with list membership—whatever the distinctive cues for that may be—and differentiation of list membership is what shows up in covert and partial intrusions that are recognized by the subject as being from the wrong list. Such recognition of list membership is obviously a fruitful concept in accounting for the lack of correlation between overt intrusions and amounts of RI and PI, and "explains" some of the discrepancy that Factor X was invented to "explain," but I am still uneasy about it and will remain so until we get a reasonable theory about what the stimulus component for list membership is—and data to support it.

The concept arose, of course, out of experiments in which the succession of two lists in time was the only extra-list contextual cue that differentiated the lists. Other contextual differences between OL and IL, such as have been investigated by Bilodeau and Schlosberg (1951) and Greenspoon and Renyard (1957), were not present. Absent also were mental-set differences such as studied years ago, and found to be powerful factors, by Lester (1932). Other things being equal, even the intra-organic contextual differences (aches, hunger, muscular tensions, etc.) that might be presumed to be the basis for discrimination of the time ordering of the lists were minimal because the lists were learned in "immediate" succession. But many other things are not equal under those special circumstances. If, as some believe, there is a perseveration of the associative processes after cessation of active practice unless there is interruption, the OL had its perseverating traces interrupted but the IL did not. Also, we know that IL could be subjectively discriminable from OL because the learning of it involved intrusions from OL and the unlearning and overcoming of them. Thus, it is possible that list differentiation may depend on some differential cues that are intimately involved in the disruption of traces and "unlearning."

This sort of speculation about the stimulus basis for discrimination of list membership gets us nowhere. Perhaps our difficulty is that we have no studies of discrimination of and memory for list membership per se, at least not in the context of rote verbal learning with varying numbers of lists, varying numbers of trials, and varying time intervals before recall. Such studies seem reasonably straightforward with a recognition method, and might give some surprising information about this particular form of differentiation. At the very least, a measure of memory for list membership which is independent of the particular resolution of response conflict at the time of attempted recall will assist in the analysis of the recall process.

So much for the concepts of response blocking, unlearning, and list differentiation. I turn briefly to the concept of generalized response competition, as introduced by Newton and Wickens (1956) and heavily exploited by Postman. I have little to say here, except to reiterate the general point of view expressed with respect to the concept of list membership. Clearly, the data force recognition of a substantial interference effect in recall, even though there is minimal specific formal or meaningful similarity between OL and IL stimuli and responses (other than all being verbal). As Postman suggests, we need systematic studies to define the necessary and sufficient conditions for this type of interference to occur. There seems to me to be a strong commonality between this effect and the problems of mental set and shift, and an independently useful contribution to the science of memory phenomena will come from systematic pursuit of the concept of generalized response interference with this commonality in mind. But in addition, it seems to me that, again, there is a requirement to try to isolate the contextual or other stimulus control of the generalization or differentiation involved in the presence or absence of such generalized response competition.

Finally, within the context of specific forgetting theory, I would like to comment on the notion of disruption of associative context, as briefly mentioned by Postman but extensively discussed and used by Postman and Riley (1959). A full discussion would be inappropriate here, but it seems to me that the introduction of such a concept in our theory of interference and forgetting is a necessary complication that can no longer be avoided. It should be an important factor in the differentiation of serial and paired-associates learning in view of the contrasting operations of these methods with respect to encouragement and discouragement of remote associations; it may well be a significant component of the contextual cues to which we must appeal for discrimination of list membership; and it may well have something important to do with the presence or absence of generalized response competition. In so far as it is a potent factor in recall under RI or PI conditions, it seems to me that it will make quite important the analyses of sequential dependencies in the recall of items during the first recall trial. We look at these quite regularly, at least in part, in our analyses of serial position effects in the recall of serial lists, but more "micromolar" analyses seem called for in both serial and paired-associates recall.

## THE NEW DIRECTION OF RESEARCH ON FORGETTING

It would be difficult to overstate the importance of Postman's extension of interference theory to the consideration of extra-experimental sources of interference in verbal learning and forgetting. It stems, of course, from Underwood's (1957) conclusion that PI is a major cause of forgetting in the usual counterbalanced, multiple-lists, verbal learning in the laboratory, and from his conclusion that forgetting should be relatively small in amount and primarily attributable to PI from extra-experimental verbal habits when a single verbal list is learned in the laboratory.

The experimental tests of this notion, as reported here by Postman and also by Underwood and Postman (1960), for letter-sequence habits and unit-sequence habits give strong support to the fertility of their conception of forgetting of new learning through the recovery of old verbal habits which were unlearned during the process of the new learning.

As I see it, there will be three extremely important consequences of this new direction of research on forgetting. In the first place, there will be a radical methodological change. No longer will the students of verbal learning attempt to devise materials for the learning task which will strip away the influence of previously established verbal habits, as was Ebbinghaus's intention when he invented the nonsense syllable and as has been the implicit intention of many of us when we carefully devised lists of unrelated nouns or adjectives. The theory and the data clearly suggest that not only could such pristine verbal materials never be achieved in fact but also the strategy was misleading. It resulted in a failure to realize that the assembly of "unrelated" consonants into consonant trigrams always involved a complex of positive and negative transfer effects depending on letter-sequence habits and that the assembly of "unrelated" adjectives into lists ignored the unit-sequence habits which would be reflected in the new learning process but without control or appreciation by the investigator. The new methodology will insist on assessment of the status of the existing language habits in the subject (or groups of subjects) prior to the new learning, the definition of the new learning task with explicit recognition of the relationships between the new associations and the preexisting ones, and perhaps in many cases the measurement not only of the retention of the new associations but also of the recovery of the old.

Perhaps a simple-minded diagrammatic representation of this critical difference in our way of thinking about our laboratory studies of verbal learning will have some mnemonic value. In Table 7-1 is shown a contrast of the old way and new way of diagramming the associative situation in a laboratory study of RI with paired associates. To avoid complicating the picture, I have not used the symbol Ax to represent stimuli that are similar to, but not identical with, stimulus A except in the description of the preexisting association structure of the subject. The dotted lines represent possible specific competing responses and the solid lines represent required ("correct") responses. Obviously, even with our simplification with respect to the stimulus-similarity factor, the design of appropriate verbal materials for the tests of our hypotheses about such factors as unlearning, mediation, spontaneous recovery, generalized competition, etc. has been greatly complicated, as has the analysis of the fate of the materials learned under our experimental control. Just as obviously, we will frequently, if not regularly, find occasion to make observations on the change of state of the preexisting verbal habits during and following our experiments.

A second consequence of this new direction of research and of the new methodology it requires will be a much closer relationship between those of us concerned with verbal *learning* and those of us concerned with verbal *behavior*. This will result in part because the students of verbal learning must become cognizant of the operant characteristics of verbal behavior, of language structure and the like. In part, it will

Table 7-1

Schematic Comparison of the Old and New Ways of Conceptualizing the Associative Complex in a Study of RI

| Concept | Subject's pre-experimental state | OL | IL | RL |
|---|---|---|---|---|
| Old way | Tabula (more or less) rasa | A → B | A → K ↘ B | A → B ↘ K |
| New way | Existing verbal habits<br>A---→B<br><br>Ax--→B<br><br><br>A---→K<br>Ax--→K<br>.......<br>A---→Z<br><br>Ax--→Z | A → B ↘ K ⋮ Z | A → K ↘ B ⋮ Z | A → B ↘ K ⋮ Z |

result from the discovery by students of verbal behavior and language that the students of verbal learning are doing experiments that result in the modification of extra-experimental language behavior and that the theories of verbal forgetting are about real-life language changes.

Finally, and perhaps of the greatest importance for psychology, this theory and new approach to verbal forgetting is, it seems to me, completely generalizable over all the varieties of human learning and forgetting. For example, the analogue of the verbal unit-sequence habits in the area of perceptual-motor skill are the "population stereotypes" (Fitts, 1951) in display-control relationships such as get involved in eye-hand pursuit tasks and many other tasks. A similar approach to the forgetting of perceptual learning will certainly find the notion of predicting rate of forgetting in terms of the compatibility of new perceptions with previously established perceptual habits to be a fertile one; likewise with affective responses, attitudes, interests, and in short, the whole gamut of learnings in complex habit-ridden organisms.

## MEMORY, FORGETTING, AND INTERFERENCE THEORY

My only general critical comment about Postman's paper relates to the complete absence of reference to the memory trace as a psychological or neuropsychological construct. In his introductory statements about the interference theory of forgetting he says, quite properly, that interference theory is the major significant analysis of the process of forgetting. But then he goes on to say that the alternative trace theory is Gestalt in origin, experimentally sterile, and may be ignored. He then proceeds to ignore the currently quite active area of research and theory which is attempting to define more exactly the appropriate properties or characteristics to be assigned to the memory trace per se and apart from the interactions of traces that lead to interference. On the basis of what we know now, and reflecting the promise I see in new efforts and techniques to describe the fate of specific memories over short periods of time after a single presentation, I am not ready to accept the notion that interference is the whole story of forgetting.

I am not, of course, defending Koffka's (1935) elaborations of Wulf's specific hypotheses about autonomous changes in the memory trace since they continue to be denied by the data (Lovibond, 1958). However, it is a mistake to reject the construct of trace because one set of hypotheses about the properties of the trace fails to stand the test of experiment. Since I have never felt that it was necessary for psychological theory to insulate itself from neurological and physiological concepts and data, and thus unfortunately insulate psychologists from neurologists and physiologists, I have no hesitancy in accepting the construct of memory trace as the carrier of $_sH_R$, association, bond, S-R connection, or S-S connection. In fact, I consider such to be one of the most primitive and necessary constructs of the science of behavior. Therefore, if one accepts such a construct, it is both reasonable and proper to ask what properties are to be assigned to it. Does it undergo decay in time, especially over short time intervals and after single presentations? Does it *require* uninterrupted continuation (i.e., perseveration or reverberation) if it is to become part of the "permanent" memory store? Must we have a duplex theory of memory, one for short-time storage and the other for long-time "permanent" storage, as suggested by Hebb

(1949)? If not, then should *all* memory traces be assumed to be permanent throughout the life of the organism, with all forgetting conceived as a consequence of interference in the utilization of the trace, or should *all* memory traces be assumed to be subject to a decay factor?

Needless to say, I do not consider the data available at this time to be sufficient to give us answers to these questions, but neither do I think that the data permit us to ignore any one of them in the development of a theory of memory, of forgetting, and of interference. My complaint is essentially that there seems to be a schism among students of memory —to a considerable extent fostered by those who concentrate on trace theory as well as by those, such as Postman, who concentrate on interference theory—and I do not think schisms are healthy. While I was completely sympathetic with McGeoch's (1932) classic attack on the Law of Disuse as it had been bandied about by early theorists, I think his major point was to assert that there had been too much neglect of the tremendous amount of variance in retention that could be accounted for by interference. He was successful in swinging theoretical attention to the interference factors, as attested by Postman's treatment of the vast experimental and theoretical literature that has developed since 1932. But during this interval, and especially in the last 15 years, new theories and methods have led to new facts. We have the new and intriguing theories of the memory trace, such as those of Hebb (1949) and Broadbent (1958). There are new and to-be-accounted-for experimental data on the effect of massive interruption of post event happenings in the central nervous system, such as the studies of Duncan (1949), Thompson and Dean (1955), and many others with electro-convulsive shock. Finally, and of the greatest importance in my thinking, there are new and fertile methods for exploration of short-term memory, such as Peterson and Peterson's (1959) analysis of the short-term retention of a single verbal unit; Pollack, Johnson, and Knaff's (1959) "running memory span"; Broadbent's (1957) technique for the study of immediate memory through the manipulation of simultaneous stimuli, and the numerous approaches to the study of short-term memory functions in complex tasks (e.g., Mackworth, 1959; Mackworth and Mackworth, 1959). Furthermore, I am in the fortunate position of knowing, at this time, that there is more to come in this diversification of method for the study of short-term memory functions (see Anderson, 1960; Lloyd, Reid, and Feallock, 1960).

To summarize, my point of criticism is simple; it is that we are not yet in a position to treat all long-term forgetting as the product of interference factors alone, even though interference factors may well be by far the most important. Nor are we in a position to develop a theory of memory or forgetting by reference only to interference factors and relatively long-term retention, when there are theorists and investigators who are asking questions about the relationship between short-term memory and long-term memory, about the properties of memory traces, and are actively inventing new methods to get an empirical hold on such questions.

But this general criticism should not, in my opinion, dim by even one JND our appreciation for the magnificent job that Postman has done of organizing fact and theory with reference to the interference component in forgetting. The lazy ones among us can only hope that he will do the same job for all theories and experiments on memory as broadly defined. Meanwhile, as pointed out in the discussion of interference theory, there are many loose ends within the theory, all of them deserving an acceleration of experimental effort if for no other reason than that the goal of understanding memory and forgetting now seems perceptibly closer, even though not yet within arm's reach.

### REFERENCES

Anderson, N. S. (1960) Poststimulus cuing in immediate memory. *J. Exp. Psychol.*, **60**, 216–221.

Barnes, J. M., & Underwood, B. J. (1959) "Fate" of first-list associations in transfer theory. *J. Exp. Psychol.*, **58**, 97–105.

Berry, R. N., & Davis, R. C. (1958) Muscle responses and their relation to rote learning. *J. Exp. Psychol.*, **55**, 188–194.

Berry, R. N., & Davis, R. C. (1960) The somatic background of rote learning. *J. Exp. Psychol.*, **59**, 27–34.

Bilodeau, I. McD., & Schlosberg, H. (1951) Similarity in stimulating conditions as a variable in retroactive inhibition. *J. Exp. Psychol.*, **41**, 199–204.

Briggs, G. E. (1954) Acquisition, extinction and recovery functions in retroactive inhibition. *J. Exp. Psychol.*, **47**, 285–293.

Briggs, G. E. (1957) Retroactive inhibition as a function of degree of original and interpolated learning. *J. Exp. Psychol.*, **53**, 60–67.

Briggs, G. E., Thompson, R. F., & Brogden, W. J. (1954) Retention functions in reproductive inhibition. *J. Exp. Psychol.*, **48**, 419–428.

Broadbent, D. E. (1957) Immediate memory and simultaneous stimuli. *Quart. J. Exp. Psychol.*, **9**, 1–11.

Broadbent, D. E. (1958) *Perception and communication.* New York: Pergamon.

Duncan, C. P. (1949) The retroactive effect of electroconvulsive shock. *J. Comp. Physiol. Psychol.*, **42**, 32–44.

Fitts, P. M. (1951) Engineering psychology and equipment design. In S. S. Stevens (Ed.), *Handbook of experimental psychology.* New York: Wiley. Pp. 1287–1340.

Gibson, Eleanor J. (1940) A systematic application of the concepts of generalization and differentiation to verbal learning. *Psychol. Rev.*, **47**, 196–229.

Gibson, Eleanor J. (1941) Retroactive inhibition as a function of degree of generalization between tasks. *J. Exp. Psychol.*, 28, 93–115.

Greenspoon, J., & Renyard, R. (1957) Stimulus conditions and retroactive inhibition. *J. Exp. Psychol.*, 53, 55–59.

Hebb, D. O. (1949) *The organization of behavior.* New York: Wiley.

Koffka, K. (1935) *Principles of Gestalt psychology.* New York: Harcourt, Brace.

Lester, O. P. (1932) Mental set in relation to retroactive inhibition. *J. Exp. Psychol.*, 15, 681–699.

Lloyd, K. E., Reid, L. S., & Feallock, J. B. (1960) Short-term retention as a function of the average number of items presented. *J. Exp. Psychol.*, 60, 201–207.

Lovibond, S. H. (1958) A further test of the hypothesis of autonomous memory trace change. *J. Exp. Psychol.*, 55, 412–415.

McGeoch, J. A. (1932) Forgetting and the law of disuse. *Psychol. Rev.* 39, 352–370.

McKinney, F., & McGeoch, J. A. (1935) The character and extent of transfer in retroactive inhibition: Disparate serial lists. *Amer. J. Psychol.*, 47, 409–423.

Mackworth, J. F. (1959) Paced memorizing in a continuous task. *J. Exp. Psychol.*, 58, 206–211.

Mackworth, N. H., & Mackworth, J. F. (1959) Remembering advanced cues during search. *Brit. J. Psychol.*, 50, 207–222.

Melton, A. W., & Irwin, J. McQ. (1940) The influence of degree of interpolated learning on retroactive inhibition and the overt transfer of specific responses. *Amer. J. Psychol.*, 53, 173–203.

Melton, A. W., & von Lackum, W. J. (1941) Retroactive and proactive inhibition in retention: Evidence for a two-factor theory of retroactive inhibition. *Amer. J. Psychol.*, 54, 157–173.

Müller, G. E., & Pilzecker, A. (1900) Experimentelle Beiträge zur Lehre vom Gedächtniss. *Z. Psychol.*, Erbd. 1, 1–300.

Newton, J. M., & Wickens, D. D. (1956) Retroactive inhibition as a function of the temporal position of interpolated learning. *J. Exp. Psychol.*, 51, 149–154.

Peterson, L. R., & Peterson, M. J. (1959) Short-term retention of individual verbal items. *J. Exp. Psychol.*, 58, 193–198.

Pollack, I., Johnson, L. B., & Knaff, P. R. (1959) Running memory span. *J. Exp. Psychol.*, 57, 137–146.

Postman, L., & Riley, D. A. (1959) Degree of learning and interserial interference in retention. *Univer. Calif. Publ. Psychol.*, 8, 271–396.

Thompson, R., & Dean, W. (1955) A further study on the retroactive effect of ECS. *J. Comp. Physiol. Psychol.*, 48, 488–491.

Thune, L. E., & Underwood, B. J. (1943) Retroactive inhibition as a function of degree of interpolated learning. *J. Exp. Psychol.*, 32, 185–200.

Underwood, B. J. (1948) "Spontaneous" recovery of verbal associations. *J. Exp. Psychol.*, 38, 429–439.

Underwood, B. J. (1957) Interference and forgetting. *Psychol. Rev.*, 64, 49–60.

Underwood, B. J., & Postman, L. (1960) Extra-experimental sources of interference in forgetting. *Psychol. Rev.* **67**, 73–95.

Whitely, P. L., & Blankenship, A. B. (1936) The influence of certain conditions prior to learning upon subsequent recall. *J. Exp. Psychol.*, **19**, 496–504.

## SUMMARY OF CONFERENCE DISCUSSION

The first question considered was concerned with the possible deterioration of the trace; i.e., does the memory trace "deteriorate" in time even in the absence of incompatible responses? Postman indicated that he would like to make the assumption that the trace does not deteriorate, although he recognized that Duncan's (1949) experiment, which showed that electric shock administered just after learning impaired retention whereas electric shock administered later did not, suggests otherwise. Peterson and Peterson's (1959) experiment was also cited to bear on this point. They tested for retention of a single consonant "syllable" (e.g., CHJ) after brief intervals filled by saying numbers. Retention loss appeared after each interval and increased over the period from three to eighteen seconds, the range of the intervals they employed for retention. Postman raised the question, how soon does proactive inhibition or interference begin? There is little evidence on the point, but perhaps its onset is very rapid. The weight of other available evidence certainly suggests that interference rather than deterioration of the trace is involved. Rehearsal may occur during such retention intervals. It was pointed out that the subject could rehearse incorrect responses, which, of course, would impair his "retention." Postman pointed out that errors made by subjects in initial recalls may carry over to later recalls. One study he did showed this to occur for nonsense syllables but not for adjectives.

Critical evidence, it was agreed, is needed on the speed with which proactive interference can set in. Likewise seen as problematic was the nature of the perseveration of the trace (Underwood). The perseverating unit is not known, either. Is it an item, the list (Underwood)? Deese suggested that perhaps the unit is seven plus or minus two items (Miller, 1956), although it can be argued that there is no discontinuity at the seven-item point. Jenkins indicated that beyond a certain point of list length, however, there is a change. Following a suggestion of George Miller's, he has presented series of digits and asked for either a recall of them or for their sum. The subject did not know ahead of time for which he would be asked. Beyond a certain length of list, the subject can do one of these tasks but not the other, having done the first one. Breaking such lists into parts containing different kinds of materials (letters, digits) was suggested as a way to study the problem further (Osgood, Deese). The additional point also was made that there is no real boundary between learning and retention (Deese).

Postman was asked by Osgood to explain how it is that he can postulate the unlearning of the first-list response during second-list learning in the A-B, A-C case, while at the same time not postulating the unlearning of the first-list response in the case of A-B, A-B', where the mediating role of the response (B) is stressed (cf. Postman's paper, pp. 153–160). Postman answered that from the start of second-list learning mediation probably takes place, so that the A-B-B' sequence leading to a correct response (B') is reinforced. This cannot occur with A-B, A-C, where there is no relation between B and C. Subjects cannot recall the B term after A-C learning has occurred under free recall. Parallel data are needed for the recall of B during the learning of A-B'. Goss reported data showing that the subject will go on learning paired associates without presentation of the response term at all if presentation of the response is discontinued after he has achieved a seven-out-of-eight criterion (under 25 per cent reinforcement). Results found by Richardson (1958) were cited as parallels to this finding.[1] Osgood suggested that recognition by the subject constituted reinforcement, without the presentation of the response. This "self-strengthening" is, Goss pointed out, found for easy lists, not for hard ones. Encoding or response integration was suggested here (Osgood, Mandler) as an explanation for the difference between the hard and easy lists, but it was mentioned that well-encoded words were employed in the study by Barnes and Underwood without necessarily being available.

There was some discussion of the point that mediational processes should take time and that various alterations in results would probably follow variation in time intervals used in these experiments.

Bousfield reported a preliminary experiment which, he suggested, shows that the operant level of verbal responses can be modified. *Chair* is the high-frequency response to the word *table*, and *legs* is a low-frequency response to *table*. In paired-associates learning, pairs like *table-legs* were learned. Subsequently, *room* was presented as a stimulus, and the frequency with which *chair* occurred as an associate to *room* was found to have declined.

This led to a discussion of the fact that pairs of words, like *table-chair* and *table-legs*, which differ in their associative linkages according to association-test norms, should also differ in their learnability (Melton). It was pointed out that the set in the learning situation is different from that in the association situation (Osgood). Deese said that sub-

---

[1] The experiments by Brown (1923) and Raffel (1934) were also cited in this connection, although they used the method of recall.

jects' ratings of the degree of association between two words predicted their learnability well (Haun, 1959). Underwood reported finding differences in the learnability of pairs like *snow-white* and *snow-powdery*, which reflect associative variation on a sensory dimension (Underwood and Richardson, 1956). Pairs in which the response is a very low frequency associate of the stimulus are harder to learn than pairs in which the response is a higher-frequency associate (Russell), but there are no differences in learning difficulty over a wide range of Kent-Rosanoff frequencies. Deese pointed out that the response is *presented to* the subject in paired-associates learning rather than *provided by* him as it is in association tests. As a consequence, frequency of association is not a good predictor of learnability. It was also stated that a Kent-Rosanoff primary to one stimulus could have a much lower frequency than a primary to some other stimulus, or even than a response of lower rank to some stimuli (Musgrave, Mandler). Deese stressed the importance of *context* in the free-association norms and urged the use of comparison procedures (Haun, 1959).

The context in which recall occurs was discussed as an important factor to the accuracy of recall. It was agreed that context is an important variable and deserves measurement and study. There is little available evidence, although studies by Smith and Guthrie (1921) and Abernethy (1940) were mentioned. Suggestions of techniques and of variables which might be important as context or in context were as follows: an added distinctive stimulus at recall (Jenkins), similarity between task and nontask materials (Postman), the social relation of experimenter and subject (Deese, Bousfield), kind of task and kind of material (Postman, Deese).

There was a discussion of the relative importance to paired-associates learning of meaningfulness ($m$) on the stimulus and on the response side. Conflict in available results was reported. Underwood pointed out that specific experiments have dealt with only a small range within the variables of association value or meaningfulness and that the relations of this variable to other variables will probably vary as a function of the sector of the meaningfulness function that is considered. Problems with the Glaze (1928) association values for nonsense syllables were mentioned, and Mandler urged the use of Krueger's (1934) materials.

### REFERENCES

Abernethy, E. M. (1940) The effect of changed environmental conditions upon the results of college examinations. *J. Psychol.*, **10**, 293–301.

Brown, W. (1923) To what extent is memory measured by a single recall? *J. Exp. Psychol.*, **6**, 377–382.

Duncan, C. P. (1949) The retroactive effect of electroconvulsive shock on learning. *J. Comp. Physiol.*, **42**, 32–44.

Glaze, J. A. (1928) The association value of non-sense syllables. *J. Genet. Psychol.*, **35**, 255–267.

Haun, K. W. (1959) Measures of association strength and verbal learning. Unpublished Ph.D. dissertation, The Johns Hopkins University.

Krueger, W. C. F. (1934) The relative difficulty of non-sense syllables. *J. Exp. Psychol.*, **17**, 145–153.

Miller, G. A. (1956) The magical number seven, plus or minus two: Some limits on our capacity of processing information. *Psychol. Rev.*, **63**, 81–97.

Peterson, L. R., & Peterson, M. J. (1959) Short-term retention of individual verbal items. *J. Exp. Psychol.*, **58**, 193–198.

Raffel, G. (1934) The effect of recall on forgetting. *J. Exp. Psychol.*, **17**, 828–838.

Richardson, J. (1958) The relationship of stimulus similarity and number of responses. *J. Exp. Psychol.*, **56**, 478–484.

Smith, S., & Guthrie, E. R. (1921) *General psychology in terms of behavior*. New York: Appleton-Century-Crofts.

Underwood, B. J., & Richardson, J. (1956) Verbal concept learning as a function of instructions and dominance level. *J. Exp. Psychol.*, **51**, 229–238.

# Chapter 8

# AN EVALUATION OF THE GIBSON
# THEORY OF VERBAL LEARNING

*Benton J. Underwood*

NORTHWESTERN UNIVERSITY

Approximately twenty years have passed since Eleanor Gibson's article, "A Systematic Application of the Concepts of Generalization and Differentiation to Verbal Learning," appeared in *Psychological Review*. It is probably not far from the truth to say that in modern times no single article has been so frequently cited by workers in the field of verbal learning as has this one. The impact of the theory can be further gauged by noting that at essentially the same time Hull *et al.* (1940), brought out another theory of verbal learning (the *Mathematico-deductive Theory of Rote Learning*) that had very little influence on research in the field. The forbidding formal elegance of the mathematico-deductive theory was no match for the lucidness and greater generality of the Gibson conceptions.

The present paper represents one evaluation of the contemporary status of the Gibson theory. More particularly, the approach will be toward an evaluation of the current usefulness of the theory. The remarks in the first paragraph make it quite apparent that I would judge the Gibson theory to have been a major force in researches in verbal learning during the past 20 years. Although a control condition is not available—what would have happened had there been no Gibson theory —I would, furthermore, tender the judgment that the area of verbal learning has been appreciably advanced because of Gibson's conceptions. The advance did not come, necessarily, because of the particular theoretical notions which Gibson chose; rather it came about because the approach represented a marked step forward in analytical thinking. By this I mean that by her way of viewing the learning situation gross phenomena could be seen as being composed of subphenomena, and to understand the gross ones a possible procedure was to try to understand their components. In short, it is my opinion not only that the theory has been highly influential but also that this influence was for the good. But the use of the past tense in the above statements indicates the general temper of the present paper. The conclusion will be that the usefulness of the Gibson theory, as originally conceived, has ended. The few notions from the theory which have survived have become public scientific property and, as such, are not often referenced.

Mrs. Gibson's theory was constructed to account for the facts of learning, retention, and transfer as these were known in 1940. Inevitably, as research proceeds, the empirical base of a science changes. What were thought to be established facts disappear with the use of more suitable experimental procedures or controls. Or, in the same sense that Gibson's conceptions represented a step forward in analytical procedures, so also have new conceptions replaced hers as analytical tools. Variables which, in 1940, were believed to be impotent, are now known to be highly relevant. It has been said that a given theory is discarded only when a better theory appears. Yet it does not seem unreasonable to expect a theory gradually to lose its attractiveness for at least two other reasons: (1) some of the fundamental predictions of the theory consistently fail to be confirmed, and (2) the level of empirical analysis reaches a point where the expectations from the theory are not very relevant.

Although Mrs. Gibson has been very actively engaged in research in related areas, she has not formally revised her theory of verbal learning. Therefore, the present evaluation can consider only the original formulation.

The paper will be divided into four general sections. In the first section the basic notions of the Gibson theory will be presented. In the second section we will look at her predictions concerning the learning and retention of a single list and see how these square with the facts as they are known at present. The third section will consider her handling of transfer. Finally, we will note briefly how analytical procedures in verbal learning have, in general, gone beyond the scope of the theory.

I will not consider specifically the adequacy of the predictions relative to retroactive inhibition. There are two reasons for this. First, the mechanisms involved in the predictions for retroactive inhibition are essentially the same as those for transfer. Secondly, methodological problems involved make it very difficult to know whether the predictions concerning retroactive inhibition are or are not confirmed.

## THE BASIC APPROACH OF THE GIBSON THEORY

The Gibson theory was formulated at Yale at the time when the Hullian approach to theory construction was attaining its zenith. As is well known, this approach was one of using principles of conditioning as basic assumptions or postulates for explaining phenomena in other areas. It was presumed that general laws held across all types of learning and that the conditioning situation, because of its simplicity, had a greater likelihood of revealing these general laws than did more complex situations. It is perhaps understandable, therefore, why Mrs. Gibson, then a graduate student at Yale, followed this approach in constructing her theory as background for her experimental work for the Ph.D. dissertation.

The basic notion in Gibson's thinking was that a fundamental part of learning was that of establishing *discrimination* among items to be learned. The phenomenon of the conditioning laboratory, used to specify differences in discrimination, was *stimulus generalization*. It is true that a second so-called law or phenomenon, *differentiation*, ostensibly has the same formal status in the theory as has generalization. In so far as I have been able to determine, however, the magnitude of differentiation is always a reciprocal of generalization. One may, therefore, merely speak of different amounts of generalization, or increases and decreases in generalization, and mediate exactly the same predictions as are mediated through the use of the term "differentiation." In any event, I will proceed as if this were true since it simplifies writing about the theory.

The paired-associates learning task is used by Gibson as the primary vehicle for applying the theory to verbal tasks, although she points out that it should apply equally to serial learning. Generalization may occur among the stimulus terms in a paired-associates list; a response learned to one stimulus tends to occur as a response to other stimuli in the list. Or generalization may occur among stimuli in different lists. The implication of generalization for learning is a matter for later discussion. There are certain matters concerning generalization per se which must first be considered.

According to Gibson's point of view, a generalization *gradient* is defined in an empirical manner in terms of decreasing tendency for other stimuli to generalize with a given stimulus. She asserts that no further assumptions need to be made about the nature of the stimulus continuum which underlies the generalization gradient but that in actual practice it is often spoken of as a dimension of similarity. Her failure to identify generalization as the behavioral counterpart of similarity exclusively has a distinct advantage for the theory. For, by not identifying it completely with similarity, she handles *meaningfulness* of the verbal material in the system. The higher the meaningfulness, the higher the discriminability and the less the generalization. Since no clear dimension of similarity parallels the dimension of meaningfulness, Gibson, by *not* limiting generalization to instances in which a dimension of similarity is present, is, presumably, able to handle the effects of meaningfulness on learning.

It seems fairly clear that Gibson (following Hull) prefers to confine her thinking of generalization to sensory or primary generalization (as, for example, along a dimension of sound intensity) as opposed to secondary generalization (as among synonymous words). However, apparently in support of her decision to use generalization as a basic explanatory mechanism, she cites studies which demonstrate generalization among nonsense syllables and also among synonymous words. The emphasis on primary generalization is implied by the stimulus terms used in her own studies (Gibson, 1941; Gibson, 1942). These stimulus terms were forms or figures which appear to have very little "meaning." Thus, the theory derives from principles of conditioning, the experiments used forms as stimuli, and yet the results of her experiments are said to be directly relevant to a theory of verbal learning. This series of extrapolations has always been a puzzle to me, although, of course, there is no puzzle if the theory actually "works" for verbal material. I do not care to become involved in an argument as to what is and what isn't a verbal item, but I would insist that it is quite possible that the laws which govern the acquisition of tasks in which forms are stimuli *could* be different from those which govern the acquisition of a task in which, say, adjectives were stimuli. I have, therefore, been reluctant to accept her experiments in which the forms were stimuli as being *ipso facto* support for her theory. That is, when she indicates that her experiments give direct support to her theory, I stumble a little. It would seem much more correct to say that the theory of verbal learning, based on conditioning principles, also appears to handle the facts (if true) of learning in which forms are used as stimulus terms. But this is not the same as saying that these experiments validate the theory for verbal material. She may have a perfectly good theory for form learning but perhaps not for word learning.

As far as stimulus generalization as such is concerned, I do not care to raise any issues when this generalization is correlated to some dimension of similarity. The evidence which Gibson cited in support of generalization among verbal units used as stimuli could be given much additional support today (e.g., Postman, 1951). However, in light of our present knowledge, Gibson's theory must be judged to be quite incomplete because of failure to include response generalization (or some corresponding mechanism). This was not an oversight on Mrs. Gibson's part; she reviewed the data available and concluded that response generalization was, at best, a minor factor in learning. One might argue, however, that Gibson's theory demanded that response similarity, if not response generalization, be made a part of the system. For, in considering transfer situations, the theory clearly predicts that there will be a difference in transfer when stimulus terms generalize, depending upon whether the response terms are identical or different between the two lists. It would be reasonable to conclude that there would be some sort of gradient between these two extremes.

One final general point may be made concerning the theory and its handling of stimulus generalization. In considering stimulus generalization between stimuli in two lists, as in a transfer situation, the theory apparently rejects identity between stimuli as being appropriate for the application of generalization theory. For example, in considering available data to check on a prediction concerning interference and degree of learning, she says, "No check on this prediction is available, since the experiments in the field . . . have used identical, rather than generalizing stimulus members in the two lists" (1940, p. 216). And yet, in reporting the results of her experiment on stimulus generalization and retroactive inhibition (Gibson, 1941), she speaks *as if* identity of stimuli was to be included in her theory as an instance of high generalization. In this experiment she had one condition in which the stimuli in two lists were identical, and she had three other conditions in which the stimulus forms had, on a previous generalization test, shown decreasing degrees of generalization. As I read the theory, it says nothing about inclusion of identical stimuli as a case of maximal generalization and, as the quote above suggests, this paradigm is not included within the scope of her theory. However, in presenting the results of the experiment she says, in referring to transfer on a second list, "The chief fact shown is the much lower degree of learning achieved in Condition I [identical stimuli], which is in keeping with the hypothesis under consideration" (1941, p. 101). I do not think this is in keeping with the theory since the theory does not handle this case. I have never been able to see why the theory wasn't originally stated so that it would include identity of stimuli as an instance of maximal generalization, but the fact is that it wasn't so stated.

Let us now examine the manner in which the theory is applied to the learning and retention of a single list. In doing this, postulates, predictions, and evaluations will be intermingled.

## SINGLE-LIST LEARNING AND RETENTION

*Rate of Learning.* The proposition with regard to learning a single list is as follows:

"If multiple generalization occurs during the learning of a list, and if the list is constituted so that the generalizing items have different responses, an increasing number of repetitions will be required to reach a given criterion of learning as the strength of the generalizing tendencies increases" (1940, p. 211).

If discrimination among stimuli is complete at the start of learning—if there is no generalization among stimulus items—the theory has nothing to say about the learning other than the fact that it will take place more rapidly than if there is some generalization. However, with perfect discriminability among stimuli—perfect in the sense that a test would show no generalization—wide differences in learning will occur as a function of other factors (such as differences in responses). The theory as originally formulated does not account for any such differences. No theory would necessarily be expected to cover all aspects of learning, and I mention this matter at this point only to show another area in which the theory is simply not relevant.

It is fair to say that within a given range of material, variations in stimulus-term similarity of paired-associates lists produce variations in learning rate which conform quite well to expectations from the Gibson theory. The greater the similarity, the longer will be required to learn the list. The greater the similarity, presumably, the greater the generalization. The relationship between stimulus similarity and learning has been shown with forms as stimuli (Gibson, 1942) and with nonsense syllables as stimuli (e.g., Underwood, 1953a; Feldman and Underwood, 1957). However, a clear inverse relationship between stimulus similarity and speed of learning has not been found with adjectives in paired-associates learning (Underwood, 1953b; Beecroft, 1956). Perhaps the use of adjectives, which in Gibson's terminology would produce secondary generalization, should not be included as a good test of the theory. But, whether the theory includes or excludes such generalization, the findings with adjectives represent a set of facts with which a theory must cope.

*Overt Errors during Learning.* It does not seem to me that the Gibson theory makes a clear formulation concerning the occurrence of overt errors during learning. It is true that in her section on explanation of terms she states that *generalization* (and multiple generalization) is a *tendency* for responses being learned to one stimulus to occur to other stimuli. But in her postulates the most relevant statement is as follows: ". . . If a right excitatory tendency and a generalized one are aroused by the same S but lead to different R's, they will interfere, the weaker tending to block the stronger in proportion to the strength of the weaker" (1940, p. 206). In any event, it is quite evident that in Gibson's mind, if not in her theory, overt errors were to be taken as an index of generalization during learning. In reporting one of her experiments in which intra-list similarity was varied, she states that "the hypothesis assumes that . . . wrong responses occur by virtue of generalization between the stimulus members" (1942, p. 191). Highly similar geometrical forms used as stimuli in paired-associates lists produced more overt errors than did forms with low similarity. However, with verbal material, even with nonsense syllables, the correlation between trials to learn and number of overt errors is not always found (e.g., Underwood, 1953a; Underwood and Richardson, 1956) when intra-list similarity is manipulated. I must quickly add that there are certain alternative methods of error measurement possible and that one's choice of method may well determine whether or not the errors are said to conform to the theory. Thus, one may find that a list with high stimulus similarity requires 20 trials to learn, and a total of 40 overt errors is made. A list with low similarity among stimuli may require 10 trials to learn and a total of 20 overt errors made. The error *rate* for the learning of the two lists is the same; the total number of errors is different and would correspond to expectations from the Gibson theory. I always seem to hold the minority opinion on this issue, for I think that error rate is the appropriate measure and not total errors. It seems to me that a theory which predicts a greater number of errors must make this prediction for error rate rather than total errors or it is a vapid prediction. Inevitably, as more trials are required to learn, more total errors will be made, even though the error rate remains the same. By error rate I mean some ratio between trials to learn and total errors, or a ratio between opportunities to make errors and number of errors made. Total errors as a theoretical prediction lacks substance because any variable which changes the number of trials to learn will also change the total number of errors even if the error rate is constant. A theory which predicts that error rate will change as a function of a given variable has uniqueness and is, in my opinion, the only meaningful kind of prediction concerning errors. If one accepts my position, there are lots of data which do not conform to expectations from the Gibson theory; if the alternative position is accepted, most available data would probably conform to the Gibson theory. Gibson's own study (1942), using forms as stimuli, conforms to expectations even by a rate measure.

Another postulate in the theory concerning generalization reads as follows:

"Generalization will increase to a maximum or peak during the early stages of practice with a list, after which it will decrease as practice continues" (1940, p. 206).

The postulate is said to have been confirmed in Mrs. Gibson's experiment (1942) where, using overt errors as an index of generalization, the errors *did* first increase and then decrease. It has also been found by many other investigators. I think it is true, as Murdock (1958) has argued, that in the usual paired-associates learning situation such an error function must necessarily be obtained. Generalization cannot result in erroneous responses until some associative strength exists between a stimulus and a response. Overt errors must, then, first increase; and if learning is carried, say, to one perfect trial, they must eventually decrease in frequency. Therefore, while such an error curve must occur under the usual conditions prescribed for the learning of a single list, the fact that it does adds nothing to predictions or expectations concerning the learning of this list. In fact, such a curve of overt errors should appear even if there is essentially zero measured similarity among the stimulus items. In the Gibson study (1942) in which the error curve is presented there was also a condition with very low stimulus similarity. The error curve for this condition is not presented; if it were, it would, if the argument above is sound, also show the same shape as the curve for the list with high stimulus similarity. Again, the failure of the theory to handle the role of responses and the development of associative connection between stimuli and responses, both of which may be intimately tied up with the shape of the error curve, indicates a clear gap in the expectations. On the other hand, I do not believe that the postulate concerning the course of errors during learning is a completely impotent postulate in the Gibson system, for it is used in predicting certain transfer effects. We will consider how these effects are handled at a later point.

*Spontaneous Recovery.* The critical postulate for predicting the retention of a list is postulate 7:

"After the cessation of practice, differentiation will decrease over a period of time, leading to an increase ('spontaneous recovery') of generalization" (1940, p. 206).

If anyone has followed the results of the studies from the Northwestern laboratories over the past several years, he will recognize that we have been unable to get confirmation of a critical proposition which follows from this postulate. The expectation from this postulate is that the higher the intra-list similarity, the greater the recovery of generalization and the greater the retention loss. We have used quite a variety of materials; we have used naïve and practiced subjects; we have both ignored and controlled differences in degree of learning before the retention interval; we have used serial, paired-associates, and verbal discrimination tasks; we have been unable to confirm the expectation by recall scores. Gibson in fact did not find confirmation in her own study (1942) in the recall scores, although she indicates she did. In our studies we have, in fact, found instances in which high-similarity lists are better recalled than low-similarity lists, but the more general finding is no difference in recall. Relearning scores would support the hypothesis, but it has never seemed to me that such scores can be used as solid support. High-similarity lists and low-similarity lists are learned at different rates originally; if the loss over the retention interval is the same, the relearning differences merely show what was shown in original learning; namely, given a certain equal level of performance, the high-similarity list will be learned more slowly from that point on than will a low-similarity list.

Our consistent failure to find support for differential spontaneous recovery of generalization as a function of intra-list similarity has provided a real puzzle. We would *like* to find intra-list stimulus similarity operating in the way the Gibson theory predicts, for it would simplify matters and also make the findings concerning retroactive and proactive inhibition more easily tied to the same principles as those governing the forgetting of a single list. But, since we have been unable to find confirmation of the expectation, we are ready to look to other mechanisms for our explanation.

The Gibson theory specifies that the *rate* of recovery will be slower, the greater the degree of learning (the greater the differential reinforcement). Since the rate is not specified in any absolute time units, there is always the possibility, of course, that longer or shorter retention intervals than we have used might produce evidence in support of the theory. We have countered this possibility by evaluating recall results in terms of degree of learning, from very weak to very strong, and still have been unable to find evidence of the recovery process. It has been noted elsewhere (Underwood, 1954) that for many materials used in learning experiments there is a reciprocal relationship between number of intra-list associations and number of extra-list associations which might interfere with recall if spontaneous recovery occurred from both sources. If this is true as a general case, it is rather surprising that the two sources would produce equal effects so frequently. It is also difficult to see how material like the Gibson forms could stand in this reciprocal relationship. We have, for all of these reasons, been forced to the conclusion that we cannot accept the spontaneous-recovery postulate as applied to generalization resulting from intra-list stimulus similarity.

Finally, concerning the spontaneous-recovery postulate, I would point out that in none of our studies of distributed practice, where short intervals are introduced between trials, have we found an increase in overt errors that could be attributed to spontaneous recovery of generalization from within the list. Such a recovery might be expected (according to the theory) on trials after the error tendencies have reached a peak during learning and are being reduced in frequency by differential reinforcement.

*Summary.* Three points may be used to summarize the evaluation of the theory as applied to the learning and retention of a single list.

1. With forms or nonsense syllables as stimuli, the theory predicts the learning rate as a function of intra-list stimulus similarity quite well. It is not satisfactory when words are stimuli and when similarity is manipulated among subgroups of these words.

2. The data concerning frequency of errors are ambiguous with regard to the theory. Whether or not error data can be said to support the theory depends to a large extent on one's convictions concerning the appropriate error measure to use.

3. There is no support for the postulate concerning the spontaneous recovery of generalization; predictions concerning recall of a single list as a function of intra-list stimulus similarity are not borne out.

## TRANSFER

The Gibson theory is relevant to only two basic transfer paradigms as a consequence of the fact that variation in response similarity is not included in the system. The two paradigms are: responses in the two lists different, with variations in stimulus similarity between the two lists; and responses in the two lists identical, with variations in the stimulus similarity for stimulus units paired with the same response. Each of these paradigms will be evaluated separately.

*Response Different, Stimuli Varied.* The proposition relevant to this paradigm is as follows:

"More repetitions will be required to learn a second list, in proportion to the strength of the tendency for items of a first list to generalize with the items of the second list" (1940, p. 213).

The reasons for the prediction are fairly obvious. The more the stimuli in the two lists generalize, the greater the conflict or interference in establishing the new association in the second list. While (as noted earlier) the transfer situation in which stimuli are identical and responses different is an ambiguous one in Gibson's writing, it can be seen that the logic of the paradigm as a whole would support the Gibson prediction. That is, with an A-B, A-C paradigm, negative transfer may be expected simply because the subject is required to learn two different responses to the same stimulus. At the other extreme, A-B, D-C, the subject is simply learning two disparate lists. Variation in stimulus similarity between these two extremes might well be expected to yield some gradient or transfer, whether attributed to generalization or not.

In my opinion there are no satisfactory tests of this prediction available, and the fact that the data which are available are somewhat ambiguous may well be due to inadequate experimental procedures rather than to the inadequacy of the theory. So far as I know, only three studies have attempted to evaluate the prediction, two of these being made by

Gibson (1941) and one by Bugelski and Cadwallader (1956). My comments on these three studies may best be made by a series of independent points.

1. All three studies used the Gibson forms as stimuli; thus, there is no evaluation of the prediction with verbal units as stimuli.

2. The three studies differ in their findings. In the first Gibson experiment (a group procedure), the A-B, A-C situation showed more negative transfer than did the other three conditions (which had decreasing stimulus similarity), but these later three conditions showed no clear differences. Thus, if the Gibson theory is applicable only to situations where stimulus similarity is varied and in which identity is excluded, no confirmation to the theory is given. In Mrs. Gibson's second experiment (in which subjects were run individually) the A-B, A-C situation again resulted in poorest performance on the second list, the A-B, D-C in the best, with the two conditions having varying degrees of stimulus similarity falling in between, but themselves not differing. In the Bugelski and Cadwallader experiment, the two middle conditions of stimulus similarity actually resulted in poorer performance on the second list than did either the A-B, A-C or A-B, D-C conditions. Thus, taking the data at their face value, no clear confirmation of the prediction is available.

3. None of the three experiments can be considered adequate tests of the proposition; all suffer the same basic methodological error. Except in the A-B, A-C condition, the stimuli in the two lists for the other conditions are different. This is necessitated by the nature of the variable being manipulated. However, it is quite possible that the second lists differed in difficulty among themselves and that the transfer measures represent a confounding of the effects of interlist stimulus similarity and differences in list difficulty. Suppose, for example, that the lists used as second lists differed in intra-list stimulus similarity (and there is no assurance that they did not); by the Gibson theory differences in learning would be expected by this factor alone. Gibson is not unaware of this possibility for she says that "internal generalization will also occur as list 2 is being learned, but the prediction as made above will not be affected, since this factor may remain constant as generalization from list 1 to list 2 is increased" (1940, p. 214). Now, it is true that this factor *may* be held constant, but the fact is that in all three experiments noted it was not known to be held constant. Furthermore, there is no knowledge concerning how the different stimuli used in the different lists may "go with" the responses used, and this may produce variation in difficulty in learning the second list. There may be other factors involved also. All of these possibilities could have been handled by counterbalancing the order in which the two lists were used; thus if all second

lists appeared first half the time, potential differences in difficulty could have then been assayed. Better still, all of the second lists should have always been used as first lists with the transfer effects being measured on a single second list—the list always used first in these experiments.

The conclusion is that no experiment has provided an adequate test of the proposition. Nevertheless, I have considerable confidence that when an adequate test is made it will be confirmed.

*Responses Identical, Stimuli Varied.* The proposition relevant to this paradigm is as follows:

"If generalization occurs from a first list to a second list, and if the generalizing items have the same responses, list 2 will be easier to learn as the degree of generalization between the two lists increases" (1940, p. 209).

There are three experiments which have, ostensibly, tested this expectation. A study by Hamilton (1943) and one by Bugelski and Cadwallader (1956) both used the Gibson forms. Both experiments showed no reversals in the transfer gradient, but the shapes of the gradients and the absolute amount of the transfer differed a great deal. If, however, one omits the identity condition, A-B, A-B, the differences in amount of transfer for the other degrees of similarity are very small. The fact that the absolute amount of positive transfer differs so greatly in two instances is probably to be attributed to the differences in the responses used. Hamilton used low-association-value nonsense syllables and obtained much more positive transfer than did Bugelski and Cadwallader, who used words as responses. It may be noted also that both studies have the methodological difficulty noted above for the paradigm in which responses were different. That is, transfer effects may be confounded by differences in intrinsic difficulty of the second lists.

The third study was done by Staner (1956), and adjectives were used as both stimuli and responses, the similarity having been determined by Haagen (1949). Possible differences in the difficulty of second lists were balanced out by having the nominal second lists occur as first lists half of the time. No condition of identity (A-B, A-B) was included in this experiment, but there were three degrees of stimulus similarity. The highest-similarity condition may be illustrated by the pairs *dirty-supreme, unclean-supreme;* medium similarity by *lazy-open, idle-open;* and low similarity by *spiral-timid, impure-timid.*

The results of this study show a very clear and sharp gradient on the initial trials of the second list. For example, on the first anticipation trial of the second list the mean numbers of correct anticipations were 3.42, 2.33, and 1.00, for the high, medium, and low conditions, respectively. However, in terms of trials to achieve one perfect recitation on the second list (there were eight pairs in the list) the values were 8.08, 8.50, and

7.96—the differential effects of stimulus similarity had completely "washed out."

On the basis of available data it must be concluded that the proposition is confirmed. However, Staner's results (in which transfer depended upon the point of measurement) suggest that the simple conception of the influence of generalization on transfer for this paradigm is not enough since other factors, either factors associated with generalization or independent factors, must be brought into the explanatory system.

*Interval between Lists.* Certain predictions concerning transfer effects as a function of time between tasks flow from the Gibson theory, with the notion of spontaneous recovery being the pivotal postulate. We have previously noted that expectations from this postulate have not been confirmed in recall measures for retention of a single list. It might be expected, therefore, that predictions concerning the effect of time interval between tasks would likewise not be confirmed. The proposition submitted by the theory is as follows:

"The interval after which a list 2 must be introduced in order to obtain the maximum interference in learning it will vary with the degree of learning of list 1, being zero if degree of learning has been carried only as far as the peak of generalization or below, and thereafter occurring the later, the higher the degree of learning of list 1" (1940, p. 219).

The reasoning behind this proposition is a little complicated, and requires a new postulate for complete understanding. This postulate (10) is:

"If differentiation has been set up among a number of stimulus items, there will be less tendency for them to generalize with new stimulus items or for new stimulus items to generalize with them, the decrease in generalization being proportional to the amount of differential reinforcement given" (1940, p. 207).

Thus, as one learns a given first list, generalization tends to increase up to a point. Then, if a shift is made to a second list whose items will generalize with those in the first, maximum negative transfer will occur immediately for any degree of learning of the first task up to the degree associated with maximum generalization. Beyond the point of maximum generalization in the first list, greater negative transfer will be obtained if an interval is introduced between the two lists so that spontaneous recovery of generalization will occur. Presumably, the higher the degree of learning of the first list, the longer must the interval be.

Let us state this expectation in a somewhat different way. Suppose we have carried a first list to a criterion of one perfect trial. With such a criterion, differentiation among stimulus items would be high. The theory says that under these circumstances there would be little generalization between the stimulus items in the first list and similar stimulus items in the second list. But, the theory continues, if a period of time elapses after learning of the first list, spontaneous recovery of generalization among the stimulus items in the first list will occur, and they will in turn, therefore, generalize with the stimulus items in the second list.

Let us push this a little further. If a list were constructed so that generalization among the stimulus items was essentially zero, although generalization with those in a second list was high, the time interval between the first and second list would be irrelevant.

The prediction Gibson makes concerning the time interval concerns an interference-transfer paradigm. However, the postulates should also apply to one in which positive transfer would be expected (responses identical, stimuli varied). Following the mechanisms through, it can be seen that if there is some generalization among items in the first list, and if there is generalization between items in both lists, and if the degree of first-list learning is high, maximum positive transfer will occur with an interval between lists, this interval allowing for maximum spontaneous recovery of generalization among items in the first list.

So far as I know, there are no data sufficiently meeting the boundary conditions of the theory to evaluate these expectations. It would appear that to make an adequate test of the theory, at least four variables must be manipulated, namely, intra-list similarity of the first list, similarity between the two lists, degree of learning of the first list, and length of interval between the two lists. However, even this complex design would be insufficient, for in discussing these propositions, Mrs. Gibson sneaks in a completely new idea which could "foul up" everything. She speaks of "the rate at which generalization tendencies are forgotten" (1940, p. 219). I am not sure I know what is meant by this. I can see how an association is forgotten (or at least interfered with), and if generalization is dependent upon this primary association, then generalization too should be forgotten, but I am not at all sure this is what is meant.

My conclusion concerning time interval between tasks would be that, while we do not have data adequate to test the expectations, the keystone character of spontaneous recovery in the predictions makes it quite unlikely that confirmation could be obtained.

*Degree of First-list Learning.* If items in two lists generalize, and if items in the first list generalize among themselves, and if a second task is presented immediately after the first, Gibson predicts that interference will first increase and then decrease as first-list learning increases. In short, the amount of interference will follow rather precisely the curve of first-list generalization errors.

It is as a test of this expectation that Gibson disallows a paradigm in which the stimuli are identical. If she did allow it, we could report confirmation of the theory (e.g., Underwood, 1949; Atwater, 1953). However, by the same reasoning which reaches the prediction concerning degree of learning and interference, it seems to me that she must also predict that in a positive transfer paradigm (in which responses are identical and stimuli highly similar) the maximum positive transfer should occur with a moderate degree of first-task learning (to correspond with the peak of generalization). Again, while available data are not definitive, internal analyses of items in the study by Staner (1956) showed that the higher the degree of first-task learning, the greater the amount of positive transfer.

*Pre-differentiation.* If a subject learns two lists which form the A-B, A-C paradigm, interference may be expected due to the conflict of learning two responses to the same stimuli. However, according to Gibson's conceptions, there is a clear positive component in this paradigm over and above learning to learn, warm-up, and any other performance factors that might be present. In learning A-B there must necessarily be a reduction in generalization among the stimulus items. This differentiation will transfer to A-C, thus producing a positive component to the performance. Gibson points out, however, that because of the unknown weights to be assigned to the two opposed factors present in learning the second list, no prediction could be made concerning the learning performance on the second list. She presumed, however, that fewer intra-list generalization errors during the learning of the second list (as compared with the first) would be evidence of the positive component.

In attempts to eliminate the negative factor inherent in the A-B, A-C paradigm, investigators have devised situations in which stimulus items in the first list could become differentiated without attaching a specific response to these stimuli which would interfere with A-C learning. Not all of these studies were devised as tests of the Gibson hypothesis, as several other theories also have something to say about transfer in this situation. In the aggregate, these studies have come to be known as dealing with pre-differentiation.

I shall not attempt to evaluate all the problems involved in adequately carrying out pre-differentiation studies, nor shall I review the evidence. Arnoult (1957) has summarized this work, and his conclusion was that there wasn't much evidence in support of the Gibson formulation. Yet it is possible that none of the studies on pre-differentiation would be considered an adequate test of the Gibson conception since none has used a strictly verbal task as the second task and avoided at the same time attaching competing responses to the stimuli which may interfere in the learning of the transfer task, and used appropriate controls for performance factors. However, work which comes close to meeting these requirements will be mentioned shortly, and these studies fail to produce a positive effect. In short, the evidence does not appear to support the notion that a reduction in intra-list generalization among stimuli in one list will transfer positively to similar or identical stimuli in a second list.

*Meaningfulness.* Gibson defines meaningfulness (meaning) as "a characteristic of a verbal or visual item which serves to differentiate it from other items" (1940, p. 205). From her discussion of meaningfulness, it is clear that, say, low-association-value nonsense syllables are more poorly differentiated than are common three-letter words. It is also apparent that she means that more generalization will occur among nonsense syllables than among the words (unless synonymous words are used). Thus, she predicts that lists with items of low meaningfulness as stimuli will be learned more slowly than lists having items of high meaningfulness as stimuli. This prediction is supported by available data (e.g., Cieutat, Stockwell, and Noble, 1958), although the effect on learning of very wide differences in meaningfulness of the stimuli is relatively small.

I do not believe that generalization in the sense that Gibson uses the term is responsible for differences in learning as a function of stimulus meaningfulness. There are two reasons for this. First, there are alternative conceptions which seem to handle the facts more simply. Second, studies which have given familiarization training to low-meaningful nonsense syllables have failed to facilitate learning when the familiarized units become stimuli in paired-associates lists (e.g., Sheffield, 1946; Schulz, 1958). The familiarization training in these studies was such that it is quite likely that if generalization were the critical factor, it should have been reduced by the familiarization training. Furthermore, adequate controls were used for performance factors, and it is improbable that the familiarization procedures developed a response to the units which would interfere with subsequent learning.

Without doubt, the two most potent task variables influencing verbal learning are similarity (intra-list and interlist) and meaningfulness. A theory such as proposed by Gibson which is intended to explain the facts of both of these variables would be very desirable. But in terms of the evidence available at present, this seems quite out of the question; to continue to think of these two variables as is done by the theory obscures very important differences and very important learning phenomena which will not yield to analysis as long as the single explanatory mechanism is applied.

*Summary.* The following points summarize the evaluation of the Gibson theory as it is applied to transfer effects.

1. Predictions of the theory for two transfer paradigms are probably adequate if these predictions are limited to transfer effects as a function of interlist stimulus similarity. However, these predictions are supported only for the initial learning trials of the second list. Other factors, apparently not handled by the theory, may obscure the transfer effects as higher criteria of learning are reached on the second list.

2. Predictions concerning the effect of degree of first-task learning and time between tasks have not been tested satisfactorily. Nevertheless, since both sets of predictions rest heavily on the notion of spontaneous recovery of generalization, and since other data have raised serious doubts about such recovery, the usefulness of the theory for predicting the transfer effects when these two variables are manipulated is minimal.

3. There is no consistent evidence to support the theory in its predictions that if stimuli are pre-differentiated, learning of a task in which the same or similar stimuli are used will be facilitated.

## A MORE GENERAL EVALUATION

At various points in the preceding discussion it has been noted that the Gibson theory simply is not relevant to certain facts of verbal learning which we now have available. One big omission was the effects of response similarity or response generalization. It is a reasonable question to ask whether or not the theory could be extended to accommodate response generalization and thus close the gap. In fact, such extensions have been made (e.g., Osgood, 1949; Underwood, 1951); and since I have been involved in some of these, it is obvious I would judge them to be somewhat successful. However, very recently evidence has been obtained which seriously questions the application of response-generalization theory to transfer studies. Perhaps that is not said quite correctly; perhaps what should be said is that it appears that with verbal material a much simpler formulation is obtained by a simple mediation theory. I shall not review the pertinent data since these have been recently published (Barnes and Underwood, 1959). However, the conception is based on the well-established principle that words which are highly similar also have strong associative connection. Using this fact, other facts of transfer when response similarity is varied can be handled by simple mediation through already-established associations rather than by generalization theory. The use of this conception broadens the range of conditions for predicting transfer effects since the critical factor now becomes associative connection rather than similarity. Thus, any items which have strong associative connection, whether they are similar in the usual sense of the word or not, will yield predictions concerning transfer when the associative connection is varied between responses in two lists.

It is my belief that this same simple mediation conception can also be applied to transfer phenomena when stimulus similarity is varied between items in the two lists. For example, Uehling (1958) has shown that when a strong associative connection is developed between two previously unrelated items, and then these items are used as stimuli in two lists, the transfer effects are quite similar to those obtained when similar stimuli are used. Whether the theory will be found applicable to stimuli of a less verbal nature (e.g., the Gibson forms, or, low-association-value nonsense syllables) is still to be determined, although I see no problems which would prevent such application.

I have also noted earlier that Gibson's theory does not grapple with the basic question of how associations between stimuli and responses are actually formed. This may be a little unfair since among her explanations of terms is one of *reinforcement*. This occurs when the subject correctly anticipates a response and thinks, "That's right." But the question of how the subject got it right in the first place is not considered. I do not mention this as a criticism, for certainly, of all the problems in verbal learning this is one of the most difficult ones to handle. However, it is a fact that in recent years, as investigators have pondered this question, certain other consequences have occurred which have relevance for the evaluation of the Gibson theory.

We have found that a useful analytical tool is to divide the rote-learning process into two stages. In the first stage (response learning) the subject must learn what the responses are, while in the second (associative stage) he must attach them to the given stimulus required by the task. These two stages may never be distinct, but certainly both are logically necessary for learning. Now if one views learning in this fashion, certain implications follow when intra-list similarity is manipulated within a list. I shall not attempt to go through all of the possibilities but a few should be mentioned.

1. High similarity of responses, hence high associative connection among responses, should facilitate the response-learning phase but inhibit the associative phase (Underwood, Runquist, and Schulz, 1959).

2. Suppose stimulus similarity is manipulated in clusters among subgroups of stimuli as has been done in several experiments, including Gibson's. Either by generalization, or by mediation through associative connections which go along with similarity, an inhibitory component should be present in the associative stage of learning. But at the same time the cluster effect should produce a certain amount of facilitation. Thus, speaking from a subject's point of view, if three of twelve stimuli in a list were *icy, cold,* and *frigid,* I would need learn initially (associative stage) only that a given response went with one of these three stimuli; whereas if the stimuli were all dissimilar, there would be no such possibilities of

stimulus elimination. To avoid this positive effect, all stimulus items in the list should be similar if the full negative effect is to be demonstrated.

3. However, the moment one makes all stimuli within a list highly similar, there is less chance that stimulus and response items will be confused. It is a fact that if the same class of materials is used both as stimuli and as responses in a paired-associates list, stimuli will be given with appreciable frequency as responses. But, one can make the stimuli less similar to the responses by increasing the similarity of the stimuli. To minimize this stimulus-response confusion, one may use a completely different class of units as responses from those used as stimuli, say, adjectives for stimuli and nonsense syllables as responses.

4. Now, if stimuli and responses interact more in a single list when they are both from the same class of material than when they are from different classes of material, then it may also follow that in the transfer situation the transfer effects will be different if different classes of materials are used. For example, suppose we set up the usual A-B, A-C paradigm, but in one set of conditions we have adjectives as responses in the first list and nonsense syllables as responses in the second, with the transfer to be compared with conditions in which the responses are from the same class in both the first and second lists.

While these are given merely as illustrations, I think they may be used to point up the fact that at our present level of analysis, we do not receive much help from the Gibson theory. We might extend and refine the theory to accommodate these new methods of analysis or new ways of looking at the learning situations, or we might start with a new basic conception. We are tending toward the latter approach.

There are other illustrations of new conceptions of verbal learning which are tending to supercede the Gibson approach because the Gibson theory is irrelevant, incomplete, or unsatisfactory for the phenomena being studied. The emphasis of Goss (1955) on response-produced cues, and Spiker (1956) on verbal mediating responses are cases in point, as is also Arnoult's position (1957) that a critical factor missing in conceptions of transfer is stimulus description.

## CONCLUSION

This paper has given one evaluation of the current status or usefulness of the Gibson theory of verbal learning. Evaluation of facts available at the present time has forced the conclusion that the theory now has very limited usefulness; to a large extent, the flow of research and the new ways of viewing phenomena have left the theory behind. A concerted effort to bring it up to date might well be successful, but if the present evaluation has any validity, such a revision would almost of necessity result in a completely new theory. However, let us not underestimate the rebound power of any theory if clever minds go to work for it. Mrs. Gibson's provocative theory has dominated approaches in certain areas of verbal learning for 20 years. One does not simply destroy the worth of such a theory overnight. The judgment that has been made—that the theory has lost its usefulness—may yet rise up to haunt, embarrass, and befuddle the present writer.

## REFERENCES

Arnoult, M. D. (1957) Stimulus predifferentiation: Some generalizations and hypotheses. *Psychol. Bull.*, **54**, 339–350.

Atwater, S. K. (1953) Proactive inhibition and associative facilitation as affected by degree of prior learning. *J. Exp. Psychol.*, **46**, 400–404.

Barnes, J. M., & Underwood, B. J. (1959) "Fate" of first-list associations in transfer theory. *J. Exp. Psychol.*, **58**, 97–105.

Beecroft, R. S. (1956) Verbal learning and retention as a function of competing associations. *J. Exp. Psychol.*, **51**, 216–221.

Bugelski, B. R., & Cadwallader, T. C. (1956) A reappraisal of the transfer and retroaction surface. *J. Exp. Psychol.*, **52**, 360–366.

Cieutat, V. J., Stockwell, F. E., & Noble, C. E. (1958) The interaction of ability and amount of practice with stimulus and response meaningfulness (*m*, *m'*) in paired-associate learning. *J. Exp. Psychol.*, **56**, 193–202.

Feldman, S. M., & Underwood, B. J. (1957) Stimulus recall following paired-associate learning. *J. Exp. Psychol.*, **53**, 11–15.

Gibson, Eleanor J. (1940) A systematic application of the concepts of generalization and differentiation to verbal learning. *Psychol. Rev.*, **47**, 196–229.

Gibson, E. J. (1941) Retroactive inhibition as a function of degree of generalization between tasks. *J. Exp. Psychol.*, **28**, 93–115.

Gibson, E. J. (1942) Intra-list generalization as a factor in verbal learning. *J. Exp. Psychol.*, **30**, 185–200.

Goss, A. E. (1955) A stimulus-response analysis of the interaction of cue-producing and instrumental responses. *Psychol. Rev.*, **62**, 20–31.

Haagen, C. H. (1949) Synonymity, vividness, familiarity, and association-value ratings of 400 pairs of common adjectives. *J. Psychol.*, **27**, 453–463.

Hamilton, R. J. (1943) Retroactive facilitation as a function of degree of generalization between tasks. *J. Exp. Psychol.*, **32**, 363–376.

Hull, C. L., Hovland, C. I., Ross, R. T., Hall, M., Perkins, D. T., & Fitch, F. B. (1940) *Mathematico-deductive theory of rote learning*. New Haven, Conn.: Yale University Press.

Murdock, B. B., Jr. (1958) Intralist generalization in paired-associate learning. *Psychol. Rev.*, **65**, 306–314.

Osgood, C. E. (1949) The similarity paradox in human learning: A resolution. *Psychol. Rev.*, **56**, 132–143.

Postman, L. (1951) The generalization gradient in recognition memory. *J. Exp. Psychol.*, **42**, 231–235.

Schulz, R. W. (1958) Paired-associate learning as a function of amount of prior experience with stimulus and response. Ph.D. dissertation, Northwestern University.

Sheffield, F. D. (1946) The role of meaningfulness of stimulus and response in verbal learning. Ph.D. dissertation, Yale University.

Spiker, C. C. (1956) Stimulus pretraining and subsequent performance in the delayed reaction experiment. *J. Exp. Psychol.*, 52, 107–111.

Staner, B. J. (1956) Transfer as a function of simultaneous stimulus and response generalization. M.A. thesis, Northwestern University.

Uehling, B. S. (1958) Frequency of associations and similarity of meaning. Ph.D. dissertation, Northwestern University.

Underwood, B. J. (1949) Proactive inhibition as a function of time and degree of prior learning. *J. Exp. Psychol.*, 39, 24–34.

Underwood, B. J. (1951) Associative transfer in verbal learning as a function of response similarity and degree of first-list learning. *J. Exp. Psychol.*, 42, 44–53.

Underwood, B. J. (1953a) Studies of distributed practice: VIII. Learning and retention of paired nonsense syllables as a function of intralist similarity. *J. Exp. Psychol.*, 45, 133–142.

Underwood, B. J. (1953b) Studies of distributed practice: IX. Learning and retention of paired adjectives as a function of intralist similarity. *J. Exp. Psychol.*, 45, 143–149.

Underwood, B. J. (1954) Intralist similarity in verbal learning and retention. *Psychol. Rev.*, 61, 160–166.

Underwood, B. J., & Richardson, J. (1956) The influence of meaningfulness, intralist similarity, and serial position on retention. *J. Exp. Psychol.*, 52, 119–126.

Underwood, B. J., Runquist, W. W., & Schulz, R. W. (1959) Response learning in paired-associate lists as a function of intralist similarity. *J. Exp. Psychol.*, 58, 70–78.

# COMMENTS ON PROFESSOR UNDERWOOD'S PAPER
## Clyde E. Noble
MONTANA STATE UNIVERSITY

The scholarly assessment of Gibson's (1940) theory presented by Underwood is a fine piece of critical work. Although I concur with and admire a large part of his paper, there are two major issues on which we have differences of opinion. I shall begin my comments with some general remarks on the influence and usefulness of the Gibson model, then proceed to specific areas of agreement and disagreement with Underwood.

### Decline of the Theory

Why is it that Gibson's theory, long an important stimulus to research in the areas of perception and learning, seems to be losing its excitatory potential? Compared with the contemporary rote-learning system advanced by Hull *et al.* (1940), there were not only more references to Gibson's paper during the decade 1941–1950 but also more psychologists who tried to utilize her postulate set. It is true that the form of Hull's theory was forbidding, yet for every expression in symbolic logic there was an equivalent English statement. Still, Underwood is correct in asserting that Gibson's theory was preferred to Hull's—at least until the appearance of the more general system outlined in *Principles of Behavior* (Hull, 1943). One might wonder, therefore, why Gibson's well-written, analytical, and objective attempt at theory construction did not make an even greater impression on verbal learning experimenters.

For one thing, there has been little use of theory in this field because of lack of interest and training in rigorous deductive techniques. Until recently, our most notable theoretical psychologists have not been associated with research on verbal behavior. Paucity of systematic data is a second deterrent factor, and I believe with Irion (1959) that this is directly attributable to poorly standardized methods and materials. Third, scientists have a natural tendency to organize data within a limited domain rather than to attempt a wide-ranging approach. But perhaps the basic criterion in any natural science is the predictive excellence of its theories or models. How well does the Gibson theory predict?

Of the 18 propositions she derived from the initial set of 8 definitions and 10 postulates, Gibson's judgment was that none was demonstrably false. As she recognized, however, empirical proof is a matter of degree. In the table below I have listed Gibson's five categories of evidence (Gibson, 1940, p. 226), together with a comparison of her evaluations and my own based on Underwood's criteria. If my interpretations are correct, and Underwood should not be held responsible for them, at least four postulates (Nos. 2, 7, 8, 9) are defective in the light of present data. But the

| Evidence | Gibson (1940) | Underwood (1960) |
|---|---|---|
| Positive, conclusive | 8 | 0 |
| Positive, inconclusive | 4 | 5 |
| None | 4 | 2 |
| Conflicting, or irrelevant | 2 | 10 |
| Negative | 0 | 1 |
| Total | 18 | 18 |

most significant fact revealed by the table is that 13 out of 18, or 72 per cent, of the theorems have failed to yield positive evidence. A batting average of only 28 per cent hits may be the primary reason why, to mix a metaphor, Gibson's theory is undergoing experimental extinction.

## Agreements with Underwood

I wish to record my endorsement of Underwood's position on the following nine points: (1) his concern over the relevance to *verbal* learning of experiments employing *visual* forms as stimuli; (2) his judgment that the theory is incomplete because of Gibson's failure to consider response factors (e.g., integration); (3) his puzzlement at her rejection of the case of identical stimuli as an instance of maximal generalization; (4) his criticism of the use of overt errors and his insistence on measuring relative errors or error rates instead of total errors; (5) his rejection of the postulate concerning spontaneous recovery; (6) his discussion of recall versus relearning scores in experiments on intra-list similarity; (7) his analysis of the two basic transfer paradigms (excluding variations in response similarity); (8) his cautions regarding interlist interval and meaningfulness predictions; and (9) his recent trend away from the concept of similarity to that of association.

### Disagreements with Underwood

Two respects in which I find Underwood's treatment faulty are these: (1) his failure to criticize the fuzzy notion of *similarity* as a "dimension" (Underwood's paper, pp. 199–200), which lies at the heart of Gibson's theory of transfer, and (2) his neglect of the operational distinction between familiarity and meaningfulness (including the laws they affect) in the discussion of pre-differentiation (pp. 211–212). The first matter is essentially one of methodological analysis, while the second concerns the interpretation of experimental facts. I shall try to show that Gibson's conception of "similarity" and all its relatives (e.g., generalization, differentiation) is ambiguous; that she gave an equivocal, non-operational definition of "meaning[fulness]" which ignored the role of motor patterning; and that, contrary to Underwood (p. 212) but paradoxically consistent with Gibson (1940, p. 222), there is definite evidence of a "stimulus–pre-differentiation effect" in recent experiments on familiarity.

*Similarity.* As I have said elsewhere (Noble, 1957), similarity is a dyadic, many-many relation which has at least two cardinal properties that prevent it from entering into scales of the ordinary unidimensional type. These properties are nontransitivity and symmetry. Define the relation "resembles" by the symbol $\sim$. Now if $S_1 \sim S_2$ and $S_2 \sim S_3$, then sometimes $S_1 \sim S_3$ (nontransitivity); and if $S_1 \sim S_2$, then always $S_2 \sim S_1$ (symmetry). But serial relations (e.g., $>$) are transitive and asymmetrical; hence similarity is fundamentally nonmeasurable. Serial relations are the stuff of which scales are made, but some psychologists appear to see seriality everywhere. I find talk about "measuring" similarity particularly confusing when "degree of similarity" is equated to numerical proximities within any scale. One measures the attribute of *familiarity*, for example, not the relation "more frequent than" (Noble, 1953; Noble, 1960). Osgood has asked whether multidimensional scaling (e.g., using pairs or triples rather than elements) is the answer. This is a complex matter because the serial relations in such parascales usually have changing referents. Since experimenter and subject may use the term differently, special caution is needed in handling the similarity concept in the field of semantic research. Similarity ratings, in other words, should always be based on some clearly specified discrimination operation. Similarity *per se* is not a quality we predicate of single events; it is a relation we predicate among two or more events (law of stimulus generalization). Certainly, similarity is not a *dimension;* dimensions are purely physical variables (stimulus defined). Perhaps multivariate similarity is best construed as a *hyperspatial attribute* which is psychological (response defined), as in configurational judgments of resemblance (Noble, 1957, p. 32). If, then, similarity is not a unidimensional variable in the usual scientific sense, what does it mean when functionalists say that transfer is a function of "similarity"? I believe "similarity" must refer here to Thorndikean common elements, i.e., to a *manipulated* stimulus dimension of percentage communality, perhaps, not to a *correlated* psychological attribute. Surely Underwood has been after S-R rather than R-R laws all these years. Considering such methodological flaws as these, we must conclude that Gibson's notions of generalization and differentiation rest on a fundamental ambiguity which renders her theory of transfer uninterpretable.

2. *Pre-differentiation.* Underwood seems ambivalent toward the foregoing difficulty with Gibson's theory (Underwood, pp. 199–200 vs. pp. 212–213), and I think meaningfulness may be the second horn of the dilemma. Is it not more equivocation than parsimony to refer the behavioral effects of variations in both communality and meaningfulness to the same intervening variable? At least we can all agree that Gibsonian "meaning[fulness]" is not operationally (unequivocally) defined; other characteristics of verbal material also produce differential responses. One of these, for which evidence was lacking in 1940, is *familiarity*. This variable is curvilinearly related to meaningfulness (Noble, 1953), it is generated by frequency of experience alone (Noble, 1960), and it produces facilitation in both serial (Noble, 1955) and paired-associates learning (Gannon and Noble, 1961). Reports of similar observations from other laboratories (e.g., Hovland and Kurtz, 1952) indicate that the Law of Acquaintance should be revived. Yet Underwood is doubtful that, if familiarization be taken as a stimulus–pre-differentiation operation, subsequent verbal transfer effects will be positive. Some of his reluctance stems from the recent work with Schulz (Underwood and Schulz, 1960), but at least one serial learning experiment (Noble, 1955) and one paired-associates study (Gannon, and Noble, 1961) appear to satisfy Underwood's (p. 211) own criteria of an acceptable design: (1) second task verbal, (2) no competing responses, and (3) controls for performance factors. Of key importance is the second experiment above, which tested five groups of subjects' proficiency on paired associates that had previously been seen

and pronounced independently either 0 or 20 times. The control group was completely unfamiliarized, whereas the experimental groups had received the four combinations $S_0$-$R_0$, $S_0$-$R_{20}$, $S_{20}$-$R_0$, and $S_{20}$-$R_{20}$. Meaningfulness was constant for all groups, with only frequency varied. The data revealed significant facilitation for the S term but not for the R term. Employing different methods, Underwood and Schulz (1960) report exactly opposite results. Future research will have to resolve these discrepancies.

On *meaningfulness* (number of associations), Underwood (p. 212) cites the Cieutat-Stockwell-Noble (1958) study as support for a Gibsonian "prediction" that high meaningfulness in the S term will produce faster acquisition than low meaningfulness. He is properly skeptical, however, that "generalization in the sense that Gibson uses the term is responsible for differences in learning as a function of *stimulus* meaningfulness" (p. 212). Taken together with some of Mandler's work, these two paired-associates experiments (Gannon and Noble, 1961; Cieutat, Stockwell, and Noble, 1958) suggest to me that frequency of experience ($n$) is sufficient as far as the S term goes (stimulus pre-differentiation), but that meaningfulness ($m$) is jointly necessary for the R term (response patterning). Since high $m$ theoretically requires high $n$ (but not conversely), I would interpret the significant S-effect Underwood had reservations about as being due basically to familiarization. That the R-effect, neglected in Gibson's theory, is essentially a result of variations in meaningfulness is shown by our latest experiment (Parker and Noble, 1960). Here we built in meaningfulness experimentally by teaching subjects 0, 3, 6, or 9 arbitrary associations to paralogs. Paired associates to new S terms of low $m$ value were then acquired significantly faster the higher the $m$ value of the R term. This supports our hypothesis that number of associations is the major factor producing the facilitating influence of meaningfulness. A replication of the experiment with more subjects and additional controls has just been completed as an M.A. thesis by Parker with confirmatory results. Sheer frequency, it turns out, cannot be used to account for the R-effect trend in these data, although there was a significant interaction between familiarity and meaningfulness.

*Conclusions.* I think Underwood's evaluation of the Gibson theory is essentially correct, but we need a new theory which is methodologically sound as well as experimentally up to date. One difficulty, to note a warning from Osgood, will be to resist the tendency to reify the S and R terms in analyzing such factors as similarity, meaningfulness, familiarity, and pronunciability. Another will be the response-scoring problem raised by Deese. Kind and degree of standardization is a third unsettled issue. Underwood's familiarization techniques are different from ours, so it is not surprising that he comes up with different "pre-differentiation" phenomena. Finally, although I suspect that the operational basis of Gibsonian "similarity" is more apparent than real to Underwood, there can be no argument with his verdict that the theory is losing its influence.

REFERENCES

Cieutat, V. J., Stockwell, F. E., & Noble, C. E. (1958) The interaction of ability and amount of practice with stimulus response meaningfulness (*m*, *m'*) in paired-associate learning. *J. Exp. Psychol.*, 56, 193–202.

Gannon, D. R., & Noble, C. E. (1961) Familiarization (*n*) as a stimulus factor in paired-associate verbal learning. *J. Exp. Psychol.*, in press.

Gibson, Eleanor (1940) A systematic application of the concepts of generalization and differentiation to verbal learning. *Psychol. Rev.*, 47, 196–229.

Hovland, C. I., & Kurtz, K. (1952) Experimental studies of rote learning theory: X. Prelearning syllable familiarization and the length-difficulty relationship. *J. Exp. Psychol.*, 44, 31–39.

Hull, C. L. (1943) *Principles of behavior.* New York: Appleton-Century-Crofts.

Hull, C. L., Hovland, C. I., Ross, R. T., Hall, M., Perkins, D. T., & Fitch, F. B. (1940) *Mathematico-deductive theory of rote learning.* New Haven, Conn.: Yale University Press.

Irion, A. L. (1959) Rote learning. In S. Koch (Ed.), *Psychology: A study of a science.* Vol. II. New York: McGraw-Hill. Pp. 538–560.

Noble, C. E. (1953) The meaning-familiarity relationship. *Psychol. Rev.*, 60, 89–98.

Noble, C. E. (1955) The effect of familiarization upon serial verbal learning. *J. Exp. Psychol.*, 49, 333–338.

Noble, C. E. (1957) Psychology and the logic of similarity. *J. Gen. Psychol.*, 57, 23–43.

Noble, C. E. (1960) Supplementary report: Familiarity and frequency. *J. Exp. Psychol.*, 59, 432–433; 60, 418.

Parker, G. V. C., & Noble, C. E. (1960) Effects of experimentally-produced meaningfulness (*m*) on paired-associate learning. *Amer. Psychologist*, 15, 451. (Abstract)

Underwood, B. J., Schulz, R. W. (1960) *Meaningfulness and verbal learning.* Philadelphia: Lippincott.

# SUMMARY OF CONFERENCE DISCUSSION

Much of the discussion concerned the notion of "similarity"; several of the group expressed the opinion that this notion has been operationally defined and that, therefore, it has, in Gibson's work as well as in the work of others, experimental significance and relevance. Noble agreed that this often is the case, but he argued that a clear-cut understanding of the nature and limitations of the concept would clarify what is actually done empirically and permit terms to be used which are more aptly descriptive than the word "similarity." Osgood pointed out that semantic distances can be derived for concepts (as in the semantic differential). Noble's objection to calling this a scale of similarity was that such a name is not as descriptive as the name *distance*. In his own case, he recognized the virtue of using the notation *m* instead of the confusing word *meaningfulness*. There was brief mention of the transfer-retroaction surface (cf. Osgood, 1953) as representing a combination of data derived from incommensurate operations; the place of "opposites" on a "scale of similarity" was given as a case in point.

In his discussion, Noble reviewed experiments which he suggests support the notion that the familiarity of the *stimulus* rather than its meaningfulness (*m*) has a significant effect on paired-associates learning, whereas for the *response* term it is meaningfulness rather than familiarity that is important. Several points were raised in conjunction with these experiments. One was that there could be errors of scoring in the case of responses of low *m* value. These would presumably arise because of the inadequate encoding (by the experimenter) of such responses, so that he might accept, as correct, responses which were erroneous to some extent. It was pointed out that Noble's interpretation of the more significant role of *m* rather than familiarity in the response term (Parker and Noble) can only be justified if the other experiment (Gannon and Noble) is considered. Evidence obtained by Mandler is at least partially supportive of this view (Mandler and Campbell, 1957), but Underwood and Schulz (1960) have data leading to different conclusions. Variations in methods and materials are probably involved in these conflicting results, and further work is required in order to determine what factors underlie the conflict. It is obvious, both in Underwood's paper and in Noble's discussion of it, that resolution of these questions would have a bearing on the evaluation of at least an aspect of Gibson's theory.

## REFERENCES

Mandler, G., & Campbell, E. H. (1957) Effect of variation in associative frequency of stimulus and response members on paired-associate learning. *J. Exp. Psychol.*, **54**, 269–273.

Osgood, C. E. (1953) *Method and theory in experimental psychology*. New York: Oxford.

Underwood, B. J., & Schulz, R. W. (1960) *Meaningfulness and verbal learning*. Philadelphia: Lippincott.

# Chapter 9

# COMMENTARY

In 1955 a conference on associative processes in verbal behavior was held at the University of Minnesota. Postman summarized that conference, and six of the eleven participants in the 1955 meeting took part in the present conference. It is rather interesting to look at Postman's summary of the earlier meeting (Jenkins, 1959) in the light of the discussions just concluded. Of especial interest are the five directions which Postman thought desirable for future research. These directions were as follows: (1) Many more grammatical categories and types of items should be used in selecting stimuli in order to stabilize and extend the available association norms. (2) the word-association experiment itself should receive careful study, in order to determine the extent to which the responses obtained are a function of instructions, specific situations, sequences of items, serial position in the list, and so on. (3) Extensions of the cognitive situations in which relations to the normative data have been shown are needed. (4) Individual differences should receive further study. (5) The logical and grammatical categories of the language have much interest and can be profitably studied.

The Minnesota Conference was more directly concerned with verbal behavior than was the present conference. Yet almost every item which Postman mentioned in his recommendations has received attention here. It is not at all clear that we have moved ahead in our knowledge concerning Postman's five problem areas since 1955.[1]

On the other hand, a number of matters have received emphatic and extensive discussion in this conference which, 10 or 20 years ago, would not have been attended to at all. One of these is the point, made very often here, that the response must be integrated or encoded before it can enter successfully into associative relations with other units. It was this point which led, in one or more sessions, to the problem of *scoring* what a subject says; i.e., it was suggested that the subject's verbalization of a poorly integrated response might be misscored, whereas his verbalization of a highly integrated response would not be. Problems of scor-

---

[1] The present conference paid little attention to analysis of problems of verbal learning and verbal behavior from a statistical viewpoint. At the Minnesota meeting this point of view was ably advanced by Davis Howes (Jenkins, 1959).

ing in verbal learning, at least in the case of discrete responses, have seldom been mentioned in the literature. It is a token of the importance which response integration has lately assumed that scoring problems should be considered here.

Another point, which would probably have puzzled Ebbinghaus and perhaps McGeoch, is that frequency of pairing as a factor in associative strength or frequency of usage as a factor making for differential learnability of words has been questioned by at least some of the participants here. This is a complex issue, and in a sense, the phenomenon of single-trial acquisition of associations is not new. It has been known for many years that subjects are able to anticipate one or two paired associates correctly after a single learning trial. But the reorientation which some of the participants seem to be undergoing concerning this problem is that single-trial association of well-integrated units is the rule and that the slow acquisition of serial or paired-associates lists perhaps represents interference or other processes not typical of the formation of single associations. It is clear that not all workers in this field share this persuasion or would conclude that list learning does not permit the observation of the formation of simple associations. But the point is a feature of this meeting, which, like response integration, might not have found its way into the proceedings of a conference held a few years ago.[2]

Another point that has had explicit recognition here is that the nonsense syllable is a complex affair. That calibrations of "association value" of nonsense syllables have been made for over thirty years is a recognition that many such syllables are "sensical." But more recently it has become clear that the sequential transitions between the letters of the syllables themselves make for difficulties. This is because such transitions deviate from the letter transitions of greater commonality in the natural language. This is an entering wedge by means of which the interactions of the subject's natural language habits with verbal learning tasks can be studied. Unit sequences, such as sequences of meaningful words, are another bridge between the language habit and verbal learning. That grammatical or syntactical factors from the language may have an influence on verbal learning is still another point expressed in this meeting in recognition that natural language habits are important both in themselves and in their interactions with verbal learning tasks. Few data concerning the influence of grammatical habits were mentioned, but the concern for their importance led to emphasis on such problems as the way in which

[2] At the time of this meeting, only two papers on one-trial learning by the method used by Rock (1957) and Rock and Heimer (1959) had appeared. The papers by Wogan and Waters (1959), by Clark, Landsford, and Dallenbach (1960), and the related paper by Bolles (1959) were published after the conference. Had all of this material been available, even more attention would, perhaps, have been devoted to this issue.

grammar is acquired, how it works, and ways of evaluating the extent of its influence.[3] The conference returned again and again to one or the other of these points. Unfortunately, there were few concrete suggestions as to ways in which these grammatical problems could be investigated empirically. There has been little progress here since Postman said we need further study of these issues. Perhaps further study of the environmental control of linguistic sequences would clarify the extent to which grammatical skills are actually operative. We can also ask, under the discriminative control of what intraverbal cues do such grammatical skills function? Some participants suggested that these skills lie outside the range of associative and reinforcement mechanisms. This in itself is enough to mark a conference on verbal learning as unusual.

The association experiment came in for a good deal of attention, along lines which Postman had suggested five years ago. Few data were presented or referred to, but there was repeated concern about the equivalence of normative constructs and experimentally established characteristics, about the situational differences between the association experiment and other experimental situations, about the possible advantages which rating procedures for the estimation of associative relation might have over the usual association procedure.

Certain other points should be mentioned as representing other considerations that appear to be reformulations of old problems. One is the idea that recall is largely a constructive or a guessing process. This has been said before, but what was different in these discussions was the postulation of association and syntactical habits as the blocks with which the constructions are made. Another item is the rejection by many participants of the idea that verbal labeling responses are reasonable to postulate in conjunction with the use and function of conceptual schemes. It appears from this that unverbalized processes must be recognized in the areas of verbal learning and linguistic functioning. The Gibson theory and the older formulation of the interference theory of forgetting, long influential in the study of verbal learning and retention, it is clear, are no longer satisfactory.

It is a fact that even among this group of specialists a number of terms and concepts caused confusion. It took a great deal of discussion to clarify the differences between an associational- and a representational-response interpretation of meaning. This difference may be summarized by saying that for the associational interpretation the associates a person gives to a word define its meaning, whereas for the representational view ratings of similarity or semantic differential ratings or even dictionaries define a word's meaning. It can be pointed out here that meaning and meaningfulness are not synonyms; meaningfulness refers to the number

_____

[3] See the addendum which follows the reference list for this chapter.

of associations which are given to a word. When the word "frequency" was used, as it often was, it could refer to the sheer frequency with which a word had been experienced, as measured, for example, by its frequency of usage in the language. But frequency was also used to refer to associations, in which case it usually referred to the number of subjects out of a given sample who gave a particular response to a stimulus. Associative strength usually refers to this latter meaning. Response integration, or, as it was often called, the encoding of a word, seems to be associated, in the views of some of the participants, with the frequency with which the word occurs in the language. That is to say, the frequent words are likely to be well encoded. To others, however, this relationship was not so clear. They seemed to think of the integration or encodedness of a response as something that either was present or was not present and as not having much relation to frequency. In any case the term integration or encodedness seems to refer to the facility with which a subject recognizes or correctly pronounces a word. If such recognition or pronunciation occurs quickly and without much effort, then the word seems to be regarded as well encoded. Perhaps also involved is the ability of the subject to say the word correctly on the basis of minimal cues which he gets from its shape, certain letters, its length, and that a well-encoded word does not have to be as clearly presented or perceived as one that is not encoded for the subject to deal with it.

These terminological problems represent a defect in the present conference, although in fact they were probably more readily overcome in this meeting than they are in many conferences. Perhaps the greatest defect of this conference was its failure to deal much with data and with the problem of what research techniques and designs can or should be used in the investigation of the many problems which were raised. It is worth noting that a number of classical problems of verbal learning were hardly mentioned. The reader will have difficulty finding in these pages references to reminiscence, length of list, distributed practice, whole-part learning, and the like. It is difficult to know what these omissions mean. There were other omissions. Little attention was paid to techniques and studies which, seemingly, have high relevance to some of the issues that arose. Among these are clustering in free recall, cloze procedure, context, partial structure and priming in the free-association experiment. Perhaps another conference would fill in some of these gaps.

### REFERENCES

Bolles, R. C. (1959) The effect of altering the middle of the list during serial learning. *Amer. J. Psychol.*, 72, 577–580.

Clark, L. L., Lansford, T. G., & Dallenbach, K. M. (1960) Repetition and associative learning. *Amer. J. Psychol.*, 73, 22–40.

Rock, I. (1957) The role of repetition in associative learning. *Amer. J. Psychol.*, **70**, 186–193.

Rock, I., & Heimer, W. (1959) Further evidence of one-trial associative learning. *Amer. J. Psychol.*, **72**, 1–16.

Wogan, M., & Waters, R. H. (1959) The role of repetition in learning. *Amer. J. Psychol.*, **72**, 612–613.

# ADDENDUM

Little attention was paid during this conference to the relations which obtain or may obtain between units of linguistic analysis and various aspects of verbal behavior and performance. James J. Jenkins, in order partially to rectify this omission, has supplied the following list of pertinent references, organized in terms of units of linguistic analysis. While the list is admittedly incomplete, it provides some useful citations to the relevant literature.

## Phonemes and Distinctive Features

Brown, R. W., & Hildum, D. C. (1956) Expectancy and the identification of syllables. *Language, 32*, 411–419.

Carroll, J. B. (1958) The assessment of phoneme cluster frequencies. *Language, 34*, 267–278.

Liberman, A. M. (1957) Some results of research on speech perception. *J. Acoust. Soc. Amer., 29*, 117–123.

Liberman, A. M., Harris, K. S., Hoffman, H. S., & Griffith, B. C. (1957) The discrimination of speech sounds within and across phoneme boundaries. *J. Exp. Psychol., 54*, 359–368.

Miller, G. A., & Nicely, P. E. (1955) An analysis of perceptual confusions among some English consonants. *J. Acoust. Soc. Amer., 27*, 338–352.

## Morphemes and Structural Units

Aborn, M., Rubenstein, H., & Sterling, T. D. (1959) Sources of contextual constraint upon words in sentences. *J. Exp. Psychol., 57*, 171–180.

Berko, J. (1958) The child's learning of English morphology. *Word, 14*, 150–177.

Berko, J., & Brown, R. W. (1960) Psycholinguistic research methods. In P. H. Mussen (Ed.), *Handbook of methods in child psychology.* New York: Wiley.

Brown, R. W. (1957) Linguistic determinism and the part of speech. *J. Abnorm. Soc. Psychol., 55*, 1–5.

Brown, R. W. (1958) *Words and things.* Chaps. I, IV, VII. Glencoe, Ill.: Free Press.

Brown, R. W., & Lenneberg, E. H. (1954) A study in language and cognition. *J. Abnorm. Soc. Psychol., 49*, 454–462.

Carroll, J. B. (1958) Process and content in psycholinguistics. In R. A. Patton (Ed.), *Current trends in the description and analysis of behavior.* Pittsburgh: University of Pittsburgh Press.

Carroll, J. B., & Casagrande, J. B. (1958) The function of language classifications in behavior. In Eleanor E. Maccoby, T. M. Newcomb, & E. L. Hartley (Eds.), *Readings in social psychology.* (3rd ed.) New York: Holt, Rinehart & Winston.

Ervin, Susan (1957) Grammar and classification. Paper read at Amer. Psychol. Ass., New York.

Lambert, W. E., & Paivo, A. (1956) The influence of noun-adjective order on learning. *Canad. J. Psychol.,* 10, 9–12.

Lenneberg, E. H. (1957) A probabilistic approach to language learning. *Behav. Sci.,* 2, 1–12.

Lenneberg, E. H., & Roberts, J. M. (1956) The language of experience: A study in methodology. *Int. J. Amer. Linguist.,* Mem. 13.

Maclay, H. (1958) An experimental study of language and non-linguistic behavior. *SW J. Anthrop.,* 14, 220–229.

# INDEX